# IS THIS YOU?

Determined to lose weight, you vowed to do it the "right" way. You stopped eating red meat, had omelets made from egg whites only, took the skin off the chicken, ate lots of pasta and baked potatoes with no butter, and oatmeal and skimmed milk for breakfast. And you stuck with it. And yet somehow it never quite felt right, and it never worked the way you thought it would.

Well, if that description fits, the probability is that you're just a normal person who's been victimized by those who don't tell you that the low-fat diet forces you to eat more carbohydrates, the very food that makes you fat.

Robert C. Atkins, M.D.

# Dr. Atkins' *New* Diet Revolution

Robert C. Atkins, M.D.

VERMILION
LONDON

This edition published in the United Kingdom in 1999 by Vermilion
an imprint of Ebury Press
Random House Group Ltd.
20 Vauxhall Bridge Road
London SW1V 2SA

Random House Australia (Pty) Limited.
20 Alfred Street, Milsons Point, Sydney
New South Wales 2061, Australia

Random House New Zealand Limited
18 Poland Rd, Glenfield
Auckland 10, New Zealand

Random House, South Africa (Pty) Limited
Endulini, 5A Jubilee Road, Parktown 2193, South Africa

www.randomhouse.co.uk

The Random House Group Limited Reg. No. 954009

A CIP catalogue record for this book is available from the British Library.

ISBN 0 09 186783 5

Printed and bound in Great Britain
by Bookmarque Ltd, Croydon, Surrey

Papers used by Vermilion are natural, recyclable products made from wood
grown in sustainable forests.

The advice offered in this book, although based on the
author's experience with many thousands of patients, is not
intended to be a substitute for the advice and counsel of
your personal physician. Always consult a medical practitioner before embarking on a diet. Neither the Author nor
the Publisher can be held responsible for any loss or claim
arising out of the use, or misuse, of the suggestions made,
or the failure to take medical advice.

# Contents

## Part Four—How to Do the Diet for Life

## Part Five—Menus and Recipes

To my loving and lovely wife Veronica,
who has unfailingly provided me with
emotional, intellectual, spiritual,
and low-carbohydrate nourishment.

# Preface

In the eight years since the hardcover edition of this book was published, there have been several developments that just might help make the rest of your life a lot more pleasant.

It wouldn't surprise me if your goal of being really slim is beginning to look like an impossible dream; and perhaps you are ready to give up trying. If so, you're not alone; the same thing has been happening to the majority of the population, and all in the last few years.

There have always been a considerable number of overweight Americans; one in four were significantly so. For generations, that 25% represented a constant, predictable measure of our obesity problem. But ten years ago, an epidemic started and spread across America like a brushfire. Every year, some two million new cases developed. When last quantified, the decade's damage was officially measured to be an increase of 32% in the number of Americans who were obese (20% or more above their ideal weight).

If you are one of this growing number of weight gainers, it may be that you have been following the wrong diet— the diet that created the epidemic. As the only physician who has steadfastly opposed the universal application of the high carbohydrate, 30% fat diet, I can state with authority that the obesity epidemic is in fact *caused* by those very instructions and by that very diet.

Think of it: the "solution" is really the problem.

Using simplistic reasoning, it would seem that reducing fat in our diet would reduce fat in our bodies. The adage "Lose weight, stay on a low-fat diet" has been repeated so often that most of us assume it is scientifically proved. But as you will learn in this book, science "proves" something quite the opposite. There is proof that obesity is due to a very specific metabolic defect. And once you have the key, a key that seems to elude even our health care policy makers, you will be able to excise obesity with the precision of a skilled surgeon who dissects away a tumor while leaving the healthy tissue intact.

Armed with this knowledge, the project of losing weight will be transformed from a hunger- and fatigue-provoking ordeal that only a handful of us can endure for life, to a surprisingly easy matter of eating abundantly, luxuriously and healthfully, yet always selectively and wisely.

Our physical urges are hard to combat. Fighting the scale armed only with willpower and determination works, at best, for only five low-fat dieters out of a hundred. But we might instead use our intellect, in the manner this book will show you, and bypass our need to rely on willpower.

Learn to unlock the secret of easy weight loss and you'll be able to lose while eating second and third helpings of traditional main courses.

Once you learn of the caloric richness and satiety that

the eating program within these pages provides, its impact should hit you like a sledgehammer. "This is not dieting," you will feel, "this is a banquet." And as weight loss and improved well-being take place, you will feel exhilaration, relief and confidence that getting and staying slim will be a breeze and that the end of your weight problem is clearly in view.

ROBERT C. ATKINS, M.D.

# PART ONE

# Why the
# Diet Works

# 1

# Dr. Atkins' Diet Revelation

Is this you?

Determined to lose weight, you vowed to do it the "right" way, until success was yours. You stopped eating red meat, had omelets made in a teflon pan from egg whites only, took the skin off the chicken, ate lots of pasta and baked potatoes with no butter. Frozen yoghurt and fruit sherbet for desserts, oatmeal and skimmed milk for breakfast, or else, granola and a banana. For lunch, white meat turkey on a roll, and a generous salad with no oil.

And you stuck with it. You knew it was the right diet because everyone was pleased to see you on it, and congratulated you on your good and healthy taste in eating. And yet somehow it never quite felt like the right diet, and it never worked the way you thought it would. You found that you weren't quite satisfied eating this way, sometimes you were hungry, you didn't feel the kind of physical pick-me-up you thought you'd get from the "right" diet, and—

worst of all—permanent, significant weight loss proved elusive. *You never actually got what you went on a diet for in the first place.*

Well, if that description fits, the probability is that you're just a normal person who's been *had*. Had by the society we live in, which encouraged you to believe in a right way that was just plain wrong for you. Had by a mudslide of media propaganda that promotes the fads of the moment irrespective of the metabolism of the people who have to go on them. But, if the person I've been describing is you, these frustrations are about to end. I have helped the 25,000 people who've come to me needing to lose weight and unsure of how to do it, and I will help you too.

Diets come and go, but what people hope to get from them remains fairly constant. Let your fancy run free. Wouldn't you rather be on a diet that:

- Sets no limit on the amount of food you can eat?
- Completely excludes hunger from the dieting experience?
- Includes foods so rich that you've never seen them on any other diet?
- Reduces your appetite by a perfectly natural function of the body?
- Gives you a metabolic edge so significant that the whole concept of watching calories will become absurd to you?
- Produces steady weight loss, even if you have experienced dramatic failures or weight regain on other diets?
- Is so perfectly adapted to use as a lifetime diet that, unlike most diets, the lost weight won't come back?
- Consistently produces improvements in most of the health problems that accompany overweight?

Too good to be true? Not at all. Simply true. Moreover, repeatedly demonstrable and scientifically unimpeachable. That's a revelation.

These are the results for better than 90% of the tens of thousands of people under my personal supervision who have adopted the diet explained in this book, and I assume a very large percentage of the millions that have done it on their own. If you're overweight, this prospect is of such a life-altering order of magnitude, that I have no doubt that you feel tempted to regard it as pie in the sky. You'll soon realize that's a poor analogy. First, I'll be taking away your pie, and second, these dietary results—far from being somewhere up in the clouds—are based on a set of well-grounded scientific facts that hardly anybody in the weight-loss business is paying attention to right now.

## Health Was the Major Goal

I've spent twenty-five years treating the overweight and yet, significantly, *most of my patients during the last fifteen years did not come to me primarily for weight loss*. The pounds they shed were a beneficial side effect of usually quite successful treatments for conditions considerably more serious than obesity.

As a doctor, it was their dawning wellness that impressed me. As a potential dieter it will be their newfound slimness that will impress you.

So forgive this chapter's title, but it fits. And, if the first half of the revelation is in the alluring promise of weight loss, the second half is in the science that backs it up. That science has overwhelming significance for people who have found through hard experience that staying at a desirable weight is not too simple.

Let me place these facts on the table from the beginning:

1. Almost all obesity exists for metabolic reasons. Most studies have shown that the obese gain weight on *fewer* calories than people without a weight problem.

2. The basis of the metabolic disturbance in obesity has been pretty well worked out by scientists over the last ten to fifteen years. It doesn't have to do with the metabolism of the fat you eat but with hyperinsulinism and insulin resistance. The insulin hormone and its effect on your blood sugar levels (which are constantly rising and falling in response to the food you eat) is far more directly related to your general health picture and to your likelihood of being victimized by killers such as heart disease and stroke than was ever suspected in the past. It is also *the single most significant determinant of your weight*. That is why, by the fifth decade of their lives, 85% of Type II diabetics are obese.

3. This metabolic defect involving insulin can be circumvented by restricting carbohydrates. When you restrict it, *you avoid the food subdivision that causes you to be fat*.

4. This metabolic correction is so striking that many of you will be able to *lose weight* eating a *higher* number of calories than you have been eating on diets top-heavy in carbohydrates. The so-called "calorie theory" has been a millstone around the necks of dieters and a miserable and malign influence on their efforts to lose.

5. Diets high in carbohydrates are precisely what most overweight people don't need and can't become slim on.

6. A carbohydrate-*restricted* diet is so effective at dissolving adipose tissue that it can create fat loss *greater* than occurs in fasting.

7. Our epidemics of diabetes, heart disease, and high blood pressure are very largely the products of the hyperinsulinism connection.

8. The Atkins diet can correct and has corrected these serious medical complications of obesity. Indeed, 35% of my patients come to me for help with cardiovascular problems. The Atkins Diet is probably the most aggressively health-promoting diet you will ever have the opportunity to be on.

Now let's get back to the word revelation. Its meaning and connotation is to make known truths that were always there. Well, if the facts I have outlined are accepted as truths by an important segment of the scientific community, and yet are not so much as suspected by the majority of the populace, then this book will indeed be an act of revelation.

During the past twenty years, it has been suggested to the public, by techniques nearly as intense as brainwashing, that the only proper and healthy diet for a human being is a *low-fat* diet. If this were true, then the course of action for each and every one of us would be obvious and direct. But it's not true: *For many of us, the bypassing of carbohydrates is our ultimate solution.*

Now let's just look at a few of the misapprehensions about diet that are still widely held.

## I Thought People Gained Weight Because They Ate Too Much.

Not so. Most overweight people do not overeat. When they do, there is almost invariably a metabolic component driving them on, most often a truly addictive craving for carbohydrates.

People eating the right foods eat what they want to eat and stay around their ideal weight. However, the normal experience as one gets older is to find that one *cannot* eat the remarkably unnatural diet of the modern world and stay slim and healthy.

Your body, which was meant to function for a long, vigorous lifetime on healthy foods becomes more and more sensitive to the actions of unhealthy ones. Your metabolism begins to creak and groan. Not only the pounds get added on but also the pains. Crushing fatigue, headaches, lassitude, irritability, depression—these are not really part of the process of reaching middle age, even though in our society they seem to be, largely because of the way we eat.

Your tough and hardy prehistoric ancestors were not eating devitalized, long shelf-life, processed foods, junk white bread, and pizza around their campfires—and they most certainly were not consuming sugar (as in our soft drinks and juices) when their bodies told them they needed water. If they had been, we never would have made it to civilization.

## Carbohydrate or Fat

It's convenient to start with overweight, not only because it's the first thing my readers want to fix but because overweight is the most visible symptom of diet. My experience in treating 25,000 overweight patients has shown me that 90% of the time the overweight was caused by a disturbed carbohydrate metabolism.

Working off of my operational assumption that a disturbed carbohydrate metabolism underlies obesity, my record of success has been rip-roaring, record-rending, and remarkably reproducible.

I'd like to mention a little ancient history. Twenty years ago, on the heels of widespread and fairly accurate reporting of my unusual success in treating overweight, I sold six million copies of *Dr. Atkins' Diet Revolution*.*

I'm writing this new book to explain to a *new generation* all the latest developments in what has been the most successful weight-loss diet of the 20th century. I'm writing it as well to explain to my critics—I never go anywhere without them—how much new scientific evidence has appeared (especially in the last ten years) supporting the basic insights of low-carbohydrate dieting, a form of dieting that has been pushed aside in recent years by the influential but, alas, ineffective school of low-fat/low-calorie dieting that I would wager every single one of you is familiar with. This has been the dominant trend in dieting for the past decade, but its dominance hasn't, by and large, done a thing to take the pounds off.

## Let's Examine the Calorie Myth

A calorie is an interesting little word that simply stands for a unit of energy—precisely the amount of heat needed to raise 1 gram of water 1 degree Celsius at 1 atmosphere pressure.

*By now the sales have exceeded ten million copies worldwide.

Now, it has always been supposed that gaining weight results from taking in more calories than you expend through exercise, thermogenesis (the body's own heat production), and all the body's other metabolic functions. And, in fact, this is quite true.

What isn't true is what many doctors have concluded from this and passed on to their hapless patients. I'm referring to the notion that the only way to lose weight is to strictly control your intake of calories. Doctors brought up in this school of thought will tell their patients that all diets are basically equal in regard to their weight-loss potential. The only thing that matters is how many calories you take in!

This just isn't so. Different kinds of diets can have different effects on the amount of calories a person's body consumes daily, and, by taking different metabolic pathways, can cause the body to *require* different amounts of energy to do its work. On a low-carbohydrate diet, there are metabolic advantages that will allow you to *eat as many or more calories as you were eating before starting the diet and still begin losing pounds and inches*.

And if you eat fewer calories—most people do on this diet—you'll lose weight very fast. It's not that calories don't count, it's just that you can, in fact, sneak them out of your body, unused, or dissipated as heat.

How does all this work on real people with real problems? Consider Stanley Moskowitz, a vigorous 64-year-old sculptor, who had survived three heart attacks in the 1980s, two "minor" and one severe. Stanley was overweight, his cholesterol levels were too high, and he had a great deal of arthritis—a very long-term problem for him. Naturally we took him off his ice-cream and his french fries, his "junk-food Americana," as he called it, and just as naturally we urged him to eat a lot of meat, fish, fowl, and eggs when he wanted them, nuts, salads, vegetables, and a little cheese. A typical low-carbohydrate diet which he thoroughly enjoyed. But what was he going to do about his body and his beleaguered heart?

Stanley soon learned to smile about his results there too. His cholesterol went down from 228 to 157—by the standard method of calculating such things, a massive reduction of 64% in his risk for another heart attack. And his weight? That went down from 228 to 190, a pretty good weight for a powerfully built six-footer, who creates all metal sculptures in his studio. Incidentally, as a side effect of his new diet, the pain Stanley was so accustomed to in the joints of his shoulders and arms improved until they felt better than they had in more than twenty years.

I asked Stanley what he thought about all this, and he said, "Well, Dr. Atkins, these are probably the most startling physical changes I've experienced in my lifetime, and, strangely enough, all I had to do was enjoy myself."

Right. Let me tell you about another patient in more detail.

## Mary Anne Evans

Before she saw me, Mary Anne had given up. I asked her to tell her own story.

"I said to myself, 'I'm simply going to be a fat person for the rest of my life.' I weighed 209 pounds when I came to see you, and I had been putting on weight steadily for twenty years—especially after each of my kids."

At 5'5" tall and 42 years old, Mary Anne's two-hundred-plus weight load was a health hazard and a half, and I told her so. She said she had tried countless diets—low-calorie diets including Weight Watchers; a hospital-based program that measured calories; and a liquid protein diet on which she lost more than thirty pounds in three months and gained it back, with interest, in four.

She had thought it made sense to watch calories in order to lose weight, but somehow it never worked. Besides, it was terribly painful. The pounds that slid off with agonizing effort slipped on again effortlessly, which didn't seem quite fair.

So what was the use? Besides, she hadn't come to me with weight loss in mind. Her problems were quite medical. Mary Anne's blood pressure was high (160/100), she had a number of allergies, and her chief complaint was the extreme fatigue she had endured for the past several years. Add her overweight to all that, and I knew she was heading into a very difficult, mid-life physical crisis. Better act now.

To begin with, I took her off all carbohydrates. At nearly zero grams of carbohydrate, the most fat-retaining body will develop ketosis/lipolysis, which simply means it will be burning its own fat for fuel. Ketosis is the secret weapon of supereffective dieting. A person in that state is throwing off ketones—little carbon fragments that are the byproducts of the burning of fat stores.

Many doctors have an unfavorable picture of ketosis, but, in fact, used as you'll use it on the Atkins program, it's going to be just as safe for you as it has been for my first 25,000 overweight patients. It's an extremely desirable state to be in, and it fully deserves the name I've coined for it: Benign Dietary Ketosis (BDK). But remember, you can't be in ketosis unless you're eating hardly any carbohydrates. For most people this means less than forty grams a day. To get you oriented, remember that an average person consumes approximately 300 gms of carbohydrates a day. And, of course, some people eat much more than that.

So let's look at Mary Anne. I wanted her to be in ketosis. She was willing to try. What did she do?

Mary Anne abandoned the crackers she ate with lunch and the potato she had with dinner, she gave up the popcorn, cake, and pizza she was used to snacking on during the day, she didn't put sugar in her coffee, she eschewed the occasional soft drink, she relinquished her breakfast orange juice, and, temporarily, she even gave up the vegetables she ate at dinner.

She was eating ham and eggs for breakfast, tuna fish for lunch, and chicken, pork chops, or steak for dinner. After the first few days, it was evident that she had had no trouble getting into BDK, and we added a salad at lunch and a salad at dinner.

"By the second week, I realized I felt really good. I had a lot more energy than I'd had on the old diet, and I wasn't hungry."

Not being hungry is a typical result of being in BDK and one of the great initial attractions of the diet.

There was soon another reinforcement to keep on the diet: Mary Anne was losing weight—ten pounds in sixteen days. After five weeks, she'd lost 21 pounds, and her blood pressure was 120/78.

It took nine months to get Mary Anne Evans to 139 pounds, which was pretty close to where she wanted to be. Leaving 70 pounds behind, she's discarded one-third of the person she'd been.

"It was so easy to do this. I lost weight without any hassle, I was eating things I really liked to eat anyway, and I was never hungry. You said if I was hungry then

I should eat as much as I wanted and anything I wanted as long as it had no carbohydrates, and that's what I did. And the change in my life was incredible. Before, my favorite position had been sitting. Now I go out camping with my youngest son, who's in the Boy Scouts, and last summer I went horseback riding in the Rockies. The people at the lab where I work can't believe the new me. I go out to lunch with some of the other women who are on diets, and they can't seem to lose weight, and *they're hungry*. And I'm sitting there eating a hamburger and a large salad."

Another two years have passed. Mary Anne's weight hovers around 142. She has a glass of wine before dinner a couple of nights a week, and she eats two potatoes weekly. Her only other carbohydrates are vegetables and salads and plenty of them. She's on a luxury diet that she perfectly well enjoys. She's full of energy, and her blood pressure is normal. She's a typical Atkins dieter.

## Is This Shocking to You?

If it is, you're entirely normal. It contradicts the mythology that says the only way to be fit, slim, and healthy is to pursue low-fat dieting, first, last, and always. That mythology is based on some well observed scientific facts poorly interpreted. This mythology is mostly harmful, because a moderate low-fat diet, which allows you to eat sugar, white flour, and other processed junk food, isn't healthy at all. And an extreme low-fat diet, which can be healthy if it excludes junk, is simply too austere for most people and infinitely more austere than the Atkins diet.

I also shouldn't have to tell you that moderate low-fat

dieting—like the low-calorie dieting that preceded it—is a complete wipeout when it comes to permanent weight loss. So big a wipeout that it's a major national embarrassment. On calorie-restrictive and/or low-fat diets, *only three to five percent* of dieters succeed in keeping their excess pounds off.

All you experienced dieters know that the test of a good diet is *keeping* the weight off. Any diet vigorously pursued can take those ounces and inches off initially. But, once a low-calorie/low-fat dieter can no longer tolerate the biologic gap between hunger and fulfillment found on such diets, what a rebound follows!

Meanwhile, the vast majority of those committed to following the Atkins diet have had little or no difficulty in maintaining their ideal weight after weight loss.

Whenever I talk about diet on my nightly radio show on WOR in New York, people call me up to tell me they've been on the diet for five years, or ten, or twenty, and they feel great. Fat? No, it never came back. I smile and congratulate them. And inside, I'm chuckling merrily. What they're telling me is that it's not just my own patients who've succeeded on the Atkins diet.

*But then, dieting success on a properly managed low-carbohydrate diet is almost inescapable.*

## What's Dieting All About?

The word "diet" comes from the Latin *diaeta* and the Greek *diaita*, meaning "way of life" or "regimen." Not something one does for two or three months and then stops but the way one eats always. That's how I'd like you to think of it, because that's the only way you'll succeed at weight loss.

Most Americans eat a typical modern diet. Forty percent of them end up overweight. Why?

The foods we eat are divided into three basic categories— carbohydrates, fats, and proteins. Proteins are found in their largest concentrations in animal foods such as meat, fish, fowl, eggs, and cheese. They are also found in vegetables, foods such as nuts and seeds, and in high-protein legumes such as beans. Fat comes in many varieties but exists in almost all animal foods and in many vegetables. Carbohydrates exist in all vegetables, fruits, starches and grains and in its purest form, in refined sugar.

If you've been fat for very long, it's almost certain you have a disturbed carbohydrate metabolism. That's what the vast majority of studies have consistently shown. This means that the sugars, the refined carbohydrates, the junk foods that are such a whopping proportion of the American diet are slow poison to you. Those foods are bad for your health, bad for your energy level, bad for your mental state, bad for your figure. Bad for your career prospects, bad for your sex life, bad for your digestion, bad for your blood chemistry, bad for your heart. What I'm saying is that they're bad.

Most of the overweight people in the world are carbohydrate sensitive—often they're true carbohydrate addicts. They need a metabolic solution, not a low-fat one. They've struggled and struggled with low-calorie/low-fat diets and consistently failed. Why do they succeed on this diet?

## This Diet Must Have Special Advantages

Yes. That is, you bet it does. Here are six reasons why the diet works.

*First:* It creates more fat mobilization than any other diet you have ever encountered. It has been *proven* (repeatedly) that it takes off more *fat* than other diets on which you would be eating an equal number of calories.

*Second:* A low-carbohydrate diet is not austere. Sheer hunger is behind most diet failure. A lifetime diet needs to be palatable, pleasant, and filling. The major austerity on this diet is the abandonment of sugar and such refined carbohydrates as white flour. But most people find that, once they shake off the sugar addiction, they feel no strong desire to go back to it. For them, a diet on which they can eat an almost limitless variety of meat and fish and salads and vegetables prepared in the most appetizing manner (i.e. with butter and cream and spices and herbs to taste) is anything but austere. The Atkins diet is a dream diet—luxurious, sane, healthy, and varied.

*Third:* This is the easiest diet on which to *maintain* weight loss. The trouble with losing weight on an ordinary low-calorie diet or on a liquid-protein diet is that the maintenance program is so very different from the weight-loss program. Thus the pounds return with astonishing speed as, unprepared for maintenance, you go back to your former way of eating. There are sound physiological reasons for this. When you restrict the calories you eat, the body tends to become metabolically committed to putting the weight back on.

Success at *maintaining* weight loss is the great plus of the Atkins diet. That's interesting, since what most people know about low-carbohydrate dieting is that you can lose a lot of weight on it rapidly. And you can. But that's *not* the point. The only useful weight lost is the weight that doesn't come back again.

For that reason, there are actually four Atkins diets. Diet 1 is the initial *Induction* diet, which crashes you through most weight-loss barriers and will generally introduce even the most metabolically-resistant person's fat-retaining body to weight reduction. Diet 2 is *Ongoing Weight Loss*—it will carry you smoothly toward your goal. Diet 3 is *Pre-Maintenance*—it begins to teach you the lessons of a style of eating that, with a modest degree of diligence on your part, will keep you slim forever. Diet 4 is the *Maintenance* diet. Even as you read this, thousands of my old patients and hundreds of thousands of my old readers are practicing this diet so that they'll never be fat again.

Let me state one crucial fact that you should always keep in mind. *On the Atkins diet, failure in maintaining weight loss is almost impossible for the committed.*

*Fourth:* Not only is this diet not austere, it makes you feel good. It's a high-energy diet. It's a quick and lasting solution to many of the commonest annoyances that patients tell doctors about in the privacy of the consulting room. Fatigue, irritability, depression, trouble concentrating, headaches, insomnia, dizziness, many forms of joint and muscle aches, heartburn, colitis, water retention, premenstrual syndrome, even tobacco addiction. For the lion's share of patients, a low-carbohydrate diet is a specific against these ills. And that's definitely a factor in keeping the weight off, because few people are willing to go back to feeling lousy once they've reexperienced the joys of feeling good.

*Fifth:* The diet is healthy. I found this out very quickly when I first began to put patients on it twenty-five years ago. They began to recover from illnesses that I had no realization I was going to be treating *that way*. I discovered that most of my patients were suffering from a condition to which I give the name Diet-Related Disorder (DRD), a condition which I'll describe in Chapters 11 to 14, where I discuss hypoglycemia, yeast infections, food allergies/intolerances, and a number of other conditions.

Correcting DRD was the key to most of my patients getting a new lease on health. In addition, hypertension, diabetes, and most cardiovascular conditions respond with extraordinary rapidity to this diet. Since I was a practicing cardiologist when I began to prescribe the diet and 30 to 40% of my large patient population is still made up of people with cardiovascular problems, you can imagine how much of my success is based on the diet's heart benefits.

*Sixth:* The diet works because, as an increasing body of scientific evidence shows, it hooks onto the basic factor in both the control of obesity and the control of most of the modern degenerative illnesses. That factor is the excessive levels of insulin, an essential hormone in the human body. Insulin governs the basic mechanism by which the body lays on fat. When found in excessively high levels—we medical folk call that state hyperinsulinism—it vigorously promotes diabetes, atherosclerosis, and hypertension.

Thus the Atkins diet—partly by serendipity, for I had no intention of attacking the modern degenerative diseases when I first developed the diet—finds itself at the center of health planning for long, vigorous life.

## This Ought to Change the Way You Look at Your Body

Metabolic defect. Hyperinsulinism. DRD. You'll understand these terms soon enough. Already they give you a hint of why you have a weight problem. For now, simply remember this: Diets high in sugar and refined carbohydrates radically increase the body's production of insulin, and insulin, as one distinguished scientist remarked, is "the best single index of adiposity." That final word is medical jargon for *fat*.

I bet you know people who eat more than you do and exercise less and yet can't seem to put on a pound. They're not lying about the amount they eat, any more than you are. They eat a *lot*. Maddening, but true.

What a revolutionary fact! In some ways, a cause for celebration. If you're overweight, you're not greedy, not weak-willed, not lazy, not self-indulgent, not *awful* but, in all probability, metabolically unfortunate. Doesn't that make a lot more sense? Overeating? So rarely is that true. Most people eat when they're hungry and stop when they're full. Well then, how could they be *over*eating? They're doing what their bodies tell them to do, and bodies have a sort of wisdom.

The critical factor is *what* you eat.

## What's Wrong with Carbohydrates?

If you mean what's wrong with a spear of broccoli or a bunch of spinach, the answer is nearly nothing, they're magnificent foods. When I speak of carbohydrates, I'm referring to the unhealthy ones—sugar and white flour, milk and white rice, processed and refined foods of all kinds, junk foods and the like. But, at least during the weight-loss portion of the Atkins diet, even potentially healthy carbohydrates such as starches and most fruits must be monitored.

Once you've lost your extra pounds, you can return to starches and fruits to the degree that they won't upset your metabolic balance and cause you to start gaining weight again. But the refined foods I've just mentioned simply aren't good for you—*ever*. Am I advocating a high-fat diet?

Not in the long run. As my critics twenty years ago were forced to acknowledge when they looked into the matter, and as Professor John Yudkin proved, this isn't a high-fat diet. The average person on a low-carbohydrate diet eats less fat than he was eating on his previous "balanced" diet—the average diet in America today.[1]

There are many reasons for that, which I'll be telling you about. But for the moment, let's consider the question of whether we are in trouble because we are gorging ourselves on steaks and hot dogs.

I hardly need to tell you about the way we eat. You've all seen the aisles in the supermarket crammed with cookies and crackers, ice cream, frozen cakes and pies, soft drinks, and junk white breads so repugnant to the metabolism that many forms of rodents—wiser than us—won't even eat them except as a last resort.

This is not real food; it's invented, fake food. It's filled with sugar and highly refined carbohydrates *and* with fat (not to mention a dreadful panoply of chemical additives). For thousands of years, human beings were in luck—none of this food existed. Now we're stuck with it. Because it's incredibly profitable, it's also widely distributed. But there isn't a person on this planet who should be eating it.

I'm ready to tell you that if you want to be slim and vigorous, you can't eat like that, but you can eat like a king or queen—and certainly a prince or princess. (When you look at the recipes in Part V and see some of the delights prepared for you by our master low-carbohydrate chef, Graham Newbould—formerly chef to the Prince and Princess of Wales—you'll see how appropriate it is that I should make such a statement.)

On the Atkins diet, you can eat the natural, healthy animal and vegetable foods that people ate and grew robust on in centuries past. You don't have to be austere or peculiar. You don't have to eat like a rabbit; you can eat like a human being. You can enjoy salads and fish, roast rack of lamb and lobster, butter and broccoli, and even that dietician's sturdy nightmare—bacon and eggs for breakfast.

Now to answer the question at the head of this section: *What's wrong with carbohydrates*? The answer is, nothing, if you're not trying to lose weight and, if they're the right carbohydrates. The Atkins diet is called a low-carbohydrate diet because during the first two stages of the diet, the only carbohydrates you eat are moderate helpings of vegetables and salads. Later, once you've reached your ideal weight, you can eat larger helpings of the healthy carbohydrate foods, as long as you stay below the Critical Carbohydrate Level for Maintenance (CCLM) that keeps you from regaining your lost weight.

The Atkins diet isn't a peculiar, exotic diet. It's *the* human diet raised to its healthiest pitch and stripped of the 20th-century food inventions that are so economically delightful and so physiologically disastrous.

The suggestion that this isn't a perfectly healthy way to eat because I don't tell you to flee in terror from a steak is amusing but also sad. There are big lies lurking in the medical forests, and one of the things this book will show is how you can detect them.

## What You Need to Do

I'd like to ask you to try the diet out for 14 days. That will be more than enough time for you to not only lose a surprising amount of weight, but to find out how wonderful you'll feel on a low-carbohydrate meal plan and how refreshing it is to lose pounds and inches even while *you eat as much as you like*.

There are lots of diets on which you can lose weight temporarily and feel lousy while you're doing it. This isn't one of them.

Of course, when I propose you try the diet out for 14 days, I'm sure you realize I don't expect you to stop there. I'm trying to lure you into your lifetime diet.

The second reason for keeping close track of what happens to you in the first 14 days is that it will help you learn the degree of your metabolic resistance to weight loss. (See the weight table in Chapter 17.)

## Metabolic Resistance—A Little or a Lot

Not everyone loses weight with the same ease, even on a low-carbohydrate diet. People with a less than average degree of metabolic resistance will lose anywhere from 8 to 15 pounds in two weeks on the diet; people with an average level, somewhat less.

However, the person who is truly metabolically resistant won't lose much at all without getting more exercise or taking nutritional supplements that help weight loss, or even slightly restricting the quantity of food he or she eats—or some combination of the three. And, if you're that rare person with an enormous metabolic resistance to weight loss, I'll show you just what you need to do. For you the program will be a little more strenuous than for everyone else.

Interestingly enough, many people who have struggled with overweight all their lives and have never been able to succeed for long on other diets have only a very moderate degree of metabolic resistance to weight loss, and lose quite quickly and easily on the Atkins diet. No one is more surprised than a person in that condition who finds the pounds swiftly vanishing. As an old pro in this arena, I have to tell you it's a particular pleasure witnessing their joy.

To all my readers I want to say: *I hope to amaze you, as I amazed millions of dieters in the past.* I want you to surprise yourself. Never think it can't be done. It *has* been done.

This is a proven diet—enlarged, refined, and, I think, made better. But still, in its essence, it is the same diet that has helped millions of people to lose weight. *No other diet in the world has its track record.*

# 2

# What This Book Will Reveal to You

If you have a weight problem, I certainly have the qualifications to help you. I suppose no diet book has ever been written by a doctor with so many weight-loss successes to his credit, including the vast majority of the 25,000 overweight individuals I have treated in my office at the Atkins Center, a clinical facility that overflows a six-story building in Manhattan. No doubt there are also successes among the millions who have read my books or healthletters or listened to my weeknightly radio broadcasts.

This level of success could not have been achieved by using a system similar to everyone else's or even a variation on the theme. It could only have been achieved by offering a revolutionary departure from the conventional diet wisdom. We went against the grain, stuck to our scientific principles, and provided a diet quite unlike all the others you may have been exposed to.

My purpose is not to be critical of other diets, for with

enough determination, all can be made to work for a number of persevering individuals. Unfortunately, in the past decade there has been a tendency to disseminate *only one diet*, as if it were the be-all and end-all for everyone—the only diet that works.

Never before in my career have I heard so many patients say, "I know what I'm supposed to eat, but I just can't make it work for me." The trouble is, they *don't* know what they're supposed to eat, but they've heard the wrong answer so often, they think it's an unchallenged truth.

You've heard the expression "fad diet." Fad refers to that which achieves a widespread, if evanescent, popularity. It conveys no value judgement on the ultimate worth of the thing described. The current diet fad is the low-fat, high-carbohydrate diet espoused by virtually every nationwide chain of diet centers, by the monthly magazine articles, the media advice-givers, professional organizations, and even by federal government bulletins. Low-fat dieting works for some people. I know that's true; I've seen it happen. But the notion that it works for everyone is sadly misinformed. And, if you delve into the medical literature, you'll discover that the apparent unanimity about its benefits is *only* apparent. Moreover, if you're overweight, you may be living testimony to the fact that it doesn't work for you. My experience leads me to say that for tens of millions of people—the majority of the overweight in America—it does not readily work. It runs directly counter to scientific evidence about the human metabolism and the actions of carbohydrate foods.

You may recall that twenty years ago, Britain's preeminent nutritionist, Dr. John Yudkin, announced that the majority of British physicians recommended a low-carbohydrate diet, and that the majority of American dieters, having read books by me, as well as by Drs. Taller,

Stillman, and Tarnower, had created such an awareness of the principle of carbohydrate restriction that such dieting was elevated to "fad" status. Before that, calorie counting had been the fad. But has there been any change in the physiology of obese humans in these years? I doubt it. The pendulum merely swings.

Another swing of the pendulum is sorely needed. The current fad is based on the kind of simplistic logic that captures the fancy of the unsophisticated: "If you don't want to be fat, don't eat fat; if you don't want cholesterol, don't eat cholesterol." It's the "You-are-what-you-eat" argument, totally devoid of any reference to known metabolic mechanisms. And the results are dismal.

The danger of the low-fat fad is clearly apparent from the study of USDA statistics. The pendulum began to swing toward fat restriction in 1975. That's when per-capita consumption of red meat began its decline, and fish, chicken, and skimmed milk showed rather surprising gains. For the last fifteen years, the movement in these directions has been steady. But the figures carry with them an ominous warning. In those 15 years the per-capita consumption of sugars (including corn syrup) has escalated from a world-leading 118 pounds a year to 137.5 pounds![1] Let's translate that into terms you understand best. We're consuming nearly 680 calories of sugar a day. And that's the average man, woman, or child, not the sugar addict. This means that, by a conservative reckoning, anywhere from ⅓ to ¼ of all the calories an adult puts into his or her body each day comes from nutritionally empty and metabolically-harmful caloric sweeteners.

If I can't convince you that this much sugar is a major potential health risk, then I would probably have a tough time convincing you to wear clothes in winter.

I'm not about to fall into the error of the low-fat dieting

devotees who claim that their diet works for everyone. I would feel rather foolish if I did. No diet works for everyone. Human biological individuality is very marked. Nonetheless, for the past 25 years, I've worked at perfecting a diet that experience has shown me is successful with the great majority of patients. And this is a diet that makes them feel better, that supports their long-term health, and that controls their weight without hunger or discomfort—sizable advantages.

## Nature's Diet

I can't emphasize too strongly that nature really did provide for us very well. Even before the onset of agriculture, the human animal was able, for millions of years, to remain strong and healthy in conditions of often savage deprivation by eating the fish and animals that scampered and swam around him, and the fruits and vegetables and berries that grew nearby. Without medicine, without expertise, without insulated housing or reliable heating, we nevertheless survived.

We were immensely aided by the fact that the dietary side of our primitive lifestyle was enormously healthy.

The dietary side of our sophisticated, modern lifestyle is enormously *un*healthy.

I'm optimistic that you'll learn to fully appreciate the fact that fresh food—unrefined, unprocessed, un-manufactured, unimproved, un-"enriched"—is splendidly right for you.

The Atkins diet that I have high hopes you'll be eating for the rest of your life contains, in its most liberal, lifetime maintenance form, most vegetables, nuts and seeds, some grains and starches to the extent that your metabolism allows, and occasional fruits. It also contains a sumptuous variety of delicious protein foods and some high-fat foods like butter and cream that you'll find stricken from nearly every other current diet.

This isn't because this is a high-fat diet. It isn't that, although heaven knows I've often had the accusation thrown in my face. At the moment, virtually everything is laid to the discredit of dietary fat, and yet its advantages for a dieter seem never to be mentioned. Fat satiates the appetite. Fat stops carbohydrate craving. And fat, in the absence of carbohydrate, accelerates the burning of stored fat. The wise dieter can use fat to his advantage.

Still the Atkins diet is not a high-fat diet, partly because some of the largest sources of fat in the modern diet are the junk foods and convenience foods I would never allow you to eat. On the Atkins diet you will be eating a larger quantity of meat, fish, fowl, eggs, and butter than you consumed before you went on it, but you'll probably be eating less fat overall.

Even though I will be showing you the benefits of fat and protein, I must emphasize that the real source of health improvement on this diet will come from excluding the typically gargantuan modern consumption of junk carbohydrates. In Chapter 3, I'll explain *hyperinsulinism* and, as soon as you begin to understand this fundamental modern concept—one of the genuine, scientific/medical breakthroughs of the last decade and a half—you'll understand why a *low-fat diet* is not a necessity for a person who's on *this* diet. The health improvements, inseparable from a diet that excludes all the possible combinations of sugar and white flour, are more than sufficient to make the Atkins diet one of the healthiest eating programs you could ever embark on.

I must make this point here at the outset because it's fundamental to everything I want you to know. You may buy this book and I may have a publishing success because you want to be a health-club knockout, and that's fine with me, but it wouldn't be a sufficient reason for writing this book.

This diet is intended to be the basis for your good health. I have *no doubts* it can be just that. My current patients aren't fools—very few people are when it comes to figuring out how they feel—and what works for them is what I'm offering *you*. The important thing is that it made them healthier. The fact that it took off their excess weight was, for most of them, merely a side benefit. But, if the emotional benefits were a side issue, the medical benefits were front and center. Overweight has complex but undeniable connections with ill health. I couldn't let my patients stay fat, *because* they had come to me to get healthy, and ideal health requires ideal weight.

In your case, you've made contact with me to get slim, and to do that, I'm going to have to make you healthier too. On the Atkins program, I don't think you could separate those results if you wanted to.

## But, Dr. Atkins, I Want to Have Fun Eating, Have Fun Living, and Lose Weight for Life

And so you shall. Do you believe that a man can go from gaining ½ pound a week to losing 3.9 pounds a week without significantly altering the number of calories he consumes? Let me introduce you to Harry Kronberg then. There are lots of Harry Kronbergs in my practice, but I didn't have to scratch my head trying to figure out which one to use because Harry happened to come in for a visit the day I was writing this chapter. I want you to pay close attention to his story and try not to give way to disbelief, because these results are real. And I think I'm going to bring Harry back to take repeated bows at a number of places in this book.

Harry Kronberg, the 39-year-old manager of a lumber yard, came to me with a heart arrhythmia, and a desperate weight problem. He had been chubby even as a child, but now things were out of hand. A few years before, he had gone to a diet center and lowered his weight from 245 to 185 on a low-fat diet. And he kept it all off, except for 95 pounds.

That's right, when Harry came to see me, he tipped the scales at 280, and on a 5'6½" frame that was ponderous. In the previous 35 months, eating a relatively starchy, low-fat diet of approximately 1700 calories a day, he had gained 70 pounds, exactly 2 pounds a month, clearly indicating that he had a metabolic problem. Then he went on my diet, the diet you're going to read about in this book. This diet has radically restricted his carbohydrates while allowing him to eat freely of meat, fish, fowl and eggs. Harry was told to eat as much as he wanted. The calorie count was strikingly similar to what he had been eating on his previous diet, but he never missed a meal, and never suffered a moment's hunger. The result was that in the first three months (to the day) that he's been on the diet, he's lost 50.5 pounds (3.9 pounds a week), and he's still losing at a steady three pounds weekly. His heart symptoms have gone away, his cholesterol has gone down from 207 to 134, his triglycerides from 134 to 31.

I think I can fairly say that Harry was impressed. In fact, he said to me, "I'm not going to stop taking these vitamins you're giving me, doctor. There's something in them that makes me lose weight." Well, there was something in them that made his experience run smoothly, but I have to confess there was nothing in them that made him lose weight.

## But Will I Be Able to Enjoy Eating on This Diet?

It will really surprise me if you can't. Let's take a look at Patricia Finley's menu. She's been on the Atkins *Induction* diet for three and a half months and she's lost 31 pounds. She has another 35 to go, but I think she'll get there. Incidentally, most of the patients I'll tell you about in the course of this book will have reached their ideal weight already, but I don't see any reason to restrict myself to them. I've had so many thousands of dieting successes that it isn't really that brazen of me to assume that a large majority of the still-in-the-process-of-losing dieters that I tell you about will also succeed.

Patricia, who used to eat quite a lot of starches and who would sometimes go on massive dessert binges when she was under pressure, has converted to a tasty low-carbohydrate diet.

For breakfast, she eats bacon and eggs, or a cheese omelet, or some vegetables with blue cheese. Lunch can be tuna fish or chicken with a sumptuous salad. But sometimes, she'll have chopped sirloin, sautéed with onions, chili powder and peppers. Patricia enjoys having olives or asparagus spears for snacks, but she puts the greatest amount of energy and attention into dinner. She finds that it isn't possible to feel deprived when you're enjoying a meal consisting of guacamole (for the uninitiated that's mashed avocado mixed with tomatoes, onion, and seasoning) and strips of chicken and steak. Add to that her passion for grated courgettes in olive oil with butter and nutmeg, her liking for broccoli with lemon butter sauce, and her homemade recipe for chicken soup, and what do you get? Starvation? *Not.* Patricia also enjoys lamb shanks with chopped onions, cooked with olive oil, herbs, and "Crazy Mixed Up Salt." And she assures me this is only a small sample of the food she finds it possible and delightful to eat—*on her diet*.

Yes, that's a strict weight-loss diet I've been describing. A diet that you can adapt to your own individual taste as long as you eat only permitted foods.

I think there's food for thought in such a food story. Now, let me mention some of the other things this book with show you:

## DIET EXPERIENCE AND WEIGHT CHANGES

- How to create an edge for yourself, a metabolic advantage that allows you to lose weight at a higher calorie intake than you've ever lost on before.
- How you'll succeed even though you may have always been hungry, tired, depressed, and unsuccessful on other diets. You won't be any of those things on this one.
- Why you won't need willpower on the Atkins diet.
- How binge eating can be stopped in a day.
- How you can reach your ideal weight by burning your excess fat as fuel—the marvelous condition of Benign Dietary Ketosis.
- How to insure that what you lose is fat and not lean body tissue.
- How you can keep those excess pounds off forever by a lifetime diet change in which you keep the same diet you lost on as your basic diet and add to it some of your most desired foods.
- How you can determine your degree of metabolic resistance to weight loss, and how to modify your diet accordingly.
- How to use the novel Atkins Fat Fast if you have severe metabolic resistance.

- How you can use nutritional medicine to help overcome metabolic resistance.

## HEALTH CHANGES

- How to overcome Diet-Related Disorder—this is the *evil* trio of hypoglycemia, yeast infections, and food intolerances.
- How you can avoid the health catastrophe of hyperinsulinism.
- How you can custom design your exercise program.
- How to improve your energy level.
- How, in conjunction with the diet, you can organize a program of nutritional supplementation that will do wonders for your health.
- How to lower your cholesterol level on the diet and improve your other blood-lipid values.
- How to use the diet to overcome medical conditions, including diabetes, heart disease, and high blood pressure, that are so often associated with obesity.

## FOOD CHANGES

- How to use the rich, sumptuous foods forbidden on other diets to make your new diet a luxurious eating pattern fit for a prince or princess.
- How to create super-palatable substitute foods for the carbohydrate items you love.
- How to function in supermarkets, restaurants, and at dinner parties after you've begun your new lifestyle.
- How to personalize your diet so it is uniquely suited to your tastes, lifestyle, and metabolism.
- How animal foods can suppress your craving for sweets.

**PERSONAL AND FAMILY CHANGES**

- How to explain your diet to family and friends.
- How to eat comfortably with them, even if their style of eating remains different from yours.

**HOW TO MAINTAIN THE DIET**

- What to do if you have cravings for sweets and starches.
- How to go on a maintenance diet that will already be second nature to you.
- How to follow the maintenance plan for a lifetime.
- How to break the diet and still survive.
- How to use dietary fat to enhance your health.
- How to adjust and return to your ideal weight if you gain weight at some point.
- How to never be more than five pounds above your ideal weight.

## This Just Might Be the Diet for You

That's an ambitious program I've just outlined, and I have wide-eyed and romantic moments in which I almost wish I could tell you it's going to be difficult and that you'll have to summon up all your reserves of energy and courage to march in step with it. But, the truth is, I can't claim anything so heroic. It's going to be surprisingly easy, and it's going to make all the difference in your life.

I've spent thirty years in the trenches with people who didn't like what fat was doing to them—young and old, some only ten pounds overweight, some two hundred. I've seen people sit down in my office and start to cry uncontrollably because they were so appalled by their repeated failures, and so despairing of help.

I hope I've finally convinced you that you're holding help in your hands right now.

# 3

## Is This You?—Three Types Who Need a Ketogenic Diet

You have a right to wonder if I'm talking about you. I've said that if you have a weight problem, there's better than a ninety percent chance I can help you solve it. Is that really relevant to your own particular, very individual weight situation? In order to help you understand where you do or don't fit in, I'll profile my typical obesity patient. It's not hard to do. There are several signature patterns about overweight due to disorders of carbohydrate metabolism that are instantly recognizable.

### Does This Describe You?
### Group A Responders

- Are you overweight despite the fact that you don't eat that much?

- Do you follow standard weight-loss diets and still make no headway losing weight or get stuck far short of your goal?
- Have you noticed that slim people definitely consume more food and more daily calories than you do?
- Are you just plain unpleasantly hungry on low-calorie diets?
- Do you find the amount of food you eat is really the least you can take in without feeling physically unsatisfied?
- Do you feel a sense of unfulfillment when you eat a normal meal?
- Do you find that when you eat the amount of food that feels just right, you don't lose—or you even gain?
- Have you often said, "I'm really very disciplined; it must be my metabolism?"

## Or is This a Better Description Of You?
## Group B Responders

- Do you have an inexplicable obsession with food?
- A habit of night eating?
- A tendency to binge?
- A craving for such carbohydrate foods as sweets, pastas, and breads?
- Do you nibble all day long when food is available?
- A strong desire to eat again shortly after you've eaten to fullness?
- Do you consider yourself a compulsive eater? Have you ever said, "I only wish I could control my eating behavior?"
- Do you have specific symptoms of ill health, such as

the ones I'm about to list, that lessen or vanish as soon as you eat? Do you suffer:

- Irritability?
- Inexplicable drops in your strength and stamina at various times throughout the day—often overwhelming bouts of fatigue, especially in the afternoon?
- Mood swings?
- Difficulty in concentrating?
- Sleep difficulties—often a need for considerable quantities of sleep, sometimes a habit of waking from a sound sleep?
- Anxiety, sadness, and depression for which there's no situational explanation?
- Dizziness, trembling, palpitations?
- Brain fog and loss of mental acuity?

## Or Perhaps This Describes You:
## Group C Responders

- Do you have a single food or beverage you feel you could not do without?
- Would you pass up an elegant meal to get your favorite food?
- Is there a specific food or beverage that makes you *feel* better as soon as you get it?
- Do you ever think, "I wonder if I could be addicted to that food/beverage?"
- Do you feel this way about a *category* of foods? (Sweets, soft drinks, dairy products, grains, etc.)

## What These Answers Tell You

Now let's see what you do with this information. First of all, let me say I would find it hard to believe there could be a significantly overweight person who had no "yes" responses. If you respond in the affirmative, then this book is about you and for you, and I probably do have a solution for your problem. If most of your "yes" responses are in group A, you have a metabolic problem, manifested either by a) a relative inability to lose weight or maintain weight loss, or by b) hunger or inability to achieve and maintain satiety.

If most of your "yes" responses were to group B questions then you probably have glucose intolerance, commonly known as hypoglycemia.

If most of your affirmatives were to the group C statements, then you probably have an addiction to the food/beverage you singled out. Other terms for the phenomenon are "food allergy" or the more accurate "individual food intolerance."

If you're a group C responder, and the food/beverage you've identified is or contains a carbohydrate, then you have a carbohydrate addiction, and this book will provide you with more answers than you've thought possible.

## These Three Responses are All Facets of the Same Problem

You A and B responders (and most of you C responders as well) have a condition that is the common denominator behind nearly all your problems, and it's called hyperinsulinism.

Before I explain the significance of hyperinsulinism and

the very good news of how easily you can tame it with this diet, I want you to reflect on the significance of eating.

Stop and ask yourself, *"What else do I do in the course of a day that constitutes such a dramatic and intense alteration of my body as swallowing the food I do?"*

Between the time you rise and the time you go to bed, you put pounds of organic matter into your mouth. Your body runs on it. Don't be surprised that if you make bad choices, you'll pay a price.

Now before I explain more about the mechanism of the metabolic problems that result, let's look at the impact of sugar and carbohydrate consumption upon real people.

## Life Without Control

Food-obsessive behavior is common, and some of the tougher cases can be difficult to cure even on this diet and impossible on any other. Certain writers in the diet area have spoken of carbohydrate addiction, and the term isn't a bad one. The men and women who binge and fantasize and often almost live for food are as much between a rock and a hard place as the addict of alcohol or narcotics. They desperately need a metabolic approach to their problem.

Gordon Lingard, a real estate executive, was an extreme example. He was 53 when he came to see me and was 306 pounds on a 5'10" frame. Gordon had progressed from a normal weight in college (when he was a lifeguard) to extreme obesity by his late twenties. His weight had gone as high as 450 pounds. He had no hormonal imbalances, and he had tried everything—stomach stapling, emetics, laxatives, and every diet from B to Z.

Gordon was as inexplicable to himself as to his many doctors. All he knew was that he had to eat. The cravings were indescribable. He told me he was constantly planning his next binge. Gallons of ice cream disappeared as swiftly as an ordinary carbohydrate addict downs a candy bar. Sugar was Gordon's master obsession.

> "There was never a moment I didn't desire it. Often I would shake until I could put some sugar in my mouth. The symptoms were totally physical, and they were really frightening. For me there was nothing else but food. I had an hour's drive from my office to my home, and I knew every restaurant, every diner, every candy machine, every soft drink dispenser along the whole route."

I bet you'd be willing to bet this was almost entirely psychological—and you'd be wrong.

Gordon Lingard's case was a special one and, for a while, treating him was no cinch. In his case, some of the vitamin aids I describe in Chapter 21 were an important part of the solution. But what I'd like you to realize is that Gordon's problem was only a more extreme version of the problems so many overweight people have. His difficulties were basically metabolic difficulties, and they were solvable metabolically. Today Gordon Lingard has nearly reached his normal weight for the first time in thirty years, and he no longer feels the drive to consume sugar.

Gordon had failed repeatedly on low-fat/low-calorie diets. And why not? His problem lay in his metabolic response to carbohydrates. To solve an out-of-control situation like this by restricting calories while not restricting carbohydrates is like marching into the surf with a firm intention of turning back the ocean.

You may have picked up this book with the secret inner conviction that you're a "compulsive eater." In all probability, you're a carbohydrate addict. How many compulsive eaters of steaks have you come across? Not too many, huh? Let me tell you, it's a rare breed.

## A Craving for Sweets is Often a Sign

Many people start off when they're kids eating the so-called "balanced" diet, but by the time they're adults, it's becoming progressively less balanced. Eating didn't seem all that important to them once, but now it does. So they look at their waistline, they look at their eating, and they realize they have a problem. Usually they notice that their taste in food has gone off in a specific direction.

Carbohydrates now form the bulk of what they eat; breads and baked goods, cakes and candies, pasta and popcorn. Surprising and illogical food cravings are typical. Do you ever have dinner with a big dessert and almost immediately afterwards find that you want some candy? That's a sign, as is fatigue, that your carbohydrate metabolism is out of whack.

It's not that you eat when you're not hungry, but you seem to be *always* hungry. And yet when you eat the carbohydrate food you crave, you feel only briefly better. Your situation is the exact opposite of the one you'll experience on the Atkins diet. There, you'll find that your appetite has diminished, but your satisfaction in the food you eat has increased.

## Do *You* Feel Like a Compulsive Eater?

Many carbohydrate addicts could no more walk past a refrigerator without opening it than Martina Navratilova could let a short lob drift overhead without smashing it.

I've heard many patients say, "It's irresistible, Dr. Atkins. I'm a slave. How can you possibly help me?"

I say, "That's alright—your compulsions have no terrors for me and soon they won't for you. When you pass that refrigerator, open it, have some chicken salad or sliced pot roast. If you eat the way I'm asking you to eat, you'll find that food is still delicious, but the compulsions will fade."

You see, your food compulsion isn't a character disorder, it's a chemical disorder called hyperinsulinism, and you have it simply because you've eaten the same unhealthy way that *most* people in our culture do.

## The Diet That Does It

There are marked similarities in the diet eaten in all the developed, modern countries of the world, so, for now, I'll just mention the statistics for the United States. Once you understand what healthy eating can be like, you'll find them as bizarre and shocking as I do.

First, and worst, there's sugar. Let me tell you just a little bit about that. Two hundred years ago, the average person ate less than ten pounds of sugar a year. Then almost exactly a hundred years ago, the lid blew off. In the 1890s, the craze for cola beverages swept the nation—which means that when we were thirsty and craved water, we got sugar as well. The net result was that the sugar intake, which had been twelve pounds a year in 1828 was nearly ten times that in 1928. The latest Department of Agriculture statistics show that the average American consumed 118 pounds of caloric sweeteners (principally refined sugar and high fructose corn syrup) in 1975 and 137.5 pounds in 1990.[1] This means that sugar and corn syrup alone form a whopping percentage of the average American's diet. Those figures translate into 170 grams of sugar (and corn syrup) a day. Since the average person eats 425 grams of carbohydrates a day, 105 grams of protein, and 168 grams of fat, sugar constitutes 40% of the carbohydrate total and nearly one fourth of our daily food by weight.

Sugar has no nutritional value and is directly harmful to your health. Despite vociferous attempts to defend it, there are hundreds of studies that clearly show how deadly its effects can be.[2] I won't go into them now, because I want you to learn about hyperinsulinism in the next chapter, and sugar deserves a whole book.

But I do want you to remember what the modern western diet consists of, especially in America. Remember too that if you don't take your sugar straight, you'll find it already inserted into a thousand different foods and beverages before they come to your table, put, for the most part, into stuff that, if it hadn't been made so sweet, you'd wrinkle your nose up at. Sugar is the American food industry's friend, and if you've allowed yourself to be overawed by the vast quantities of anti-fat propaganda issued forth in the guise of nutritional education during the past ten years, you may almost have forgotten what's *really* packed on to those supermarket shelves.

Let me assure you that eating meat, fish, and fowl isn't a health hardship—it's what the human carnivore has eaten for millions of years.

Look at the way people ate in the 19th century. They were liberal in the use of butter and lard, they were beef and pork eaters, and their eggs were unrestricted. Yet hardly any one died of heart attacks. Paul Dudley White, who was Eisenhower's personal cardiologist, recalled that he didn't see his first heart attack until after his first year of postgraduate training in the 1920s. If you want an even more illuminating fact chew on this one: The Frenchman of today with his butter-, cheese-, and goose-liver-pâté-laden diet has a heart disease rate 60% lower than his American peers.[3] (The Frenchwoman does even better—she has the lowest heart disease rate in the western world.)

So what caused the avalanche of degenerative diseases? The only thing I ask is that you observe how our diet actually changed in the last century. Not only were colas invented in the 1890s, but to make matters worse, the mills that could refine wheat into a white, nutritionally barren flour were developed in the same decade. Once that flour was put together with sweetness and saltiness, we had the makings of the junk food culture of America and many of the other developed countries—but not all of them.

Let's look at the Frenchman again—the fellow with his teeth buried in the *pâté de foie gras*. As anyone who's been to France or who watches *Sixty Minutes* knows, the French are far less afflicted by obesity and heart disease than Americans. Yet their diet is *higher* in fat. (They eat comparable amounts of meat and fish, four times as much butter, and twice as much cheese as Americans.) What does it all mean? *Could it have anything to do with the fact that the American per capita consumption of sugar is 5½ times that of the French?*

Yet we all know that fat is the source of all ills. Don't we?

## Keep Your Eye on Your Metabolism

Sugar, you see, activates certain metabolic processes that are both harmful to your health and folly for your waistline. Sugar is a metabolic poison.

You could, of course, ignore this fact and attempt to control your overweight by calorie counting and eating only so many pieces of this and only so many grams of that. That is, you could direct yourself to the quantity instead of the quality of your diet. Isn't that what conventional dieting advises you to do?

But I want to tell you that *the likelihood that you'll permanently lose weight by controlling your calories is almost nil.*

Bet you guessed that before now. Common sense dictates that when a lot of people try the same answer to the same problem and they all fail, there's something wrong with their solution. You may have tried a low-calorie diet. I'm sure you've seen other people try it. After a promising start, they end up as failures. Perhaps there is no sense beating your head against the wall.

Melissa Jackson, a 35-year-old insurance executive, came to me weighing 223 pounds on a 5'4" frame. She had tried literally every diet that she read about or that anyone proposed to her since she was 16. She had been fat even as a child. The situation had always tormented and obsessed her, because not only did fat interfere with her life, it was something she simply couldn't handle. She tried diet pills and liquid-protein diets, and then Weight Watchers and a long list of other low-fat diets. By the time she was in her thirties, she was used to being told after months of conscientious struggle that she was "plateauing at 200 pounds."

"The situation was out of my control and because of that I didn't like myself. It got to the point where I would be hungry all the time on low-fat or low-calorie diets, and I'd lose maybe two pounds a month. Then I couldn't even lose that. I would literally starve myself to the point of collapse, and after four or five days of eating nothing I'd find I'd lost half a pound."

Melissa Jackson went on the Atkins diet and lost 77 pounds in a year. Without hunger. She has always liked—and during a large part of her life had craved—cake, candy, soda, and pasta, and she gave those foods up. But everything else she enjoyed eating, she ate. After the first few weeks, she didn't miss what she wasn't having. She had more energy, needed less sleep, her cholesterol level went down, and her ratio of HDL to LDL cholesterol went up. She used to wear a size 20 dress, now wears a size 8 or 10.

If all this still seems mysterious to you, I can only say, *read on.*

I said one whole large category of obesity, which we agreed to call group A, was metabolic. Let's learn in what specific way.

# 4

# Insulin—The Hormone That Makes You Fat

I'm going to talk to you about the hormone whose name you've heard many times—insulin. Even though this chapter is going to cover some technical points, I think you ought to read it carefully, because for many of you, the answers are here.

Almost everyone has heard of insulin because it's given to certain kinds of diabetics to help control their blood-sugar levels. This insulin hormone is one of the most powerful and efficient substances that the body uses to control the use, distribution and storage of energy.

Your body is an energy machine, never resting, always metabolically active—and it powers its operations mainly through the use of glucose (a basic form of sugar) in the blood. It *must* have the glucose, and even under conditions of starvation it will continue to obtain it so long as there's anything in the body it can convert into glucose. Thus, even on a prolonged, total fast, the body can maintain its glucose level within a rather narrow normal range. As a general rule, of course, the body obtains its principal supply of fuel by eating.

## Eating a Meal

Dinnertime comes. You sit down at the table and consume a three-course dinner. What does your body do? Somewhere between chewing and excreting, it absorbs certain substances from your food, mostly across the surface of your small intestine. At that moment, the food is actually entering your body for use.

From the carbohydrates you eat, your body will absorb simple sugars, all of which either are, or quickly and easily become, glucose. From fats, it absorbs glycerol and fatty acids, and from proteins it absorbs amino acids, the building blocks of protein.

Obviously, if you eat a lot of carbohydrate, you'll produce a lot of glucose in your blood. Sounds good doesn't it? All that energy coursing through your system. Eat sugar and starches and fruits and you're going to get those blood-sugar levels up fast, aren't you?

If you love candy bars, perhaps you're saying, "That's great, the more I eat, the stronger I'll be."

Alas, a bad mistake. You see, your body was designed way back in pre-Neanderthal days when they didn't have any candy bars. Your body's capacity to deal with unrefined foods as they occur in nature is quite adequate; its capacity to deal with an excess of quick-energy, simple sugars is pretty poor, which is the true reason why our 20th-century diet gets us into trouble.

If you don't understand this yet, then let's look at what

insulin and the other energy-controlling hormones do when you eat.

## As Your Blood Glucose Rises

If your blood-sugar levels go sharply up, as they do soon after you eat carbohydrate, your body makes an instant decision. How much of that pure energy is it going to use for immediate needs and how much will it store for future requirements?

*The instrument of its decision is insulin, because insulin governs the processing of blood sugar.*

Insulin is manufactured in a part of your pancreas called the islets of Langerhans. As the sugar in your blood goes up, insulin rushes forth and converts a portion of that glucose to glycogen, a starch stored in the muscles and the liver and readily available for energy use. If all the glycogen storage areas are filled, and there is still more glucose in the blood beyond that which the body needs to function, insulin will convert the excess to fatty tissue called triglyceride, which we carry on our bodies as the main chemical constituent of adipose tissue—the stuff you're reading this book to get rid of. That's why insulin has been called "the fat-producing hormone."

Insulin is a pretty efficient worker. If it were not, your body could not process glucose, its basic fuel, and blood glucose levels would escalate while the body searched for other fuels—first your fat stores, and then your muscle tissue itself. That's what happens in insulin-deficient diabetes when no insulin is present. On the other hand, suppose insulin is too effective, or in too great a supply. It would process too much, leaving too little to circulate in the blood to fuel the brain. The body attempts to adjust by liberating counterregulatory hormones—mainly glucagon, adreno-corticoids and adrenalin to raise the glucose level, but a stiff dose of insulin can overpower the lot of them. Fortunately for most of us, this glucose balancing act takes place automatically and our blood sugar stays in a fairly narrow, normal range of between 65 and 110 mg per 100 cc of blood.

## Hyperinsulinism

It's easy to see that there's a relationship between the kinds of foods you eat and the amount of insulin in your bloodstream. Carbohydrate food, especially simple carbohydrates such as sugar, honey, milk, and fruit, which contain glucose, and refined carbohydrates like flour, white rice, and potato starch, which, because they are readily absorbed through the gut, speedily convert to glucose, require a lot of insulin. Proteins and fat, on the other hand, produce almost no alteration in the insulin level.

As an overweight person becomes fatter, the insulin problem expands too. Numerous studies have shown that the obese (and diabetic) individual is extremely unresponsive to the action of insulin. That's where you will see the term "insulin resistance." Carbohydrates are triggering the release of large quantities of the hormone, but the body is incapable of utilizing it efficiently. The body responds by putting out yet more insulin. Consequently, overweight and high insulin levels are almost synonymous.*

What appears to happen is that the insulin receptors on

*And, to confuse the cart-before-the-horse issue a little more, it has been shown experimentally that high levels of insulin can themselves *increase* insulin resistance. This means that the high insulin levels can be the *cause* of the entire vicious carbohydrate—insulin—insulin resistance cycle.

the surfaces of the body's cells are blocked from carrying out their function, which in turn prevents insulin from stimulating the transfer of glucose to the cells for energy use. It's one reason why overweight individuals are tired much of the time. Because insulin is not effective in converting glucose into energy, it transfers more and more into stored fat. You'd like to slim down, but your body is, in fact, becoming a fat-producing machine.

Your body's hormonal system is now in desperate straits. Insulin—your fat producing hormone—is now being secreted all the time to deal with high sugar levels, and it is doing its job less and less effectively. In time, even the insulin receptors that convert glucose to fat start getting worn out—this forecasts diabetes. In severe cases, the pancreas itself becomes exhausted by the effort required to produce so much insulin—and a high-insulin diabetes changes into the insulin-dependent type.

To have your insulin levels more or less permanently high and yet to be resistant to the effects of insulin is what's called *hyper*insulinism.

## Diabetes to Follow?

The next step in this tragic process is indeed diabetes, a disease that's *epidemic* among the overweight.[1]

In this situation, the first sign of diabetes is often that the obese person, who's never been able to lose weight, starts losing weight inexplicably. That's because blood sugar is no longer being converted into energy *or* body fat. Insulin, that crucial fat-producing hormone, has been reduced to impotence.

Diabetes is a heavy-duty illness, not only vastly increasing the risk of heart disease, but having long-term adverse effects on the eyes, kidneys, nervous system, and skin.

## A Few More Insulin Problems

Not all fat people reach diabetes, but afflicted as they are with hyperinsulinism, they are in a pre-diabetic condition that has its own significant perils. Those of you who responded "yes" to the B group of symptoms should recognize yourselves.

First, and most noticeable, the persistent bouts of daily fatigue that overweight people can't seem to do anything about; then shakiness and hunger often traveling in company with depression, irritability, and poor mental function. Not only are fat people tired because their cells are not effectively taking in energy, but off and on throughout the day, they are the victims of hypoglycemia, or low blood sugar, the ironical consequence of consuming too much sugar.

As a man or woman goes deeper into carbohydrate-induced metabolic disorder, hypoglycemia becomes more and more ingrained. Just a touch of glucose will send insulin pouring forth, dropping blood-sugar levels to an abnormal low. If you are a group B person, you become tired, irritable, and hungry. A mid-afternoon attack of hypoglycemic exhaustion is very typical. This, of course, makes you hungry, you eat more, and the whole sad process goes on. Thus you see that what you thought was compulsivity, a behavioral problem, is really a glucose-triggered mechanism, a metabolic problem. So don't feel so guilty.

There is more to say about hypoglycemia and I'll be doing that in Chapter 11, when I describe it as one of the branches of a very prevalent modern epidemic, which I call Diet-Related Disorder.

Meanwhile, let me point out that your high insulin levels have other sad results.

- Insulin increases salt and water retention—a recipe for both hypertension and continued overweight.
- Insulin aggravates hypertension by increasing the responsiveness of arteries to the effects of adrenaline.
- Insulin affects the body's supply of neurotransmitters and can cause sleep disorders.
- Insulin provokes the liver into producing more LDL cholesterol. It may be one of the most significant components in the cholesterol/heart disease connection. Since obesity and high insulin travel in company, this is probably the reason why overweight is such a major risk factor for a heart attack.

## This is Why You Can't Lose Weight

The last few pages recount a horror story which might be headlined: *Innocent Possessor of Human Body is Turned Upon by Own Hormones!* But we did it to ourselves, you know. Remember, no culture in world history has ever consumed even a fraction of the amount of sugar that we Westerners do now.

Perhaps you've been overweight for a long time. Once there was a stage in the progress of your metabolic disease when you could lose weight pretty well, if you sharply cut your caloric intake. You'd gain the pounds back, but at least at the price of hunger, you could take them off for a while, if you really needed to.

Now you may be past that stage. If you are, insulin has

really closed the trap. The pancreas, faced with your abuse of simple and refined carbohydrates, has become so efficient at secreting it, that just a touch of blood sugar will release a flood.

*Mediated by high insulin levels, your body has become intent on saving fat.* And, in so doing, group A responders will recognize the role that excess insulin plays in preventing weight loss, either directly by lowering your apparent caloric needs, or indirectly, by giving you a constant sensation of hunger that can be satiated only by constant overeating.

Now that you've reached this understanding of metabolic overweight, imagine the fat person who goes into his doctor's office and is told, "Well, if you just had a little more willpower . . ." Sad, isn't it.

To lose weight, you're going to need the low-carbohydrate diet offered in this book. You may also need the two other legs of the Atkins Program triad: exercise and nutritional supplementation.

## How It's Done

I know I've produced a really heart-sinking analysis of why the fat stays on your body. So, what does one do now?

One makes an end run around insulin.

One needs glucose for fuel, but one doesn't need to get it from one's diet. It's time to turn off the insulin spigot. Weight loss? The answer lies in two golden words: KETOSIS and LIPOLYSIS.

# 5

# The Great Fat Meltdown— The Secret of a Ketogenic Diet

Once you've been fat for some time, you're in a metabolic trap, a sort of high-walled box created in large part by high insulin levels.

You may already have noticed that you're trapped. Certainly, trying diet after diet and failing on all of them is depressing. I know from personal experience and from the comments of thousands of my patients just how tightly the lid of metabolic obesity seems to press down. Ketosis—the Benign Dietary Ketosis I'm talking about— opens the lid up.

The term ketosis, when it applies to the benign diet-induced type we're talking about, is really a shortening of the term ketosis/lipolysis, which is enough of a tongue twister that you can see why it is commonly referred to only by the name "ketosis," and why the diet that is responsible for this remarkable (to dieters) achievement is called the "ketogenic diet."

The definition of lipolysis sounds like Nirvana to dieters and diet doctors alike. It means "the process of dissolving fat." Now, isn't that exactly why we're all gathered here today?

When your fat is used up metabolically, it breaks down into glycerol and free fatty acids, which in turn break down into pairings of two-carbon compounds called "ketone bodies," leaving a newer fatty acid, shorter in chain length by the two-carbon fragment that entered the metabolic pool to be used as fuel. Apparently this is the *only* metabolic pathway for fat breakdown (lipolysis).

Therefore, there is no lipolysis without ketosis, no ketosis without lipolysis. The two terms are biologically linked, and therefore, it is appropriate that they be linguistically linked.

How does the process actually work? Are there any drawbacks? There are plenty of laypeople and even physicians who think there must be. Burning one's fat off sounds like a faddish trick. These folks give a skeptical shrug and say, "I'm sure people lose some weight on your diet, Dr. Atkins, but don't they gain it right back again?"

The interesting thing is, not many do. The Atkins weight-maintenance diet, though more indulgent, is quite similar to the Atkins weight-loss diet, and weight regain is not very common.

As for the weight-loss portion, that is simple and overwhelmingly effective. I don't see any reason why I should understate the facts. Ketosis is one of life's charmed gifts. It's as delightful as sex and sunshine, and it has fewer drawbacks than either of them. Many low-carbohydrate diets have been proposed over the years. They work with some degree of effectiveness for some people. However, many of them do not bring carbohydrates down to a level—generally less than forty grams a day—that will permit BDK.

For people who are metabolically obese and have great difficulty losing, that is a grave weakness.

The Atkins ketogenic diet, on the other hand, is state-of-the-art in weight loss. The safest, healthiest, most luxurious way to start the slim, second half of your life.

## Going For It

You've heard me say you can burn the fat off your body. How does ketosis/lipolysis work?

Being in ketosis simply means that you're burning your fat stores and using them as the source of fuel they were meant to be.

When your body is releasing ketones—which it will do in your breath and your urine—that is a chemical proof that you're consuming your own stored fat. Once more, for emphasis: *When a person on a safe low-carbohydrate diet such as mine is releasing ketones, he or she is in the fat-dissolving state known as BDK, or ketosis/lipolysis, which is simply the most efficient path ever devised for getting you slim.*

The more ketones you release, the more fat you have dissolved.

BDK is the physiologic method of weight loss—the exact opposite of the process that got you fat to begin with. It can be your life raft, gaining you not only slimness but health, putting you at a good healthy distance from the obese person's perils of diabetes, heart disease, and stroke.

Most of all, of course, it is the achievement of your goal—to use up the fat stored on your body.

The phenomenon of ketone formation as the major alternative fuel system is so scientifically well-studied that it is simply not disputed in academic circles. It is as agreed upon as any scientific fact can be. In fact, Dr. George Cahill, the Harvard professor considered to be the preeminent teacher of metabolic-pathway research, after noting that brain tissue utilizes ketones more readily than glucose, announced that ketone bodies were a "preferred fuel" for the brain.[1]

Why, then, are you likely to hear or read that ketosis is undesirable or in some way bad for you? My only answer can be that there are too many "experts" who don't do their homework. Making a statement that benign dietary ketosis is anything other than beneficial is like wearing a sandwich board that says "I'm an expert," on the front panel, and admits "I don't know my field," on the back.

True, there is confusion in the minds of laymen (and some ill-informed doctors) between BDK and the ketosis of diabetic ketoacidosis. The latter is the consequence of insulin deficient subjects having their blood sugar levels out of control. The two conditions are virtually polar opposites and can always be distinguished from one another by the fact that the diabetic has been consuming carbohydrates and has a high blood sugar, in sharp contrast to the fortunate person in BDK.

Let's see just how BDK is the dieter's best friend.

## Why Does Ketosis Work?

Ketosis is the reversal of the biologic pathways that are involved in obesity. You'll remember that insulin was there to convert all your excess carbohydrate into your body stores of fat. As you gained more weight, your pancreas released more insulin to carry out this process.

Most obese people become so adept at releasing insulin that their blood is never really free of it, and, even at night, when weight loss most naturally occurs, they're still not able to use up their fat stores. In a normally functioning body, fatty acids and ketones are readily liberated from adipose tissue and converted into fuel during those hours. But the overweight subject is overweight because the high insulin levels prevent this from happening to him or her—or to you.

Now, with very little carbohydrate in your diet, your insulin levels will become normal—perhaps for the first time in years or decades.

Back in 1971, Drs. Neil Grey and David Kipnis convincingly demonstrated that insulin levels drop as carbohydrate intake is lowered. When carbohydrate drops to ketogenic levels, an abnormality in insulin can no longer be detected. Numerous studies over the past two decades have reconfirmed that the insulin levels drop on ketogenic diets.[2]

In ketosis, you burn the fat placed in storage by insulin when the obesity cycle began, and this fat powers your brain and your other vital organs.

The reason that BDK can take place so smoothly, if you know the "secret" to unlock its latent power, is that your body elaborates specific substances to sustain and facilitate the process. Back in 1960, three English researchers, Dr. T. M. Chalmers, Professor Alan Kekwick, and Dr. G. L. S. Pawan, whom I'll be telling you about in the next chapter, isolated the most significant of these, a Fat Mobilizing Substance (FMS), from the urine of animals and humans who went on ketogenic diets containing virtually no carbohydrates.[3] When they injected that urinary fraction into nondieting animals and humans, the recipients *lost weight without dieting*. Subsequently, other researchers discovered other substances that have similar effects, and a class of compounds called lipid mobilizers was identified.

Presumably what happens is that in the absence of carbohydrates to fuel the body, a signal is sent out to release a symphony of lipid mobilizers. The burning of stored fat in the absence of dietary carbohydrate is a *natural* mechanism of our bodies—it's what sustains hibernating animals—and our bodies provide natural messenger substances to ensure that the process of fat mobilization, heralded by ketosis, takes place smoothly and is self-sustaining. For you, this is a sort of biologic utopia. Once you reach a state where fat mobilization is supported by blood-borne enabling substances, the process of losing weight becomes as painless and hunger-free as "eating naturally" was in the days when you were gaining weight.

## Yes, No Hunger

This is one of the most attractive features of any low carbohydrate, ketosis-producing diet. Frankly, it first attracted me because back in the 1960s, when I was a young doctor with an ever-increasing paunch, I wanted to diet but didn't want to be hungry. I knew very well that I couldn't stand being hungry for very long. I had too big an appetite and too little willpower, two facts which haven't much changed.

When I found out about Kekwick and Pawan's work and realized that the body could satisfy its hunger by burning its own fat as fuel, I thought I saw an escape hatch. Ketosis turned out to have certain metabolic similarities to fasting. After the first forty-eight hours on each, the body suppresses hunger and lowers appetite.

There was still another advantage. A prolonged fast can be dangerous and has one severe metabolic disadvantage: When fasting, the body not only burns fat for energy, it also burns protein. This means that it burns off some of the body's lean muscle tissue, which is clearly not desirable. Investigation has shown that on a high-protein, ketogenic diet, virtually no lean tissue is lost, only adipose tissue. And that's why I am able to put extremely overweight individuals in ketosis/lipolysis for six months to a year (and longer), knowing that they will suffer no ill effects of any kind.

These enlightened people are able to consume their own fat for energy and feel good while they're doing it.

## The Message of Smooth and Happy Weight Loss

The beauty of BDK is that it bypasses the agony of low-calorie dieting, which is carried out with the help of almost no lipid mobilizer support. And ketosis is not only pleasurable, but frequently essential. People who've been fat for a long time or who've tried many diets often find it very nearly impossible to lose much weight *unless* they're in ketosis. I've treated people who, on 700 or 800 balanced calories a day, couldn't lose weight. That's less than half the normal caloric intake of an average woman. And yet they lost weight when they were placed on ketogenic diets of even more calories.

When I make this claim, that you can lose more weight on a higher number of calories, I seem to be breaking the law—one of the hallowed laws of thermodynamics. Many powers-that-be get terribly provoked when I repeal their laws. But the calorie theory is a false law that is meant to be broken, and ketosis/lipolysis is the instrument for breaking it. You'll see exactly what I mean in the next chapter.

# 6

## The Metabolic Advantage— Every Dieter's Dream

I can't wait to get you started on the convincer—the real clincher—the 14-day trial on the *Induction* diet. That experience will be worth a thousand chapters.

But before I do, I have something designed to increase your enthusiasm to a fever pitch. Are you ready for this?

*You can lose more weight and more fat, calorie-for-calorie, on the Atkins diet than on any other diet you've ever tried.*

In other words, this diet will give you an edge, what in scientific lingo would be called a *metabolic advantage.* That's what will enable you to lose weight on the Atkins diet eating the same number of calories you used to gain on. And, if you're eating fewer calories on this diet, as you probably will be, it will enable you to lose with considerably greater rapidity. You'll remember I pointed out that the calorie theory, as an explanation of weight gain and weight loss, has enough loopholes to render it invalid.

Nothing could be more evident to anyone who has spent a long time working in this field.

But let me tell you right here and now that the enormous dietary bonus I call metabolic advantage is an area of controversy and has remained so in spite of innumerable studies affirming its reality. I began describing this surprising phenomenon long before I ever heard the expression *metabolic advantage*. In 1973, the term was thrust upon me by the American Medical Association. Annoyed by the extraordinary success that *Dr. Atkins' Diet Revolution* was having in promoting a low-carbohydrate diet at just the time that they themselves were choosing to side with the supporters of high-carbohydrate, low-fat diets, the AMA put together a council of carefully chosen nutritionists to attack low-carbohydrate dieting and, in particular, my book, as the most prominent example of that trend.

Virtually all of their criticisms were inapplicable or easily refutable merely by reviewing the scientific reports already published at that time, but one of the stray arrows they fired off is fascinating since it called *my* attention to one of the most striking pluses provided by low-carbohydrate dieting for weight loss. Their commment was, "no scientific evidence exists to suggest that the low-carbohydrate ketogenic diet has a metabolic advantage over more conventional diets for weight reduction."[1]

Since I had scoured fifty years of scientific research on ketogenic and low-carbohydrate diets and found only confirmation of the phenomenon I'm about to demonstrate to you in some detail, I must admit I was more than taken aback by their statement. Were they suggesting that none of the studies had actually been done or that none that were done had any validity? Since the AMA has never bothered to retract the palpably erroneous statement I quoted above and since metabolic advantage remains one of the most spectacular pluses that an overweight low-carbohydrate dieter has in his favor the minute he goes on the Atkins diet, I've decided to lay out for you the actual scientific evidence that undergirds the advantage you'll be experiencing on the diet.

I know many of you are not of scientific bent and are put off by doctors talking medicalese to you. But, if you pay close attention to what follows, I promise you that you'll be privy to some of the most exciting scientific studies a person interested in weight loss ever gets to learn about. And, before the chapter's over, I'll give you a small reward by demonstrating, through one of my patients, just how the concept works in the case of a flesh and blood person and his diet.

Let me start by introducing you to the academic achievements of two brilliant, painstaking British researchers, Professor Alan Kekwick and Gaston L. S. Pawan, whose seminal experiments on mice and on obese humans provided the breakthrough concept, the mechanism and rationale, and the irrefutable experimental evidence that a low-carbohydrate—yes, even a high-fat—diet has a significant metabolic advantage over balanced or low-fat conventional diets. Let me point out that my intellectual allies in this pseudo-controversy were not mad scientists writing in the Podunk Medical Journal, but rather represented the top echelon of British obesity research, both serving as chairmen of many international conferences. Professor Kekwick was Director of the Institute of Clinical Research and Experimental Medicine at London's prestigious Middlesex Hospital and Dr. Pawan was the Senior Research Biochemist of that hospital's medical unit. The AMA's panel of experts could not have been unaware of their research or of its far-reaching significance.*

---

*They did acknowledge reading one of the Kekwick/Pawan papers.

The Kekwick and Pawan saga began in the early fifties when they were struck with the many studies that suggested that differently composed diets provided differing rates of weight loss. They had read the exciting clinical studies of Dr. Alfred W. Pennington on employees of the Dupont Corporation, as well as German and Scandinavian papers showing success in dieters who restricted carbohydrate. So they did a study on obese subjects and found that those on a 90% protein, and especially on a 90% fat diet lost weight, but when they were given a diet of the same number of calories, 90% of which came from carbohydrate, the subjects *did not* lose.[2]

Kekwick and Pawan were so impressed with the potential importance of their unexpected findings that they devoted nearly two decades of their collaboration to learning why and how the theory that all calories are equal seemed to be so patently wrong. They then replicated an animal study of theirs on humans and found the same phenomenon: A low-carbohydrate diet of 1000 calories worked well for weight loss and a high-carbohydrate 1000-calorie diet took off very little weight.[3] They then showed that their subjects did not lose at all on a balanced 2,000 calorie diet, but, when their diet was mainly fat, these same obese subjects could lose even when as much as 2600 calories were given. A typical example was their subject, JB, who lost 9 pounds in 3 weeks on the 2600-calorie low-carbohydrate diet, yet not an ounce on the 8 days he was on the balanced 2000 calorie diet.

Skeptics with the calorie-is-a-calorie mindset were in a state of shock and set out to disprove this intellectual bombshell that Kekwick and Pawan had dropped on them.

A spate of studies followed. One, by T. R. E Pilkington and his associates, was published in Lancet in 1960.[4] But the study dealt with the 1000-calorie level, a level at which nearly everybody loses weight, and only 3 of the subjects in the study were kept as low as 32 grams of carbohydrate, the upper limit of intake to provide a ketogenic diet. But if you look at their data, you'll see the same striking accelerated weight loss on restricted carbohydrates that Kekwick and Pawan showed, except that the Pilkingtonians blithely eliminated the first 12 days of the low-carbohydrate diet from their mathematics, which just happened to be the only way they could make their conclusion—that all low-calorie diets give the same result—fit their data. Their reasoning? They said the low-carbohydrate diet causes water loss. How did they know? Unlike Kekwick and Pawan, they did no water balance studies to prove their point. With the ivory tower complacency Galileo's contemporaries showed when they insisted the Earth could not possibly move around the sun, Pilkington and his associates concluded that their preconceived dogma must certainly be true.

I'm embarrassed for the nutritionists at the AMA who, in their desperate search for ammunition, even cited that study. If you did something like that too often, you could get a reputation as The Gang That Couldn't Think Straight.

But Kekwick and Pawan stuck by their guns. Their data had shown water loss to be only a small part of the total weight loss. For the next two years, they embarked on a study of mice in a metabolic chamber. By measuring the loss of carbon in the feces and urine, they were able to show that the mice on the high-fat diet excreted considerable unused calories in the form of our friends the ketone bodies, as well as citric, lactic, and pyruvic acids. At the end of the study period, they analyzed the fat content of the animals' bodies and found significantly less fat on the carcasses of the high-fat-diet mice. Nevertheless, the AMA's team of scholars didn't even bother to review this study although it was published in the prestigious American journal *Metabolism*.[5]

There is more to the Kekwick and Pawan story. During the time they were proving the reality of the metabolic advantage of ultra-low-carbohydrate dieting, they detected and extracted a substance from the urine of the low-carbohydrate dieters which, when injected into mice, caused the same metabolic events they had observed in the mice on low carbohydrate, indicating that fat was melting off the body. The carcass fat decreased dramatically, the ketone and free fatty-acid levels rose, and, most significantly, the excretion of unused calories via urine and feces rose from a normal 10% to 36%! This substance was named fat-mobilizing substance (FMS). FMS is the instrument of your metabolic edge; it enables you to sneak out some unused calories from your body that you wouldn't be able to remove so easily on a low-fat diet.

Kekwick and Pawan attributed hormonal properties to FMS, and at least four other research groups coming at the subject from a variety of directions felt they had identified fat mobilizers. Thus, the idea that you have a metabolic ally in sustaining weight loss has been demonstrated by a plentitude of researchers.[6]

## The Struggle Continues

There were two more studies that the AMA panel of experts reviewed on the subject of metabolic advantage. One was by Olesen and Quaade, which again showed extremely favorable weight loss on a low-carbohydrate diet.[7] Like the Pilkington study, this favorable result was attributed to water loss, and once again no attempt was made to document the water-balance dynamics. The other study by Sidney

Werner simply did not apply, being a study of a 52-gram carbohydrate diet—far too much for demonstrating ketosis and lipolysis.

Now let's look at the studies that were deliberately excluded from the AMA critique. First let's look at the study done by Frederick Benoit and his associates at the Oakland Naval Hospital.[8] Impressed with the Kekwick and Pawan success, they decided to compare the 1000-calorie, 10-gram-carbohydrate, high-fat diet with fasting in seven men weighing between 230 and 290 pounds. On the 10-day fast, they lost 21 pounds on average, but most of that was lean body weight; only 7.5 pounds was body fat. But on the ketogenic diet, 14 of the 14.5 pounds lost was body fat. Think of it. By eating foods such as bacon, whipped cream, cream cheese, and mayonnaise their subjects lost their fat stores almost twice as fast as when they ate nothing at all! Benoit's other exciting discovery was that on the ketogenic diet, the dieters maintained their potassium levels, while there were major potassium losses when fasting. You may recall that about a decade later, many dieters were to lose their lives on very-low-calorie formula diets that were very much like fasting, presumably due to potassium losses leading to heart arrhythmias. Had the medical establishment accepted the Benoit study for what it was—the needed confirmation of the Kekwick and Pawan research that should have made the ketogenic diet the treatment of choice for the overweight—these lives might have been spared.

Benoit presented his findings at the Golden Anniversary session of the American College of Physicians and his paper was published in the *Annals of Internal Medicine,* both in 1965. Hardly an obscure study. Why was it not included in the AMA's critique? I admit that trying to explain that without using the words "intellectually dishonest" is difficult.

Actually the Benoit study set off quite a furore in the minds of establishment spokesmen such as Francisco Grande, who knew that Benoit's data had to be wrong because it contradicted the calorie theory.[9] Grande calculated that 640 grams per day (the amount of fat the ketogenic dieters actually lost), if multiplied by 9 calories a gram will equal a 5760 calorie deficit, and no one could lose that much weight. What he was saying in effect was, "Don't bother me with data, I've already calculated the results."

But this confirmation of metabolic advantage continued to be replicated, sometimes from the most unlikely sources, such as Dr. Willard Krehl, a determined opponent of low-carbohydrate dieting.

Krehl went on to study two obese women, average weight 286 pounds, for 10 weeks on a 12 gram, 1200-calorie low-carbohydrate diet and recorded weight losses averaging a half-pound *daily*.[10] He then described this as "commensurate with caloric restriction and exercise." (Three hours a day.) But is it? To lose a half pound per day, a woman would have to burn up 1750 calories a day, over and above the 1200 calories she was eating on Krehl's diet. That means that Krehl assumed these women, one of whom had a basal metabolism 18% below the norm, would normally burn up 2950 calories a day. The accepted theory, however, is that the average obese woman does *not* lose weight on 2000 calories a day. Therefore, to me, Krehl's figures conceal a metabolic advantage of 950 calories a day or more.

Still not convinced? Try this one. The AMA panel of nutrition experts, most of whom certainly read the *American Journal of Clinical Nutrition,* failed to acknowledge an important paper by Charlotte Young, professor of Clinical Nutrition at Cornell University, published in that journal just two years before.[11] This time, the subjects were overweight young men, and the three diets compared were of

1800 calories, all with some degree of carbohydrate restriction. The diets contained 30, 60, and 104 grams of carbohydrate and were followed for nine weeks. Young and her colleagues calculated body fat through a widely accepted technique involving immersion under water. Those on 104 grams lost slightly better than 2 pounds of fat per week, out of 2.73 pounds of total weight loss—not bad for 1800 calories. Those on 60 grams lost nearly 2.5 pounds of fat per week, out of 3 pounds actual weight loss—better. Those on 30 grams, the only diet which produced ketosis and, presumably, FMS, lost 3.73 pounds of fat per week—approximately 100% of the weight they were losing each week.

We should forgive Dr. Young for editorially concluding that she preferred the 104-gram diet she had been working with for twenty years. After all, she had published the fourth peer-reviewed medical study demonstrating the metabolic advantage of the ketogenic diet and quantitated it rather accurately. Look at her figures. These young men, by dropping 74 grams of carbohydrate and replacing it with 300 calories of protein-based food, will lose an extra 1.7 pounds of body fat each and every week. In other words, if they were to replace their cereal, banana, and skimmed milk with a ham and cheese omelet every day for 30 weeks, they will lose 51 more pounds of fat than if they stayed with the cereal.*

That's the edge the frustrated, struggling dieter needs. That's what metabolic advantage provides. That's what has enabled most of my patients to succeed. That's what has made the Atkins Center a success, and that's what will make you a success.

Before we leave Charlotte Young, I've got good news

*Providing the rest of the diet contained 1500 calories and 30 grams of carbohydrate.

for those of you who have been trying to lose weight with the major commercial plans. Most of them have been trying to get you thin with diets containing 60% or more carbohydrate. Dr. Young's *highest* diet was only 35% carbohydrate. But what I, in treating 20,000 weight-loss patients, and Charlotte Young in her meticulous research, and virtually every other scientist who has actually studied low carbohydrates diets have discovered, is that *the more the carbohydrate, the less the body fat lost*.

Here's the part of the story that has hurt you the most. What do you think happens to exciting, breakthrough-potential medical research when it runs afoul of the medical establishment? Does the truth come out, no matter what? Can the establishment win even though truth is not their ally? The answer to that can be deduced from recent history. Power wins. Once the AMA spoke out, no further research on the question of metabolic advantage was ever done in the U.S. And that's one of the major reasons why you're struggling with your weight and getting nowhere. *The proper, easy solution is not being offered as one of your options*.

Fortunately for the world, German science is not as inhibited by AMA position statements as is American research, and on the European continent, metabolic advantage continued to be explored. One example was a study done at the University of Wurzburg on 45 patients who were studied in the hospital for 5 weeks.[12] Once again the low-carbohydrate diet demonstrated a significant metabolic advantage, this time an extra 9.24 pounds was lost on the low-carbohydrate version of the 1000-calorie diet. Moreover, careful water-balance studies demonstrated that the proportion of those extra pounds that could be set down to water loss was not significant. Five other German studies[13] make the score:

Number of studies showing metabolic advantage—10
Number of studies showing no advantage on ketogenic
diet—0

Perhaps you will now understand how Harry Kronberg, the patient I mentioned in Chapter 2, was able to lose fifty pounds in three months on a diet containing an abundance of calorically-dense foods, even though in the previous three years all he had been able to do on a moderately-low-fat balanced diet was gain 70. This does not contradict reason, but it is an outstanding example of metabolic advantage.

Let's look at the mathematics and then you'll understand that Harry isn't losing all this weight because he's restricting his calories.

It works like this. To lose a pound a week one has to be eating 500 fewer calories a day than one burns up in energy. To gain a pound a week, one eats 500 calories a day more. Harry had been gaining half a pound a week for 35 months, which means he was taking in 250 calories a day too many. He was eating three full meals with chicken and fish for dinner and he was taking in 2129 calories a day.

## HARRY KRONBERG'S BEFORE AND AFTER MENU

### A TYPICAL PRE-ATKINS DAY

| *Breakfast* | *Calories* |
|---|---|
| Cheese Danish | 308 |
| Coffee (decaf with half 'n' half) | 2 |

| *Lunch* | |
|---|---|
| French Fries (3 ½ oz) | 175 |
| Pastrami/Corned Beef (4 oz cooked) | 410 |
| Rye bread (2 slices) | 140 |
| Pretzels (3 oz) | 220 |

| *Snacks* | |
|---|---|
| Nestle Crunch Bar (1 oz) | 138 |
| Orange | 71 |

| *Dinner* | |
|---|---|
| Herring (4 oz kippered) | 217 |
| Vegetables (1 serving cabbage) | 24 |
| Salad (lettuce/tomato/no dressing) | 80 |
| Crackers (4 rye thins) | 52 |
| Diet Soda | 0 |
| Vanilla Ice-cream (1 serving) | 290 |

| Total: | 2129 |
|---|---|

### A TYPICAL POST-ATKINS DAY

| *Breakfast* (Brunch) | *Calories* |
|---|---|
| Tuna Salad (1 serving) | 240 |
| ½ grapefruit | 41 |
| Decaf Coffee (black) | 0 |

| *Lunch* | |
| --- | --- |
| Grilled Chicken (light meat, 6 oz) | 280 |
| Small Green & Tomato Salad | 80 |
| Salad dressing (1 oz) | 170 |
| Diet Soda | 0 |
| | |
| *Dinner* | |
| Rib Steak (6 oz) | 490 |
| Summer Squash (1 serving) | 19 |
| Small Green & Tomato Salad | 80 |
| Salad dressing (1 oz) | 170 |
| Seltzer | 0 |
| | |
| *Snacks* | |
| Almonds (1 oz) | 176 |
| Coleslaw (with Sweet 'n' Low) | 174 |
| Cucumber (1/2 medium) | 8 |
| | |
| Total: | 1928 |

Now on the Atkins diet, Harry was losing 3.9 pounds a week, which means that according to conventional calorie theory, he would have to be taking in 1950 fewer calories a day than he burned in energy. We already know that at 2129 calories a day, he was taking in 250 calories a day too many. Thus Harry's break-even point is 1879 calories a day. To lose 3.9 pounds a week, he should be taking in 1879 calories minus 1950 calories, or minus 71 calories a day—clearly an impossibility since you can't eat less than nothing.

You've seen Harry's menu. In fact, that menu calculates out to 1928 calories a day. Harry is eating 49 calories a day over break-even point and therefore, according to calorie theory, he should be gaining ⅒ of a pound a week, and after 13 weeks on the Atkins diet he should have gained 1.3 pounds, not lost 50.*

All the calories Harry eats over and above minus 71 is metabolic advantage. That means he has a metabolic advantage of 1999 calories a day. Impossible? Not according to the research that's been done on low-carbohydrate dieting, and not according to the facts of Harry Kronberg's case.

The metabolic advantage is there. It can't be disguised, evaded, put down to water weight, or wished away.

I would have no difficulty going into my charts and finding hundreds of other such examples.

Back when I wrote my first book, I described a patient of mine who lost 5 pounds a week for 17 weeks, 85 pounds in all, while consuming enough meat that his documented food intake was 3000 calories per day (2½ pounds of red meat, plus a cheese omelet.)

By not eating carbohydrate, this patient, like Harry Kronberg, had stimulated the release of FMS to sustain the breakdown of his fat stores. This lipolysis (fat dissolving) became his major metabolic event. He, too, had created a metabolic advantage.

I have followed 25,000 patients on the program you're about to learn—better than 90% of them showed some measure of metabolic advantage. Now it's your turn.

From studying the medical literature, which, as you've seen, is in surprising agreement on this point, and from studying my own patients, I can safely say that the bonus benefit of switching from high-to ultra-low-carbohydrate diets of the same caloric content varies from one half to

*Incidentally, for those of you who aren't familiar with how diet research is done, 13 weeks is a very long time to test out a diet; there's nothing short-term about such results.

three pounds per week. This may not seem like a lot, but done for a year that calculates out to from 26 to 156 pounds of extra body fat lost.

Henceforth, the AMA will never be able to say metabolic advantage doesn't exist. The strongest statement they can make in the future is: "Well, yes, there is a proven advantage, but why would you want it?"

To have an edge, a bonus, the vigorish, the odds on your side. Would you want that? You could bet the ranch you would.

May the Edge be with you.

# PART TWO

# How to Do Your Fortnight Diet— 14 Days to Dieting Success

*You have just ahead of you what I believe will be a remarkable experience. Fourteen days of healthy, hearty, hunger-free eating will rapidly begin to take your excess pounds away and will show you the first outlines of a new you. It will be a "you" that is slimmer, more energetic, less driven by cravings, and very possibly freed of innumerable minor symptoms of a nutritionally inadvisable lifestyle. It will be a you that begins to understand through his or her own body what I can only sketch out for you in words. The flesh teaches faster than the pen. If you are metabolically obese, if you have been driven hither and yon by the lure of carbohydrates, then I have great surprises in store for you. Welcome to a whole new world!*

# 7

# In the Beginning— Getting Your 14-Day Diet Off on the Right Foot

I know you want to get into the 14-day *Induction* diet, so I'll make this chapter fairly brief. Here are two pre-diet steps well calculated to prepare you for success. In spite of your impatience to start dieting, I believe you should consider them.

I assume your weight and your physical well-being are both extremely important to you. It follows from that you're going to make a sincere attempt to abide by the not-so-very-difficult requests that I'll be making of you. I won't be angry at you if you don't—after all, we won't have met—but if you're not willing to try, you really should be angry at yourself.

With my own patients, I'm sometimes very frank. A patient of mine named David French—a 52-year-old stockbroker—had by his own account tried 6,000 diets and failed on all of them. He came to me somewhat reluctantly, nagged by his wife and children, I think, expressed his skepticism, groaned at the thought of taking a lot of vitamins, and looked to me like someone who would never make it off the ground. He weighed 206 pounds on a 5'8" frame, and his only real symptoms were fatigue and a clearly observed tendency to have a hard time with even very mild physical exertion.

"Let's at least check your blood chemistries, Mr. French," I said, "and then we'll have some idea of whether you have anything to worry about."

Those blood tests were quite enlightening. He had a whopping cholesterol level of 284 and a nearly incredible triglyceride level of 1200. At our next meeting, I leaned forward and, coming on a lot stronger than I normally would, let him have it with both barrels. *"I'd say you're probably going to die in the next year or two, Mr. French."*

That caught his attention. In all probability, I remarked, a heart attack or a stroke would be his undoing. He also showed signs of being a borderline diabetic. His condition was completely reversible, but it was apparent he wasn't going to make the effort to reverse it.

Six months later, Dave French weighed 162 pounds, his cholesterol level was 155, and his triglycerides were 90. He had been a heavy-carbohydrate eater his whole life, someone who always hit the coffee carts for bagels and rolls, liked to stop on the way home from work for a calzone, and drank soda pop every day.

He thrived on my diet, reassured by the fact that there was no limit to the amount he could eat. "If you're hungry, eat," I said. "That's what God gave you a mouth, tongue, and lips for."

Getting into BDK was no trouble at all for Dave French. I got him to do a half hour of exercise four times a week. He found that he slept better, and he felt far less tired during the day.

Physical exertion was no longer beyond him. Of course, it shouldn't be when you're only 52. Quite simply, he became a slim and healthy man. But let's let him have the last word.

"I have a picture that I keep on the desk in my office that shows the maximum me—I look like I'm having a baby. I keep it right there where I can see it, to remind me of what I'll never be again. Nowadays, I don't even look like the same person."

He's right, too, he doesn't look like the same person.

## The Pre-Diet Steps

Now let's look at those pre-diet steps. They're both important. *You should not do the diet without considering these questions carefully.*

1. Stop taking any *unnecessary* medications.
2. Arrange to have a medical checkup, so you can determine your general state of health—and so you will be aware of your levels of cholesterol, triglyceride, glucose, insulin, and uric acid before you start the diet. These are the blood tests that often change with drastic dietary change. Since these levels are at the center of controversy about what constitutes a healthy diet, you may regret not having a "before" level to compare with the "after" level.

## Medications

The list of medications that inhibit weight loss is a long one. If you are on one or more of them, you will be disappointed in your diet results. For a more extended discussion of these pharmaceutical diet impediments, please turn to Chapter 18.

But there are also some drugs that combine with this diet to produce a dangerous overdose. They are the diuretics (the diet is itself a potent diuretic) and the anti-diabetes medications, including insulin. The insulin requirements invariably change on this diet. If you fall into either of these two categories, you stand to benefit more than most people. Without knowing how much and how fast these medications can be decreased, you could get into serious trouble. You or your doctor should call or write the Atkins Center for Complementary Medicine for specifics.

## Checks and Tests

### NOW FOR THAT MEDICAL CHECKUP

My second recommendation was that you get a medical checkup.

Even if you're not on any medication, this is a wonderful opportunity for you to take a look at your overall physical condition. If you have a personal physician, then he or she will be the best guide to interpreting that condition for you.

Obviously, if you're under 35 and have no evident health problems, then you don't have to have that checkup, but I still recommend it. There's something else I recommend at the same time and that's getting your blood chemistries done.

What an advantage it is—for me and for you—to know these numbers before you begin!

If you choose to keep track of those hidden physical changes that are measured in your blood—and these numbers your doctor can best interpret for you—you'll find, after you go on the diet, that they begin improving steadily. I'm talking about uric acid levels, cholesterol and triglyceride levels, glucose and insulin levels.

You may be startled because there's a whole body of published literature suggesting that you ought to be terrified of a diet that allows you to eat as much eggs, meat, fish, and fowl as you desire. The most common question I'm asked when I tell a patient what I expect him to eat is, "But won't my cholesterol go up?" I have no hesitation in answering, "No, it will go down."

A low-carbohydrate diet has a plentitude of health advantages that I'll explain in Part Three of this book. Meanwhile, if you have your blood chemistries done, you'll discover that the "experts" on low-carbohydrate dieting— those physicians who never studied a low-carbohydrate diet in their lives—will be proved wrong yet again. For them, being wrong must be habit-forming.

Here's what you should expect: Your uric acid levels will be normal, your kidney function will be excellent, your blood glucose and insulin levels will have stabilized, your triglyceride level will almost certainly have fallen sharply, and your cholesterol level will already be starting to go down.

I suggest you get these blood chemistries, and quite possibly the glucose tolerance test, measured before you start the diet, so you'll have a baseline. If you're obese, many of these measurements will not be too good before you start the diet, and, if you haven't been seeing your doctor for regular checkups, you probably don't have any idea what they are. Most of the conditions that get revealed through lab work are quite insidious—your numbers can be highly abnormal and yet you will have no symptoms referrable to them.

I don't want you to do the lab work a few weeks into your new diet, because then you may think any remaining abnormalities are the result of your dieting. I treat dozens of people every month who have high cholesterol two weeks after they start on the diet, but they had *even higher* cholesterol before they started.

While checking your lab work, get your entire state of health estimated. Make sure to have your blood pressure done. High blood pressure is known for its insidiousness, and overweight and hypertension go together like, oh, like pancakes and maple syrup. What happens to blood pressure on the diet? Just this: Nothing is more consistently and rapidly observed on the Atkins diet than normalization of blood pressure.

Certainly, you're also going to want to know about your thyroid function. A sluggish thyroid is one of the legitimate causes of metabolic obesity other than hyperinsulinism. If you are one of the approximately one in ten overweight subjects who needs thyroid, your weight problem will suddenly get very much easier, once you take it.

## A Very Special Test

Let's talk about the most illuminating and specific laboratory test of all—*the five-hour glucose-tolerance test (GTT) with insulin levels*. I hope I've convinced you that the metabolic defect in obesity is hyperinsulinism and that some combination of pre-diabetes, reactive hypoglycemia, and diabetes itself are found in the *majority* of significantly overweight people. Wouldn't you want to know if that applies to you? If you're really overweight, wouldn't you want to know the *extent* to which it applies to you?

Since your reading of this book is *a priori* evidence of superior intelligence, I'm going to assume that your answer to the above questions is, "Yes." But you may legitimately ask, "When?" Should I do it now or later?

First, let me tell you why I drive the car consistently rated number one in consumer satisfaction. My wife and I wandered into their showroom never having heard of this make of automobile. The salesman said nothing to us except, "Here are the keys. Why don't you take it for a test drive?" Eight blocks later, I said, "Where do I sign?" You can be sure that I cannot wait to get you to test drive the 14-day *Induction* diet. I know you'll sign on immediately.

So I don't want to impose an inconvenience, or a delay in getting started on the program, which would also be a delay in getting on with the best part of the rest of your life. After all, performing a GTT properly involves having blood tests drawn seven or eight times in one morning, and you must schedule it with a doctor or a commercial medical lab. Fortunately, it is covered by most major medical insurance policies, so for most of you, finance will not be a problem.

There is one point I must make. The test results are not considered accurate unless you are on full-carbohydrate intake (200 grams a day for four days), so you cannot decide in the middle of this diet that you are finally ready to take the test. This leaves you only two intelligent choices.

1. Do the test (with all the other lab parameters) *before* you begin the 14-day *Induction* diet.
2. Start the diet and promise yourself that before you commit to a lifetime on the Atkins program, you will

get this and the other tests done properly. That sounds like your best option, but remember once you experience how great it feels to rid yourself of your carbohydrate addictions, you won't *want* to go off your new diet and get re-addicted again!

The other option—never getting the test done—is not intelligent unless the following conditions apply: You are young, you have less than 15 pounds to lose, and you do not have a pot belly (upper body obesity connects strongly with hyperinsulinism).

Whatever you have decided to do about your GTT, this is the information you will need:

The glucose-tolerance test traces your sugar (glucose) level over the course of 5 to 6 hours after you take in a test dose of glucose with no other food or beverage. Any variation from the perfectly normal response may be viewed with suspicion. If the highest reading is over 160 mg, it may suggest pre-diabetes, a drop 25% below the baseline, or below 60 mg% suggests reactive hypoglycemia, a delta (difference between the highest and lowest readings) over 90 points suggests an abnormality, as does any hour in which the sugar drops 60 points or more. And many other criteria exist to show deviations from normal—all of which take on more importance if the symptoms (the group B responses) are characteristic.

But to really be informative (and to make your mini-ordeal worthwhile) insulin levels should be drawn along with the glucose levels, at least for the first 3 hours. After all, it is hyperinsulinism that *is* the laboratory correlate of obesity. The fasting insulin should be below 30 units, but the level drawn two hours after the glucose drink is a very important reading. In Western cultures this number seems to go up with age. This may not be a healthy change, but it is usual. My rule of thumb is that it is significantly elevated if it is 1.5 times your age, up to the age of 50. Thus, 75 is a high reading for anyone.

Now it is obvious that doing a lab test doesn't make you any healthier, but by providing you with a *bona fide* laboratory confirmation of your medical condition, it may motivate you to a degree you just haven't reached by looking in the mirror at a gradually expanding waistline.

And now for the 14 days that will change your life.

# 8

# The Rules of the Induction Diet—This is Your 14-Day Test Drive

First of all, let me welcome all the new arrivals who will be trying to start the book at this point. The *Induction* diet printed here is the prelude to the Atkins diet, not the Atkins diet itself, although it will probably be analyzed and reanalyzed as if it were and as if these words were never written. My critics, who realize they can't win on a level playing field, will seize this opportunity to prove it is an unbalanced diet, as if that magic word "balanced" represented a virtue rather than a handicap.

This *Induction* diet is a corrective diet; it's primary purpose is to correct, as expeditiously as possible, an unbalanced metabolism. *An imbalance cannot be corrected by adding balance; it can only be corrected by counterbalancing with an unbalanced correction.*

Let me show you my favorite diagram.

An unbalanced modern metabolism with a) an unbalanced (low-carbohydrate) diet and b) a standard balanced diet applied to it.

a)

unbalanced
metabolism

unbalanced
corrective diet

balanced
result

b)

unbalanced
metabolism

balanced
diet

unbalanced
result

Which looks like the better solution to you?

The diet below is called the *Induction* diet because its purpose is to induce a successful weight-loss by creating ketosis/lipolysis and thus summoning the body's own production of FMS and other fat-mobilizers.

These are the things the *Induction* diet will be doing for you:

1) Efficiently switching your body from a carbohydrate-burning to a fat-burning (your fat!) metabolism.
2) Stabilizing your blood sugar and abruptly halting a myriad of hypoglycemia symptoms that cause fatigue, moodswing, brain fog, weak spells and the like.
3) Stopping your cravings through abstinence, rather than moderation.
4) Breaking addictive eating patterns to chocolate, sugar, wheat or corn derivatives, alcohol, caffeine, grain gluten, or whatever you may have developed an allergy/addiction to.
5) Letting you experience metabolic advantage first-hand.
6) Knocking your socks off by demonstrating how much

fat you can burn off, while eating liberally, even luxuriously, off the fat of the land.

Nonetheless, attractive though it is, the *Induction* diet is
not going to be your lifetime regimen. That regimen will
be determined by a series of steps I will teach you to take,
so that the diet is eventually geared to create the best possible balance between your metabolic responses, your food
tastes and lifestyle, and your total health profile as it relates
to diet, which it most often does.

In permanent dieting, once the 14-day test drive you are
about to begin now is over—once, in fact, you're a dieting
success and you're enjoying the even-more-luxurious, lifelong Atkins *Maintenance* diet—the *Induction* diet will still
serve a purpose. It will be a start-up mechanism allowing
you—when necessary—to get back in stride by resuming
the diet at the level you were originally successful at. Thus,
when you've broken your permanent maintenance diet for
whatever good (or bad) reason, you will return to the *Induction* diet, and, like the ignition mechanism of an automobile, it will turn your engine over and start you rolling
down the road again. For this latter purpose, in the fine
days to come when you've reached your ideal weight and
then just slipped out of it for a moment, it won't be necessary to stay at the *Induction* level for two weeks. You'll
only have to do it until maximum ketosis/lipolysis takes
place, as evidenced by a full measure of appetite suppression. What *that* is you'll learn this first time around.

## The Rules of the Induction Diet

1. *Your diet must contain no more than 20 grams of
   carbohydrate a day.* For most people, induction of
   ketosis/lipolysis can be achieved on this intake. This

allows for approximately 170 g (6 oz) of salad vegetables (loosely packed) or 120 g (4 oz) of salad plus 130 g (4½ oz) of cooked vegetables in the below 10% carbohydrate category.

2. You are no longer on a quantitative diet. Therefore you should adjust the quantities to your appetite. When hungry, eat the amount that makes you feel satisfied but not stuffed. When not hungry, eat nothing or just a small protein snack to accompany your vitamins.

3. You are, however, on a qualitative diet. This means that if the food is not on your diet, you are to have absolutely none of it. Your "just this one taste won't hurt" rationalization is the kiss of death on this diet. Addicts will find this rule builds character in a hurry.

4. Your diet will consist of pure proteins (not many of those in nature, however), pure fats (this means butter, olive oil, and mayonnaise are permitted), and combinations of protein and fat (this is the mainstay of your diet). Foods which are protein-and-carbohydrate or fat-and-carbohydrate are *not* on this diet, because carbohydrate is not on this diet.

5. Using a carbohydrate gram counter, one could find other combinations totalling less than 20 grams of carbohydrate. One would be using foods like nuts, seeds, olives, avocados, cheeses, cream and soured cream, lemon and lime juices, and low-carbohydrate diet foods. Don't assume these foods are low, unless you absolutely know the carbohydrate content of the portion you are eating. In the Carbohydrate Gram Counter on page 307, I will include the carbohydrate content in grams of the foods you may include on this 14-day *Induction* diet as well as on more liberal levels of the diet that you will be doing as your lifetime diet plan.

## FREE FOODS:

| MEAT | FISH | FOWL |
|------|------|------|
| Beef | Tuna | Chicken |
| Pork | Salmon | Turkey |
| Lamb | Sole | Duck |
| Bacon | Trout | Goose |
| Veal | Flounder | Cornish Hen |
| Ham | Sardines | Quail |
| Venison | Herring | Pheasant |
| *in fact,* | *in fact, all fish* | *in fact, all fowl* |
| *all meat* | | |

| SHELLFISH | EGGS | CHEESE |
|-----------|------|--------|
| Oysters | *Scrambled* | Aged and fresh |
| Mussels | *Fried* | Cow and goat |
| Clams | *Poached* | Cream cheese |
| Squid | *Soft-boiled* | Cottage cheese |
| Prawns | *Hard-boiled* | Swiss |
| Lobster | *Devilled* | Cheddar |
| Crabmeat | *Omelets* | Mozzarella |
| *in fact,* | *in fact,* | *in fact, almost** |
| *all shellfish* | *all eggs* | *all cheeses* |

*Exceptions 1) luncheon meats with nitrites or sugar added*
*2) products that are not exclusively meat, fish, or fowl, such as imitation fish.*

---

*All cheeses have some carbohydrate content, and quantities are governed by that. (See Carbohydrate Gram Counter.) No diet cheese, cheese spreads or whey cheeses. Those with a known yeast infection, dairy allergy, or cheese intolerance must avoid cheese. Imitation cheese products are not allowed, except for Tofu (soy cheese)—but check carboydrate content.

## OTHER INDUCTION DIET FOODS:

Vegetables of 10% Carbohydrate or Less

**SALAD VEGETABLES**

| | | |
|---|---|---|
| Lettuce | Mache | Celery |
| Romaine | Bok Choy | Jicama |
| Escarole | Chives | Posse Pied |
| Arugula | Parsley | Alfalfa Sprouts |
| Endive | Cucumber | Mushrooms |
| Radicchio | Radishes | Morels |
| Chicory | Fennel | Olives |
| Sorrel | Peppers | |

**SALAD HERBS:**

| | | |
|---|---|---|
| Dill | Basil | Rosemary |
| Thyme | Cilantro | Oregano |

For salad dressing use the desired oil plus vinegar or lemon juice and spices. Grated cheese, chopped eggs, bacon, or fried pork rinds may be added.

**VEGETABLES IN ADDITION TO SALAD VEGETABLES:**

| | | |
|---|---|---|
| Asparagus | Scallions | Sauerkraut |
| String or Wax Beans | Leeks | Collard Greens |
| Cabbage | Spinach | Dandelion |
| Beet Greens | Summer Squash | Greens |
| Cauliflower | Courgettes | Christophene |
| Chard | Okra | Broccoli |
| Aubergine | Pumpkin | Spaghetti |
| | Turnips | Squash |

**VEGETABLES IN ADDITION TO SALAD VEGETABLES:** (*continued*)

| | | |
|---|---|---|
| Kale | Avocado | Celery Root |
| Kohlrabi | Bamboo Shoots | (celeriac) |
| Tomato | Bean Sprouts | Brussels Sprouts |
| Onion | Water Chestnuts | Artichoke Hearts |
| Rhubarb | Snow Pea Pods | Hearts of Palm |

**SALAD GARNISHES:**

Crumbled Crisp Bacon          Sour Cream
Grated Cheese                 Minced Sautéed Mushrooms
Minced Hard-boiled Egg        Anchovies

**SPICES:**

All spices to taste, but make sure sugar is not in the seasoning.

**BEVERAGES:**

Water
Mineral Water
Essence Flavored Seltzer
   (must say "No Calories")
Decaffeinated coffee or tea
Diet Soda (read label)*
Iced tea with artificial
   sweetener*
Cream (whipping or single);
   note carbohydrate con-
   tent
Natural and artificial orange
   soda* products have
   some carbohydrate—they
   may be one of your op-
   tions for a few grams

Herb tea
   (no barley, dates, figs, sugar)
Caffeine is not allowed.
   Limit caffeine for one
   week (to break possible
   addiction). Then it may be
   used sparingly.
Carbohydrate free, artificially sweetened powder
   for making fruit-flavored
   drinks*
Clear broth/bouillon (not all
   brands)
Grain Beverages (i.e. imitation coffee substitutes) are
   not allowed

*Contains aspartame.

**BEVERAGES**: (*continued*)
Spring Water
Club Soda

Lemon or lime juice
(note: each contains
2.8 gm carbohydrate
per oz)

**FATS AND OILS:**

Many fats, especially certain oils, are essential to good nutrition. Include a source of GLA (gamma-linolenic acid) and omega-3 oils (EPA, salmon oil, linseed oil). Monounsaturated oils, such as olive oil, avocado, macadamia, and hand-pressed canola oils are especially valuable. All vegetable oils are allowed. The best are canola, walnut, soybean, sesame, sunflower, and safflower oils, especially if they are labeled "cold pressed." Butter is allowed, margarine is not. Margarine should be avoided not because of its carbohydrate content but because it is a potential health hazard. Mayonnaise is permitted unless you are on yeast restriction. The fat that is part of the meat or fowl you eat is permitted.

Avoid the seeming paradox provided by today's "diet foods." Understand why cream is allowed but not skimmed milk, why soured cream can be used but not yoghurt, why low fat chicken breading is not allowed even though chicken may be panfried. The answer common to all these seeming inconsistencies lies in the higher carbohydrate content of the low fat dieter's foods.

**ARTIFICIAL SWEETENERS:**

The safest choice comes from a natural shrub; it is called Stevia. It should be used as a pure white powder. For best results, use Stevia in conjunction with a blend of other non-caloric sweeteners.

Dieters must determine which artificial sweeteners agree with them, but the following are allowed: saccharine, aspartame*, cyclamate acesulfame-K. Sweeteners such as sorbitol, mannitol, and other hexitols are not allowed, nor are any natural sweeteners ending in the letters -ose, such as maltose, fructose, etc.

**COMMON MISTAKES TO AVOID:**
1. Note that the 14-day diet contains no fruit, bread, grains, starchy vegetables, dairy products other than cheese, cream, or butter.
2. Avoid diet products unless they specifically state "No carbohydrates." Most dietetic foods are for fat-restricted, not carbohydrate-restricted diets.
3. The word sugarless is not sufficient. The product must state the carbohydrate content, and that's what you go by.
4. Many products you do not normally think of as foods such as chewing gum, cough syrups, and cough drops are filled with sugar or other caloric sweeteners and must be avoided.

---

## How to Fashion a Diet From the Above List

Once you know what you can have, the meal plan should leap out at you. You should instantly see that for breakfast, a ham, cheese and mushroom omelet, or bacon and scrambled eggs, or a mixed selection of smoked fish with cream cheese would start the day off on the right note.

For lunch, the typical chef salad with ham, chicken,

*Although most published scientific studies have proclaimed aspartame (NutraSweet, Equal) to be safe, clinical experience often indicates otherwise. Headaches, irritability, failure to lose weight or to control blood glucose have all been reported and I have confirmed this in many patients. It is likely to cross-react with those who cannot tolerate MSG. The best advice is to use it sparingly, preferably by blending it with other sweeteners. Remember, too, that aspartame loses its sweetness when heated.

cheese, and hard-boiled egg on a bed of greens, covered with a creamy garlic dressing will qualify, as will a bacon cheeseburger without the bun. Or maybe a charbroiled half chicken with a salad, or a scoop of tuna salad with a scoop of chicken salad.

Dinners should be your favorite protein main courses— rack of lamb, poached salmon, roast chicken, filet mignon, buttered lobster tails, seafood mixed grill, or whatever you fancy, plus a salad. You might have included an appetizer such as prawn cocktail with a mustard and mayonnaise sauce (the red sauce has carbohydrates), or pate, or steamed mussels. And for dessert, assorted cheeses or diet jelly with whipping cream.

Remember, the purpose of these 14 days is to improve your health, not to win a gourmet eating contest. Of course, gourmet eating is more likely to be achieved on this diet than on the low-fat diets currently making the rounds. But, for the moment, I merely want to introduce you to the notion that gourmet dieting will be yours once you master all the possibilities offered by a diet allowing butter and cream sauces. That's a beautiful prospect of eating to come. Here and now, your attention should be totally focused on whether you feel you are in control of your eating and whether you feel healthy.

Now that you have the rules of the diet, you may benefit from some pointers. It's one thing to know the rules of chess or backgammon, but it takes some instruction to become a master player. Two of the major pointers I'm going to explain here and now as part of the diet rules: nutritional supplements and lipolysis testing strips.

The first will build up your health while you pare off your weight, and the second will make it possible for you to obtain confirmation of the fact that your fat is melting away—that is, that you're in the state of ketosis/lipolysis.

## Dietary Supplements

In starting people on the diet, I have found that their vitamin and mineral reserves are often so depleted that it frequently takes a week or two of supplementation to build those reserves back up again. This is one of many reasons that by the time you complete your 14-day trial period on the diet, you're likely to experience a burst of energy.

Some critics of low-carbohydrate dieting have made the suggestion that the Atkins diet is so restrictive in certain areas that I have no choice but to advise everyone who goes on it to take vitamin and mineral supplements. There's only a smidgen of truth in this. When you go down to a very low level of vegetable consumption during the first 14 days—the strictest portion of the diet—you'll certainly be consuming inadequate portions of certain nutrients.

## I Recommend Supplements for Everyone

The more I learn about nutritional supplements, the more I discover nutritional components that can help nearly everyone. A typical example is the anti-oxidant group of nutrients, which is showing absolutely well-documented effects in protecting against heart disease, cancer, and aging. Now who wouldn't benefit from that? Multiply that health stimulating benefit by the number of nutrition breakthroughs that have accumulated in the last two decades, and you can easily see why my average patient takes over 30 vitamin pills a day. And in order to make it possible to obtain the maximum benefit at that level, I had to develop a system of Targeted Nutrition (TN) so that I would only be prescribing what each individual needed for the conditions or metabolic findings that were peculiar to him or her.

In this chapter, however, all I want to do is provide adequate nutritional support for a 14-day diet, not the lifetime program my face-to-face patients get after a two-hour evaluation. When you opt to become a lifetime Atkins dieter (notice, I didn't say "if") you will have to familarize yourself with Chapter 22.

So for now, this is what you do:

1. Find a very broad multiple vitamin, a model for which you can find in Chapter 22, "Nutritional Supplements," where I give the breakdown of my Dieter's Formula, Basic #3. Such a formula should contain considerably more than the RDA of B complex factors and of vitamin C and should contain at least 40 different nutrients. Don't expect to take fewer than four pills a day. Ideally, chromium picolinate, 200–600 mcg, should be included.

2. If you have sugar cravings, you must include L-Glutamine 500–1000 mg before each meal.

3. If you are concerned about an elevated cholesterol level from the very beginning, you should be sure to include two borage oil capsules, 2 tablespoons of lecithin granules per day, and pantethine 300 mg before each meal.

## Lipolysis Testing Strips

### *How to Get and Use LTS*
Using lipolysis testing strips, which hereinafter will be referred to by the acronym LTS, to measure your degree of ketosis/lipolysis is in another category from nutritional

supplementation.* You don't necessarily have to do it, but it can be an extremely convenient aid to doing the diet. And, if you're not getting the results you expect, then they will surely help you to clear up the mystery of why that's so.

After all, the clear basis for going into the strict *Induction* phase of the diet, the first 14 days, is that you be in ketosis. I'm going to allow you one medium-sized tossed salad a day to start. After you've used up your 48-hour supply of stored carbohydrate—it's called glycogen—you'll almost certainly enter ketosis.

Your LTS will help to measure how deeply you've done so. After the first two weeks, as you increase your carbo-hydrate, your LTS will help to insure that you don't increase them too much and fall out of the effective state of ketosis/lipolysis.

## What Are Lipolysis Testing Strips?

Lipolysis Testing Strips are urine test sticks that when placed in your urine change color depending on what they find there. If you're excreting ketones in your urine, then the LTS will turn purple. The more ketones excreted, the darker the purple.

LTS are moderately inexpensive, and you can ask your pharmacist to order them for you if they are not readily available. My patients often tell me that LTS are

---

*Lipolysis testing strips is a generic term for a variety of products available for determining, semi-quantitatively, the presence of ketone bodies in the urine, thus heralding fat breakdown. You can buy lipolysis testing strips (which may be referred to as ketone testing strips or simply urine testing strips) from your pharmacist. Some brands, designed to warn of Ketoacidosis in diabetics, can also serve as lipolysis testing strips.

psychologically supporting. To see them go from beige to purple (depending on the brand you use) is to receive in chemical code the message, *I'm losing weight.*

## What If They Don't Turn?

Well, basically, they must, unless you're not doing the diet correctly or you have very severe metabolic resistance. First, make sure that none of your foods—except that salad—have carbohydrate. No hidden sugars, no breading, etc. Then follow the diet for five days, using the LTS each day. If they still haven't even changed to at least the color of lavender, then cut out that one salad. It's the only significant source of carbohydrate that you're consuming. As soon as the LTS turn purple, put the salad back in the diet again.

Do your LTS testing at the same hour each day. Usually the evening works best, because that's when you generally get the deepest reaction.

For the vast majority of you, there will be no difficulty getting your LTS purple at this stage. You'll have more interesting variations as you go up the carbohydrate scale later in the diet. At that point, in the *Ongoing Weight-Loss* phase, you'll be testing out where your Critical Carbohydrate Level lies.

## Critical Carbohydrate Levels?

This is an interesting aspect of the diet. The diet aspect of the Atkins program has four stages. First, there is this, the 14-day *Induction* diet for fast weight loss. Next, there will be the stage of *Ongoing Weight Loss* (OWL). Then, there will be the *Pre-Maintenance* diet, a stage of transition to your lifetime diet, which will take place while you're losing your last few pounds. Finally, there will be the lifetime *Maintenance* diet.

For each of these levels of the diet, there is a Critical Carbohydrate Level that pertains to you. Your individual metabolism has a certain quantity of carbohydrate beyond which it will cease to lose weight, or—after you've reached your ideal weight—beyond which you will begin to gain it back. Therefore, in Part Four, I'll tell you all about those very critical levels.

## What Does This All Mean Metabolically?

Principally, of course, your purple LTS and your capacity to stay below your Critical Carbohydrate Level for Losing will mean that you've found the very easiest method of losing pounds and inches.

Your LTS are evidence for the fact that you've carved out a different metabolic pathway. The first fuel your body burns for energy comes from the carbohydrates you eat and drink. Now that you've lowered your carbohydrate consumption to a level that can't finance your energy expenditures, you must burn your stored fat. Easily, if you're metabolically average, reluctantly, if you're metabolically resistant, your body draws upon those stores of fat. A new metabolic pathway for supplying energy has been successfully taken. And, at that moment, your body converts from being a carbohydrate-burning engine into being a fat-burning engine.

You really are doing the diet now. I'm very happy for you. This should be the last diet you'll ever have to do.

# 9

# Doing the Strict Level of the Atkins Diet at Home and at Work

The 14-day *Induction* diet is primarily about losing weight and feeling good. You now know how to do it, but let me add one necessary caution before you begin: If you have serious health problems, seeing your doctor is *essential*.

The Atkins diet has a strongly positive effect on virtually all conditions, but it *is* a major lifestyle change, and, if you have a serious medical problem, you should monitor your changing metabolism with a physician's aid and counsel. Enough said. But please don't forget.

Also, I must insert a crucial warning: *this phase of the diet is not appropriate for pregnant women and people with severe kidney disease.*

Now, how about my other suggestions?

Have you laid in your stock of vitamin supplements and lipolysis testing strips as suggested in Chapter 8?

What about those blood tests I spent so much time urging

on you? Have you had them? I hope so, but, if you're young and healthy, and you just haven't been able to get your act together and do them, so be it. It's a pity to remain uninformed, but it would be a far greater pity to remain fat.

But don't think I'm letting you off the hook here. I do strongly, intensely, urge you to do them. If money is a problem, then be aware that the federal government conducts cholesterol screening programs that you can participate in and that will give you at least your cholesterol and triglyceride levels.

## Dieter's Morale

Psychologically, have you made a firm commitment? Don't start something this important with the shallow notion that "Oh, well, I'll give it a whirl." At the least, you should have decided that you'll give two weeks of your life without deviation and without compromise to this diet.

If you can commit yourself to that, then quite frankly I expect great things for you. By the end of your 14 days, you'll be walking with new energy, getting out of bed in the morning with new zest, and joyously anticipating your every encounter with the bathroom scale.

## Blast Off! You've Begun—Munch Away

Naturally, you begin by eating—something you've always done with some degree of guilt. But don't hesitate as you plow into the spare ribs or the roast duckling. If you're an experienced dieter, you may have to suppress an involuntary shudder as you begin downing high calorie food you always thought would make you fat.

Once again have faith. In the absence of carbohydrates, the body has no choice but to burn its own fat. Moreover, at this stage of your dieting, eating the rich, fatty foods your last dietician advised you to flee from can only be advantageous.

You're starting off at the most extreme low-carbohydrate end of the diet, and I'm encouraging you to eat as much as you like.

I want you to be totally, shockingly unafraid of fat during these two weeks. Fat is much more ketosis-inducing than protein. After all, 58% of protein will become glucogenic amino acids, i.e. convertible to glucose, but only 10% of fat will become its glycerol portion which is similarly convertible. The ease of getting into deep ketosis/lipolysis is based on the ratio of fat to carbohydrate. The higher that number, the more ketosis. Thus, you should strive for the maximum amount of fat during this initial period, and in doing so, you will almost certainly find yourself experiencing the deepest, sharpest, most appetite-suppressing aspects of the diet.

As an overweight person, you're very likely to be resistant to ketosis, since ketosis means parting with your fat, and that's just what your body has obviously been reluctant to do. During your fortnight trial diet, we're taking no chances. We're going to make those LTS turn purple.

## Have the Food on Hand

Stock the refrigerator and the cupboard with the food you're going to eat. Go to the supermarket and check out the protein goodies you're fond of. Naturally, avoid the aisles where the carbohydrate temptations are found. I had a nineteen-year-old patient named John Connors, who, standing 6'4", dropped his weight from 290 to 209 in six months. He used to tell me how he'd go to the supermarket on some legitimate food errand, get sucked into one of the sugar aisles, and end up walking out of the store with a package of candy bars. In the course of his journey home, self-control would reassert itself, and he'd lower the car window and throw it into the street!

What permitted foods do you like to have in front of you when you open the refrigerator door? Deviled eggs, turkey, chicken, prawn salad, your favorite cheese?

If you live alone, don't keep the things you won't be eating. Invite some friends over to finish off the ice cream. Have a final party. Give away all your forbidden foods to a neighbor or an in-law. (Blood relatives may share your inherited metabolic disorder.) Or just throw them away. Alter your mental picture—for you, that food doesn't exist.

If you don't live alone, then it almost always makes sense to prepare your significant others for the "shock" of your new diet. Unless you come from a family of vegetarians, it actually shouldn't be too shocking. You're planning to eat things you've always eaten.

If you do the cooking, unless you can convince your household to share the Atkins diet experience, you'll have to cook for yourself and make additions for them. They may want bread, potatoes, and dessert. There's a little problem with temptation here, but if you really want to lose weight I think you'll bite the bullet and not the breadstick or the banana. You have this comfort: Human beings are remarkably adaptable, and, in as little as a week, your tastes will start to change. Soon you'll find that sugar and refined carbohydrates don't tempt as much as they did. And the appetite suppression I've told you so much about will be your constant ally.

If, for the first few days, you find it a bit of a downer

watching other folks eating foods that you're fond of and can't touch, then comfort yourself in your own way. Take a double portion of what's permitted. Remember, weight loss is now your destiny; these moments of temptation are just momentary afflictions. Make sure you tell family members that you need a strong show of support and understanding. You certainly don't want them tempting you with illicit food and saying vile and inappropriate things like, "Don't worry, this tiny piece of cake won't harm you." *It will!*

Tell people in advance that you take your diet seriously, and you'd appreciate their doing the same. The Atkins diet is a breeze, the most luxurious diet you'll ever be on (and the last), but we all know what a tricky, emotion-laden, family-connected, downright passionate business food is.

I understand that the other people in your house may not automatically be entranced with your new diet. In the nicest possible way, tell them it's your diet, not theirs, and they don't need to be entranced. All they need to do is show respect for the major decision you've made. You're about to lose a lot of weight and gain a lot of health. After you've done the diet, you won't need to request respect for it, the results will speak for themselves.

But above all, remember: If other people are going to be impressed with your resolve, then you yourself must take your diet seriously. Do so! Go at it, as if it were a life and death matter. For overweight people, over the course of years, that's exactly what it is.

## What's the First Thing You Notice?

You're not hungry.

Indeed, how could you be? Ketosis, just like a fast, always induces appetite suppression once the body's two-day supply of glycogen is burnt off.

Two days are past. Your glycogen is gone. You're solidly into ketosis/lipolysis. At this point, you're finding out that this appetite suppression is the *most striking thing* that has ever happened to your appetite in your entire life.

Suddenly, you find yourself eating quite moderate quantities of food and feeling no hunger pangs.

You certainly know you're in ketosis when you find yourself saying: "You mean lunchtime was an hour ago?"

You may be a person for whom incessant, almost hourly food cravings have been a way of life. I'm sure you remember Gordon Lingard, the patient who came to see me at 306 pounds. He used to say, "I'd always be planning the next binge. I'd be in a business meeting, very serious, a lot of money at stake, and one half of my brain would be figuring out what I would eat, how much I would eat, when and where I would eat. Food seized my brain."

Now that's enslavement to food. Yet in the end, Gordon succeeded, and if he could do it, almost any one of you can, too.

Willpower is not required on the Atkins diet, only the wisdom to put yourself into a position where you won't be needing it.

## What's the Second Thing You Notice?

Unless you have an exceedingly high energy level, the next thing that will strike most of you is a feeling that you've latched onto some misplaced, long-lost energy. Typically, this feeling arrives around about the third or fourth day. Some people experience a slight euphoria. Most simply find that those dreary, weary hours that used to hit them two or three times a day have been reduced to mere occasional moments.

Conversely, there are people who experience fatigue during their first week on the diet. Most often this means that the diet is going too fast for their particular metabolism—they're losing weight too fast, losing water and minerals too fast, and their bodies aren't adjusting to these quick changes very readily. Usually, I advise patients who have these problems to back off and slow down. I suggest they add a second salad or a helping of vegetables with their evening meal. Though their bodies would almost certainly adjust during the second week, there isn't any good reason for feeling washed out and sickly for five or six days.

I'm happy to say that with most people it's the energy lift they experience. It tends to send them roaring on through the diet because it's such clear evidence of the satisfying influence their dietary change is having on their metabolism.

## This is Your Diet Wherever You Go

It's true I began by talking about eating at home, and for a reason. The person in his or her own habitat, living with the refrigerator, is the basic prototype. This is the world in which food is always there for the asking, this is the land of temptations, and often gluttony. Sitting at the kitchen table and wondering, *What shall I eat?*

The answer is always the same: Eat as much as you want of the *permitted* foods. If you've spent a whole lifetime plagued by food cravings—usually, I know, straightforward carbohydrate cravings—then the pleasant truth is that hunger isn't going to occupy as much of your time and thought. Oh, yes, you'll still have an appetite, and you'll still eat with pleasure and delight, but the days of obsession are on the way to being past. What a joy not to always be hungry and always be tired and always be searching for some satisfying physical solution that you've never been quite able to reach. That's the lifestyle of the carbohydrate addict, which so many of you are, and it's a profoundly exhausting and irritating lifestyle that you'll be eternally happy to be rid of.

But what about when you're not sitting at the kitchen table? Well, I hope it's clear to you just how easy this diet is to follow in all the circumstances of life. On weekends, in restaurants, on the job, when you travel a lot—unless someone imprisons you in a candy store—you really have nothing to worry about. Of course, the diet is not completely adaptable to dinner parties given by hostesses with fixed ideas about what everyone should eat. You'll need a little ingenious diplomacy to get you out of that one.

Of course, there are also the airlines—the Last Final Frontier of Junk Food. I'll have some further remarks on airlines in my chapter on eating in the Real World, but for the moment, I have a suggestion to make that applies just to your 14 days on the *Induction* diet. I think you should try to choose a two-week stretch in which you're not traveling, not vacationing, and not attending other people's dinner parties. These first two weeks are important, so why make them difficult?

## Outside Eating

Let us consider eating outside the home. If you eat five lunches a week at work or in a restaurant that's no problem at all. And certainly the Atkins diet is wonderfully accommodating to the needs of those of you who like as many weekly occasions of restaurant dining as you can manage.

If you eat out a lot at restaurants, or at your office caf-eteria, then you must become familiar with the possibilities of the menu, and you must be alert for hidden pitfalls. If the eating establishment is one you go to often, talk to the waiter or the maitre d' and be quite clear about the fact that you're on a diet that doesn't permit you to eat sugar in any manner, shape, or form. A surprising problem can be sugar in salads. Sometimes fruit juices are used as a sugar sub-stitute. For your diet, this is absolutely not permissible.

Go right down the list and make sure that your appetizer, main course, and salad all qualify for the diet. Avoid sauces, breading on your meat, bread crumbs, flour as thickener. Such carbohydrate ingredients can be hidden in surprising places. There may be flour or grain in your ham-burgers, or breadcrumbs in your crab cakes.

Eating out requires alertness. Otherwise, one meal can destroy your weight-loss program for the day and set it back for the week. Your first week's results won't look so good, if, instead of losing three quarters of a pound on Wednesday, you gained half a pound that day.

If the choices are really limited at the cafeteria or lunch-eonette where you dine, then you may prefer to pack a lunch. Bring along some finger food—chicken drumsticks, hard-boiled or deviled eggs, slices of ham, cheese, and chicken roll.

At this point in the diet, you're simply looking to have what it takes to stabilize your blood sugar and avoid hun-ger. Make sure, if you're bringing your own food, you have enough food with you. Don't allow for even the slim chance that you might be hungry enough to turn to the carbohydrates.

More information about doing the diet with your family and in the outside world can be found in Chapter 23.

## Special Situations

Once the diet begins to become a habit, you won't have to think about eating the right foods, because you really won't think about eating any other way.

Cynthia Marlborough, who for many years was executive secretary to one of the top corporate chairmen in New York, had battled mood swings and fatigue for years when she first came to see me. Cynthia, a chocaholic, had recently quit smoking.

"I had been overweight since I was a child; I can remember dieting when I was twelve but this was different. The weight was really piling on. And worse yet, it was a tense, stressed-out time at work. It got so I didn't know how I could handle the pressure and my poor physical state simultaneously. This actually began to depress me to a degree that people noticed. After lunch, I could have slept for hours. Instead I had to work through the fatigue. My job, which is one of the central things in my life, was just becoming torture."

Yet Cynthia Marlborough easily lost weight, cured her sugar cravings (it was a lot easier than quitting smoking), and went from a size 16 dress to a size 6 in less than six months. She also acquired an uncanny sensitivity to the foods she was eating. Two weeks into the diet, she had dinner at a girlfriend's house. She found herself eating some sliced filet mignon, a green salad, and a helping of horseradish.

"As soon as I ate the horseradish, I knew something was wrong, and I stopped and asked my friend if there was sugar in it. She said there was, and, of course, I didn't eat another bite of that. By that time I had a lot more energy, and I'd lost seven pounds, and I'd already become very careful what I put into my mouth."

This sensitivity to the taste of sweets is not uncommon among people who are curing themselves of sugar addictions. It's a good, protective sensitivity that will help you out in some of the situations I described above. Sugars and refined carbohydrates have gotten you into a bad physical pickle, so be wary of them.

## A New You

This introduces us to an idea I want to emphasize right here at the end of this *Induction* diet chapter. *It's a lot easier to change diets than you imagine*.

I know that some of you are still hesitating about doing the Atkins diet because you're thinking, This isn't really the way I eat—how will I live without my favorite foods? Psychological attachment is more important here than physical. We're attached to ourselves, our habits, the customs of our lives, our cultural and culinary traditions. Sharp changes are like the rending of old attachments, the breaking of friendships.

All I can tell you is that it must be done. You'll find after you change the way you eat that the essential you is still intact. And since that will be true, what you must look to is the salvation of the physical you.

You *can't* afford to be fat and unhealthy—it's as simple as that. This is a path that will cure you; for many of you, it will be the only path. You may imagine that your tastes won't change, but you're wrong. The body, faced with the necessity of cating, the passage of days, the inevitable renunciation of old habits, adapts. This is it, simple, almost humiliatingly basic: *The body adapts.* The body learns new tastes and forgets old ones. And since much of the desire for carbohydrate food is metabolic addiction, once the path of renunciation is completed, the desire for the old goodies is really very small.

Look at Ernie Kingman, who came to me for the oddest of reasons. At 55 years old, Ernie still felt pretty healthy, but he had one problem: He was carrying 290 pounds on his 6'1¾" frame. He had tried a liquid-protein diet in the 80s and gotten a temporary weight loss of no long-term significance, except, after the lost pounds came back, he found it was even harder to lose again.

Ernie didn't know what to do because he had developed a weight-related lifestyle problem. His children rode horses, and three years before, he'd taken it up to have something to do with them and found he loved it. He felt he needed to be agile and limber for horseback riding, and, as he put it, "At my weight, it isn't fair to the horse and it's dangerous for me."

His best friend, who's fair comment had been, "All you can do is get on and pray," was a patient of mine and urged Ernie to come, too. "Another diet doc," Ernie said. "Oh, I don't know."

Soon after, Ernie was taking a business trip to Florida and while he was waiting in the airport, the public address system paged him to a phone. It was his friend, and what he had to say was, "You have an appointment with Atkins next Thursday at nine o'clock."

My patients aren't usually sent to me as forcibly as that, but I was glad to have Ernie, who is a charming guy, and who was definitely in need of a little lifestyle improvement.

I looked at his diet, which had more than its share of cakes, cookies, ice-cream, and sweet goodies, and which, amazingly, nobody had attempted to change in the direction of carbohydrate limitation; not even his previous doctor, who had told him, "You're an accident waiting to happen."

You won't be surprised to hear Ernie was a resounding success. He got his weight down below 240 in eight months and his pounds are still falling off, slowly now, but steadily.

Where he used to have cake and coffee in the middle of the afternoon, he now has a slice of turkey on swiss cheese. Ernie had been so afraid he wouldn't be able to bear life without his sugar-loaded carbohydrate diet that I made him promise he'd call me up, if he felt he was going to quit.

It never came to that. Ernie got used to his change, he adapted, and moreover he noticed that "I feel better when I have protein, lots of protein on my diet. I'm really glad that I don't want to go back to eating the way I ate before." Ernie was an overweight person with typical glucose intolerance and an addiction to the very carbohydrates that made his condition worse. A couple of weeks eating the Atkins way pretty well took away the urge to eat the sweets and starches that were at the root of his weight problem. Ernie admits that now and then in a restaurant, he'd like to reach for a roll or order up a gushy dessert, but the urge is hardly irresistible.

Some people go even further and simply find their former urges aren't there at all. Marjorie Burke, an excellent chef and a woman who had craved starches her whole life long, found after a month on the diet that starches no longer filled a spot in her imagination. She could cook delicious breads for other people without so much as a desire to taste them.

Such a complete conversion is rare, and I don't recommend that any Atkins dieter become a baker. Nor do I recommend going back at some later stage to eating those white flour foods or those dreadful sugars, especially if you were addicted to them. But if you weren't addicted, it is possible to enjoy an occasional indulgence, as you'll see in the *Maintenance* chapter.

# 10

# Time to Review
# Your 14-Day Results

You've gone through 14 days on the Atkins diet. For approximately 90% of you this will have been a highly satisfying experience. You're taking stock of the successful
loss of considerable girth. How did you do it? By eating
luxuriously and without stint! You'll remember I promised
you a diet fit for royalty? That's what you've been eating.

At the same time, you probably noticed that though self-
indulgence reigned supreme, you weren't eating as much
as you had expected to. Your metabolism changed mark-
edly after the first few days. *Your appetite became controllable, and, for some of you, that will have been a new
experience*.

Now you're at the end of your diet fortnight, and you
have choices ahead.

## Do I Go On?

This is the logical time for you to make a decision, and I hope you will join the vast majority of dieters who choose to go on with the Atkins diet. They do this for a number of reasons. First, they're losing weight easily. Second, in direct contrast to the experiences they've had on so many other diets, they're not only feeling no pain, they're also feeling more vigorous and energetic than they did before they began. Third, a significant percentage of dieters, especially those who are over forty, have discovered that a variety of nagging minor physical ills, from headaches to body aches, have completely vanished.

Those are impressive general results. But as an individual, you may want more information to help you in making your choice. I suggest you get a second round of lab tests done at the 14-day break point. In just two weeks, blood chemistries can change a lot.

I think it's important for you to realize that not only do you feel good but good things are happening inside you. This is especially important because *high*-carbohydrate dieting has been elevated to the status of a religion during the last decade, and you're bound to feel a slight uneasiness over going against the grain—and against the potatoes, for that matter.

Your real decision ought to be not whether or not to have repeat blood tests done, but whether to continue with the diet while you're waiting for results or go off the diet and see what those results are first. If you haven't done your initial blood tests, particularly your glucose/insulin blood tests, you certainly should go off the diet, spend at least four days on your previous eating pattern, and then have the tests done.

Most people go right on to the next level of the diet, a

vote of confidence I'm vain enough to appreciate, but, in all honesty, each of these decisions has its advantages. You have a whole lifetime in which to take the weight off and keep it off, and a week or two of reflection will do you no harm.

## Some Questions to Ask

- Did you experience any hunger?
- Did you have any problems with constipation?
- Did you like the food?

If you were hungry, then you weren't following my counsel to eat as much as you wanted. If you were constipated, then you'll do better as you progress to an easier phase of the diet, as your body learns to adjust, and as you accustom yourself to eating some of the low-carbohydrate bulking agents or bowel preparations we'll discuss in Chapter 22. A certain amount of constipation is common during the first week, but it almost always gets solved a lot more quickly and easily than your weight problem.

As for liking the food, that's a classic difficulty of any major dietary change. Fortunately, most people enjoy protein food. If your tastes run to the vegetarian line, you can still do the diet but not without major efforts. The lack of selection on a diet that's low in carbohydrate and simultaneously excludes animal food is a serious taste difficulty. It's theoretically possible to construct a healthy low-carbohydrate vegetarian diet, but there aren't a lot of foods on it. In general, I've found that a person who will not eat any animal food at all will not stay on the Atkins diet indefinitely. The narrow range of selection is too boring.

The rest of you can enjoy a very delicious diet. What you'll chiefly regret is the loss of some favorite carbohydrate foods. Pasta and bread, as well as fruit and juice, are very often missed in the first few weeks.

So why do bread lovers continue on the diet? Simply this: The upside is much larger than the downside. Weight loss, of course, but feeling physically better and in control of your eating are paramount issues, too. I've told you about these improvements so many times that I hope you're beginning to understand I'm not talking through my hat. Feeling good is a major part of the Atkins diet.

At this point, I'd like to take inventory of your 14-day experience. You may well start with the quiz below. If you feel better in a number of these areas, that should provide strong support for the idea of going on with the diet.

## 14-Day Quiz

| Problem | Worse | Same | Better | Much Better |
|---|---|---|---|---|
| Energy Level | — | — | — | — |
| Anxiety | — | — | — | — |
| Depression | — | — | — | — |
| Headaches | — | — | — | — |
| Premenstrual Symptoms | — | — | — | — |
| Sleep Function | — | — | — | — |
| Comfort with Appetite | — | — | — | — |
| Concentration | — | — | — | — |
| Willpower | — | — | — | — |
| Mastery of Eating Behavior | — | — | — | — |

Other Symptoms:

1. _____

2. _____

3. _____

*Scoring Your Quiz*

**SCORE:**

−1 for worse

−1 for a new negative symptom

0 for same or does not apply (you didn't start with the symptom)

+1 for better

+2 for much better

A score of +4 should encourage you to stay on the diet.

A score of + 8 should mandate you to.

---

# Medical Indicators

Now, assuming you've taken my advice, let's look at the results of your blood tests.

First, let's look at the cholesterol reading. Lipolytic low-carbohydrate diets have been well studied in this regard, and even the extreme high-fat version of such a diet generally drops the total cholesterol level a little bit in the group starting with readings over 200. But this process usually takes 4 to 8 weeks. During the first week the cholesterol may be elevated, a phenomenon reported on all diets that act quickly in using up fat stores. Even zero food, i.e. fasting, has that effect.*

---

*The biphasic cholesterol response is so well known that one has to take notice of the study by Rickman purporting to show that a low-fat and low-carbohydrate diet such as the one proposed by Stillman is a cholesterol elevating diet, even though Rickman's study covered less than two weeks on the Stillman diet. That study, which has been quoted many times because it served the purposes of those who wish to criticize low-carbohydrate diets, must be classified as either an incompetent and poorly thought out investigation, or as an intellectually dishonest hatchet job.

Now, since you will be doing this test after only two weeks, you may get unpredictable results. Unless the cholesterol has shot up considerably (over 20 points), it may be assumed that it would be lower by the time another reading is taken after 3 to 4 more weeks. If the cholesterol has not gone to a healthy level, yet you were satisfied with the diet's advantages, you should make it a point to remain on the diet, take the cholesterol-lowering nutritional supplements outlined on pages 147–149 and repeat the test within a month.

On the other hand, if your triglyceride level was elevated, or even high normal (over 140 mg%), it will plummet down dramatically. Drops of 40–80 mg% are commonplace. If you don't get such a response, make sure you followed the diet correctly; or else, repeat the test making sure you wait 14 hours after your last meal before the blood is drawn.*

The other lab parameters should remain as good as before, except that there may be an elevated uric acid level. Should this happen, know that you can control it by going to a higher level of the diet and slowing your weight loss to less than two pounds per week.

## Practical Problem Solving

If, however, you simply don't seem to be losing much weight on the diet, then you need to turn immediately to Chapter 18, *Metabolic Resistance*. Sometimes, some very simple problems can give adverse results. Simple problems usually mean simple solutions. When I say that only two

*And you should be aware that many scientists regard elevated triglyceride levels as perhaps an even better marker for the risk of heart disease than cholesterol levels.

percent of dieters are unable to succeed on the Atkins diet, I mean precisely that—two percent—one dieter out of fifty. I think that means the odds are good that Chapter 18 will correct your difficulty.

On the other hand—I suppose there always is another hand—too much success can sometimes masquerade as failure. When the diet works too well, and the weight loss is too rapid, there can be weakness or other slightly debilitating symptoms, presumably caused by sodium or potassium shifts, that can be corrected by the simple measure of tripling or quadrupling the vegetable intake and slowing the weight loss down. Whenever weight loss exceeds one pound per day, you should suspect that you may experience some symptoms. Another problem that people occasionally experience is leg cramps at night. This is due to a rapid excretion of calcium and almost invariably indicates that the dieter has not followed my recommendations on vitamin supplementation. See Chapter 22.

## Success and Long-Term Satisfaction

The Atkins low-carbohydrate diet has many levels, and is made for many different types of people. The high-fat, deep-ketosis form of it that you've just experienced is not *the diet* but an extreme variation of it. And the fact is most of the time spent on the Atkins diet is not spent on this level. This first level, the *Induction* level, is to be used whenever ketosis/lipolysis must be induced, but I do not advise staying on this level for any length of time, unless it is the only level that works.

Instead, I want you next to find the level of carbohydrate restriction that works best for you as you're making your passage through the pleasant waters of long-term weight loss, whether that passage is 6 weeks to lose twenty pounds or 10 months to lose a hundred. Later on, you'll go one step further and find the level of carbohydrate restriction that works best in sustaining you at your ideal weight level once you've attained it.

All you gung-ho types may think the ideal level is simply that which takes the pounds off fastest, i.e. the diet you've just been on for the first 14 days. But why, in heaven's name, should that be true? Fast weight loss isn't a very important consideration when you're going to be solving your weight problem for the rest of your life. What *is* an important consideration is being comfortable, contented and healthy. I want you to feel at ease on the Atkins diet. Physically well, satiated, pleased with your daily menu, confident in your body. The vast majority of you will find that the level of carbohydrate consumption that achieves that best is *not* the first level.

In Part Four of the book, I'll show you how you go on through the four Atkins diets, passing from the *Induction diet*, to the *On-going Weight Loss* diet, and then to the *Pre-Maintenance* and *Maintenance* diets. On the last of those diets, you'll learn how to find and work with the lifetime carbohydrate level that's right for you.

Now it's time to look at some of the health advantages of the diet you've already discovered has the capacity to take weight off more efficiently than any diet you've ever been on before.

# PART THREE

---

# Why the Diet
# Makes You
# Healthy

# 11

## Diet-Related Disorders and You

Now that many of you have experienced the remarkable improvements in well-being that accompanied your 14-day diet experience, I will assume that I got your attention. I promised you weight loss while taking in lots of food, and since I prepared you for it, you're probably not surprised. But I'll wager that many of you were quite surprised to see that symptoms you have never connected to weight loss cleared up too.

Twenty-five years ago, I reasoned that if a diet could predictably clear up a cluster of symptoms, then that symptom cluster must have been partly caused by whatever diet my patients had previously been on. I was convinced I was seeing hypoglycemia, and I so stated.

But over the next few decades I witnessed thousands of patients whose symptoms promptly cleared up on their new diet, but who were not hypoglycemic. I classified the whole lot of them—patients whose symptoms came and went *ac-*

*cording to whether they were consuming carbohydrates*—
as people with Diet-Related Disorder. And, over time, I
realized that was a category of illness in its own right. Besides unstable blood glucose, the two other principal car-
bohydrate-based conditions that are part of the Diet-Related
Disorder syndrome—DRD—are a) individual food intolerances, and b) the yeast syndrome, the condition caused
when the organism Candida albicans gets numerically out-
of-control in your intestinal tract. Less commonly, we
found nutritional deficiencies or addictions to certain foods
as other contributing causes of the disordered body har-
mony that clears up when carbohydrate is sharply restricted.
These are the elements of Diet-Related Disorder.

A pretty intelligent question, and the one you are probably asking, is: "Why did you feel you had to invent a
disease you call Diet-Related Disorder? Why couldn't you
just identify who has hypoglycemia, who has yeast overgrowth, and who has specific food intolerances?"

The basic answer to that question is that there is considerable confusion among those doctors clinically expert in
these conditions as to which symptoms should be attributed
to which conditions. For example, when the hypoglycemic
complains of abdominal bloating is it not his/her yeast syndrome? If a chemically sensitive individual craves sweets,
is it not his/her hypoglycemia? When a yeast patient reacts
to dairy products, is it not his/her food intolerance? More
and more doctors have come to recognize that they must
deal with all of these problems in a single individual because they are so frequently found together in individuals.

Interestingly enough, the majority of people on the ke-
togenic/lipolytic diet feel better even before weight loss
mounts up to more than a handful of pounds. That's one
of the reasons why this section will be important to you.
It's going to have a major positive impact on your lifelong

commitment to the diet. After all, if you know that the diet corrects a specific condition or conditions that you have, that will inevitably motivate you to stay on it. All diets are not alike, and all do not correct Diet-Related Disorder.

In these next five chapters, let's see how much you can learn about yourself.

# 12

# The Sorrows of Hypoglycemia and the Perils of Diabetes

I assume you recall that in Chapter 3 I talked about hypoglycemia as the symptomatic aspect of the hyperinsulinism that correlates so strongly with the presence of obesity. Now here I am talking about it as the cornerstone of DRD.

I won't be repetitive, but I do want you to know the vast extent of the scientific discoveries that justify your considering the real probability you may have or may eventually develop disturbances of your glucose and insulin metabolism.

A brief review is in order:

1) If you are, or have been, significantly overweight, or if you have an eating (behavior) disorder, chances are much greater than 50–50 that you have insulin resistance and hyperinsulinism.
2) Insulin resistance and excess are the first abnormali-

ties on the way to developing glucose disorders (gly-copathy).

3) Hypoglycemia, pre-diabetes, and type II diabetes are stages of the same disease—glycopathy. All begin with insulin resistance/excess.

4) Insulin and glucose disorders accelerate the development of atherosclerosis, the mechanism leading to heart attacks.

5) Therefore, stop the insulin-based chain of events, and you can protect your heart and extend your life.

First, I'd like to stress the symptoms you may be experiencing right now. Let's look at hypoglycemia first.

## Why Do People Feel So Much Better So Fast on the Atkins Diet?

The correct answer certainly is (most of the time) that the diet deals with the unstable levels of blood sugar that we speak of, somewhat loosely, as reactive hypoglycemia. This instability produces symptoms, such as:

- Frequent bouts of fatigue—sometimes overwhelming—often in the afternoon.
- Sleep difficulties, usually combined with a need for considerable amounts of sleep. Awakening from a sound sleep is a specific example.
- Emotional instability, mood swings, sadness and weepiness for which there's no explanation or cause. Inability to concentrate, irritability, anxiety, brain fog and confusion. Becoming easily obsessed with annoyances.

This list of symptoms, some of which obviously share common ground with mental disorders, could be expanded. My patients often don't want to talk about them. They think it's their fault, just like being fat. I hear them make remarks like this:

*Maybe I should be seeing a psychiatrist.*
*I just don't seem to care anymore. Life can do what it wants with me.*
*I don't have any control over my life.*
*I'm so weak-willed that I don't know why I even try.*
*Sometimes I feel suicidal.*

These remarks, coming from people who quite clearly have nutritional disorders, arouse my suspicion that a fair percentage of the "mental illness" that doctors diagnose would vanish if only people would eat right.

I'm sure you'd like to avoid these symptoms as well as the physical ones, but following a low-fat diet isn't necessarily going to do that for you. I've seen many people who go on this current fad diet and feel worse because they're consuming more fruit, fruit juices, frozen yoghurt, and Gatorade. The knee-jerk reaction in favor of low-fat dieting simply doesn't address many of the actual diet-related problems of body and mind that a sizable percentage, perhaps even a majority, of human beings have.

## Coming Alive Again

Let's look at the physical first. I'm sure you remember what it was like being a kid, bouncy with energy and sure of your physical capacity to meet any challenge. Well, how would you like to have part of that back again?

Changes come quickly once you alter your blood glucose dynamics, and those changes are one of the reasons people stay on the diet. There's no doubt that feel-good changes can make their appearance in Atkins dieters long before there is significant weight loss. Over the years, I've seen thousands of people come into my office with expressions of lethargic weariness and plop themselves down in chairs in a manner that makes me wonder if a crane and derrick will be required to lift them out again.

Yet when I see them next, two or three weeks later, the change is generally remarkable. They have pep, and the air of helplessness I noticed at the first visit is gone. I had a patient, whose story I recounted at length in my last book, who had been suffering from fatigue for the previous twenty years, had gotten no help from a half dozen doctors, and had then come to me and cleared up all his symptoms in less than a week on the low-carbohydrate diet. A few weeks later, as he recounted at an office visit, he went out to dinner at an Italian restaurant with a client, ate a lot of pasta and bread, and afterwards, driving home alone, stopped for a red light. The next thing he knew a policeman was waking him up. The fatigue induced by his meal had put him to sleep right there in the middle of traffic.

## And What If the Problem Seems More than Physical

Direct physical results are most common, but the complexity of human beings can produce more complex and serious problems than fatigue. For instance, Phillip Rossi, a 35-year-old wrestling promoter, came to me because for years he had been the victim of extreme panic attacks. Various doctors blamed it on "nerves" and some of them helpfully prescribed Valium, which Phil dutifully took, occasionally supplementing their soothing effects with self-prescribed marijuana joints.

Naturally, drugs, whether prescribed or recreational, were no cure, though there were times when they toned down the situation. Yet, Phil still had panic attacks, which were so frightening and upsetting that, as he put it, "My whole day consisted in trying to stay calm."

Many of us when confronted with a grown man who has attacks of trembling, cold sweats, heart palpitations, and absurd overwhelming fear—and has these grim things inexplicably and repeatedly—are perhaps tempted to dismiss these problems as simply too bizarre and irrational to understand. Yet they are utterly real and overwhelming. Phil's anxiety was so great that "big things scared me and little things scared me. Driving scared me and being in the dark scared me."

By 1988, Phillip Rossi had become so dependent on his drugs and so disgusted with himself that he decided to go "cold turkey." He went off everything, and the result was an anxiety attack so severe that he didn't leave his house for three months. "Even the sound of the phone ringing terrified me."

I know you're thinking, "Are you really going to tell me this is *all* hypoglycemia, Dr. Atkins?" My answer is, no, I wouldn't necessarily say that. But I treated it as if it were! And with success!

Though I suspected what the major diagnosis would be, the GTT was, of course, the giveaway. His fasting glucose was 122, going up to 166 in a half hour and plummeting to a low of 45 after three. The difference between the high and the low is called the delta, and a delta of 121 is a definite indication of blood sugar abnormality.

The results of treating Phil's panic attacks with a low-carbohydrate diet were very satisfactory. It's true he had to dump his Oreos and his banana barges, but in compensation, within two weeks, his anxiety became manageable and his panic attacks were very, very rare. He says he has about four a year now.

And since this is a weight-loss book, I may as well mention that when Phillip Rossi came to see me he weighed 224 pounds, and, after four months on the diet, he weighed 180, which is a region he's remained in ever since.

Phillip Rossi's comment? "My life has changed; now I feel up to manufacturer's standard."

## Enormous Effects

So you see that when we talk about blood sugar disorders, we have a condition that can radically affect an individual's physical and mental states. Women with severe pre-menstrual syndrome often find, for instance, that a change of diet will correct the underlying hypoglycemia that can fiercely exacerbate this hormonal condition. When their next menstrual period comes around, they often find they've dramatically improved.

But let's look at hypoglycemia and its frequent follow-up disease, diabetes, in some sort of logical order and try to understand their mechanics.

## First There's "Low Blood" Sugar

As I mentioned earlier, your blood glucose powers most of what your body does, as well as fuels your brain. Anytime you're feeling good, you can take it as given that your body is working off of optimal quantities of glucose (or ketone bodies, if you're in ketosis).

Hypoglycemia (low blood sugar) is not a good thing, but what is hypoglycemia? The word itself is Greek, derived from *hypo* meaning "under," *glykis* meaning "sweet," and *emia* meaning "in the blood." *Too little sugar in the blood.* That sounds clear, but what it demonstrates is that the word *hypoglycemia* is actually a misnomer.

Stick with this literal translation, and you will assume it's the opposite of diabetes, which you probably remember involves too *much* sugar in the blood. You may have heard it said of a diabetic that he's "spilling sugar in his urine." That is indeed the product of excess—and yet the fact is that, far from being opposites, hypoglycemia and diabetes are actually successive stages of the same disease.

The proper term for describing the hypoglycemic's real problem is "unstable blood sugar," for it is the over-reaction of the glucose mechanism (going up too high and then dropping too far and too fast) that explains the hypoglycemic's problems.

One of the most intriguing evidences for the hypoglycemia-diabetes connection was found by scientists in the 1960s[1]. These researchers studied the offspring of *two* diabetic parents—people who were almost by definition, pre-diabetic. They found a classic series of abnormalities in these patients. First came hypoglycemia—a sharp drop on the glucose tolerance curve I showed you in Chapter 4. Years would pass. Then these subjects, still hypoglycemic, showed elevations of their blood sugar readings within an hour after glucose was administered. These elevations lasted 2 hours, then 3 hours. Finally, the very high blood-sugar readings of early diabetes occurred throughout the test and throughout the day.

What happened was this: In the early stages, these individuals, genetically sensitive to any abnormalities of blood glucose, were reacting to the high levels of serum glucose that their diet produced by manufacturing large quantities of insulin and forcing the glucose down. This led to the typical hypoglycemic curve in which blood sugar rises fairly quickly after eating and then falls in the third, fourth, or fifth hour to an unpleasantly low level. It's this *fall*, too rapid and to somewhat too low a level that constitutes hypoglycemia, rather than a low level of blood sugar, *per se*.*

This early stage is typical of people with insulin resistance—the very people who tend to become fat. People of normal insulin sensitivity tend to stay thin, because just a touch of the "fat producing hormone" is enough to lower their blood glucose to a normal level and more insulin need not be released.

If you're insulin resistant—and you probably are, if you're reading this book to lose weight—then your body at some fairly early stage in your life lost the capacity to respond quickly to insulin. It "resisted" the insulin, and so the pancreas had to secrete more. The metabolic dynamics of glucose and insulin are thrown awry by this abnormal effort, and the body generally loses its capacity for fine tuning in this essential area. Consequently, too much insulin is secreted, and the blood-glucose level is temporarily knocked down to an undesirably low level. The unpleasant symptoms I mentioned at the outset of this chapter are either caused by the fact that the glucose level is too low to supply the brain's needs, or by the adrenalin-like activity

---

*I make this point because critics of hypoglycemia have attempted to obfuscate the issue by suggesting that something called *low blood sugar* is really very rare. As a permanent state of affairs, of course, it is. It's a response to glucose rather than a constant deficiency such as you have when your potassium or iron levels are too low.

initiated to counter-regulate the precipitously falling sugar level.

This is a first step in an unhealthy metabolic path. Eventually, the body can absolutely lose its capacity to produce insulin in the quantities required or its capacity to employ the insulin that's being produced, so that high blood-sugar levels result, and the early stages of diabetes are reached.

Lifelong students of diabetes have suggested that the potential for the disease exists in 20% of the population.[2] Keep in mind that most of that 20% is found among the overweight, since, when the final tally is made, 80% of all diabetics are obese. Some studies have suggested that, *if you're significantly overweight*, your chances of becoming diabetic will be one in two.

## And After Hypoglycemia, Diabetes?

Amazingly enough, many specialists have managed to suggest precisely the wrong diet for their hypoglycemics, pre-diabetics, and diabetics. I have treated hundreds of patients with Type II diabetes who were put on low-fat, high-carbohydrate diets and consequently had to be on insulin—sometimes as much as a hundred units a day—to cope with the unnecessary and *avoidably* high glucose levels that resulted.

I hate to be so cynical as to suggest that proper diet might adversely affect the thoroughly profitable administration of insulin and oral diabetic drugs, but I will certainly say that if sugar were denounced from the scientific pulpits as if it were sin, it would seriously compromise a mutually supportive food and pharmaceutical industrial culture.

It is difficult to avoid the damning implications of a high-carbohydrate diet, especially with regard to hypoglycemia and diabetes. As far back as 1970, Muller, Faloona, and Unger wrote in *The New England Journal of Medicine* of the effectiveness of a low-carbohydrate diet in preventing excess insulin production.[3] Four years later, two German doctors, E. F. Pfeiffer and H. Laube, at an International Symposium on Lipid Metabolism, Obesity, and Diabetes Mellitus presented the result of research indicating that diabetes might not occur at all, if it were not for the effects of sugars and starches on insulin levels. (And for T. L. Cleave's brilliant work on the relation between refined carbohydrates and diabetes, see Chapter 16 in this book.)

In 1972, in an intriguing study, A. M. Cohen described in the prestigious American journal, *Metabolism*, how he and his associates had been able to create an entire strain of diabetic rats in just a few generations by feeding them sugar and selectively breeding the most sugar-susceptible rats.[4] Is this not what is effectively happening to a significant percentage of our 20th-century human population? I do not know if any studies indicate overweight people tend to marry other overweight people, but if that were the case, then they would be selectively breeding for a susceptibility to diabetes provoked by our culture of refined carbohydrates.

Other studies, especially a number carried out on rats from 1964 to 1982, have demonstrated, almost beyond the possibility of contradiction, how the whole process begins with a deterioration of glucose tolerance generally compensated for by hyperinsulinism and continues grimly on toward diabetes.[5]

## But for You, That Will be the Road Not Taken

This process, which may already have begun in you, must be counteracted and put to rest. Let's get practical and see how it's done.

Suppose you know from your symptoms, confirmed by your GTT, that you are a reactive hypoglycemic. Suppose you know from your medical experience that you are diabetic. Suppose you are even on medication or insulin. What is the complete how-to for you?

You must have gathered by now which diet will be best for you. My experience numbers 15,000 patients with documented abnormalities of the GTT (hypoglycemics and diabetics) and over 99% showed improvement ascribed to the Atkins diet.

There's a good deal more you must know, but before I tell you about it, let me discuss a patient who went from eating the wrong foods to eating the right foods.

John Parlone, a 58-year-old real estate consultant, is a good example of what the program can do for a Type II diabetic in the early stages. John had already been diagnosed before he came to see us (his fasting blood sugar was 315) and put on glipizide, an oral diabetic medication.

Treating John wasn't difficult. Look at how across-the-board his improvements were! He started the Atkins diet two months before he came to the Center for a checkup, and by then, his blood pressure, which had been dangerously high for nearly a decade, had already fallen to 140/80. We eventually got it down to 116/70. In the two months before John came to the Center, he had also got his weight down from 225 to 204 using the low-carbohydrate diet. (John is 5'8".) In the next six months, we took it down from there to 169. John's cholesterol was 296 when he came to the Center; in five months we took it to 251. His triglycerides were 187; they fell to 77.

As for his diabetes, it proved to be eminently controllable. By his third month on the diet, John Parlone's blood sugar had fallen to 80, and we were able to take him off his medication.

John had been a big sweets eater with a passion for cake. He adjusted very well to his new diet and adjusted even better to the fact that his pants size had gone from a 40 to a 34. He felt better than he had in years and looked a heck of a lot better. What you see in John Parlone's results is a reflection of the fact that diabetes is a disease of carbohydrate metabolism completely bypassed by a low-carbohydrate diet. You may think I chose to write about John because he improved so rapidly and so thoroughly, but in reality, he's just a typical case.

## Start With the GTT

Let's see how one diagnoses blood glucose problems and the possibility of eventually developing diabetes.

I told you on page 75 that you must demand a 5-hour test and that drawing insulin levels is imperative if you are 15% above your ideal weight. But how does the test get interpreted?

Your doctor will tell you if you are abnormal, right? Maybe right and maybe wrong. The prejudice against the diagnosis and management of reactive hypoglycemia by the medical establishment represents one of its most prolonged failures to practice good, responsive medicine. For the past forty or more years, nearly a majority of physicians have taken a hypoglycemia-doesn't-exist attitude and, for them, presenting grossly abnormal results done at a proper medical lab will get you nowhere. It will get you angry denials, sometimes replete with expletives.

## Who Are These Doctors

By and large, these doctors represent the mega-orthodoxy within the profession—doctors who worship medicine with religious fervor, but not the process of medicine, rather the conclusions of its Holy Synod, the amorphous but all-powerful medical consensus.*

It is consensus medicine that denied the existence of reactive hypoglycemia even though GTT testing has always revealed deviations from the normal, or ideal, picture in the majority of obese subjects. The scientific rationale for their position is a series of studies on so-called "healthy normals," many of whom showed abnormalities that fulfilled most criteria for the diagnosis of reactive hypoglycemia. Their conclusion: If healthy normals show it, then the lab test has no meaning. But these healthy normals were not screened for family histories of diabetes, obesity, or heart disease, nor for symptoms like sugar craving, food addiction, or academic underachievement. Just how normal were the ones with the abnormal lab findings? Suppose someone had studied the same subjects for their cholesterol level? Would all of them have been below 200 mg %? I doubt it. Yet, if someone had concluded that those healthy normals with cholesterol elevations were to be treated without concern, he would have been drummed out of the corps.

The real diagnosis of reactive hypoglycemia is based more on symptoms than on the GTT results. The bottom line for the diagnosis is the correction of the symptoms by a diet known to stabilize hypoglycemia. And for overweight, symptomatic people, that's this one.

---

*I have discussed the matter at length in my second book, *Dr. Atkins Superenergy Diet*, and those of you running into difficulties with physician close-mindedness will find it of value.

---

**How to Measure a Normal Glucose Tolerance Test**

Use this as unequivocally normal:

Fasting 70–100 mg%
Peak (30–60 minutes) 120–160 mg%
Nadir (2–4 hours) 60–90 mg%
Delta (difference between lowest and highest reading) 30–80
  mg%

Without going into all the criteria for ferreting out abnormal values that I published in 1977 (*Superenergy Diet*), let me call your attention to one criteria—the delta.

If the delta is over 80 points, and you are overweight, you most probably have hyperinsulinism.

If the delta exceeds 100 points, you have fulfilled *my* official criteria for abnormality.

If it exceeds 125 points, you've got it, baby.*

---

## What About the Diagnosis of Diabetes?

Here you can get help from your personal physician. The medical profession does recognize diabetes. For cases in

---

*Remember that during glucose tolerance testing, when hyperinsulinism is present, there is usually a "free fall" of the glucose just before it hits its low, at which time adrenalin release raises it very quickly. It only stays at its real nadir for two or three minutes. Therefore, the lab's chance of drawing blood (on a once an hour basis) that reflects that real low is about 1 in 20. Consequently, the *rate* of fall in any given interval is an important criterion.

the grey area, the criteria given in the box on this page have been agreed upon.

---

**The Glucose Tolerance Sum System:**

Add the first four numbers in your GTT together. This means the numbers at fasting, 30 minutes, 1 hour, and 2 hours.

If the total (in mg%) is below 500, that is considered normal. If the total (in mg%) is above 800, that is considered diabetic.

The gray area, between 500 and 800, is called impaired glucose tolerance, and nearly half of the significantly obese fall into that area. So you see, there's a very good chance I'm talking about you. The closer your total approaches the 800 mark, the more probable it is that you will eventually be classified as a true Type II diabetic. But there is still some good news for you. Even if you are considerably into the diabetic range and are obese, the normalization of your weight by the lifelong curtailment of carbohydrate can get you to, and keep you in, the normal range for life.

---

## Special Nutrients for Glycopaths

If you do have one of these glucose/insulin disorders, there is a great deal that can be done *in addition to going on the diet*. First and foremost is the use of chromium supplementation.

Chromium is an essential part of the Glucose Tolerance Factor (GTF), and GTF has such a profound effect on facilitating sugar metabolism that several researchers suggested it be elevated to vitamin status, meaning that it is *essential* to health. I certainly believe it to be an essential nutrient for those with overweight tendencies.[6]

The problem was finding a source that the body assimilated well. For years the only effective source was brewer's yeast, which posed problems for the many people with the yeast syndrome that you'll be learning more about in the next chapter. But with the recent availability of chromium polynicotinate, a biologically available source has become available. In the three years I've been using nicotinate, and before that picolinate, I have seen a definite further benefit in the glucose metabolism of patients with both hypoglycemia and diabetes. Even more striking is the benefit of lowering the cholesterol and raising the HDL levels, a fact that strongly points to the value of controlling cholesterol by way of controlling carbohydrate metabolism.

The effective dose range of chromium (in either form) is 200–700 mcg per day.

## Zinc

The second most important mineral for diabetic/hypoglycemic individuals is zinc.[7] I have had cases in which I used zinc orotate (one of those hard-to-find zinc salts) and found blood glucose improvements in diabetics of 20–30 mg%.

An effective daily dose of zinc is 100–150 mg. Note, also, that two other minerals probably advantageous for diabetics are magnesium and manganese.

Vitamins, especially vitamin C and the B complex, facilitate most of the metabolic pathways that diabetic subjects use and must be a liberal part of any nutritional supplement. A single paper on one B complex constituent, biotin, in doses 100 times greater than you get in a good multivitamin pill, looked very promising.[8]

Other promising nutrients to help the diabetic are coenzyme $Q_{1}0$, pyridoxine alpha ketoglutarate (PAK), and the essential fatty acids, GLA and EPA. (You can learn more about these in *Dr. Atkins Health Revolution*.)

The newest nutritional concept for diabetes management may prove to be the use of selenium plus vanadyl sulfate. It is too early to tell whether they are safe in effective doses. They were effective in animal studies done by J. H. McNeill in Vancouver University of British Columbia, but the doses were greater than those used in human trials.[9] However, I do recommend 200–300 mcg of selenium daily for adult diabetics.

And although my mind does not readily run along the lines of prescribing pharmaceuticals, particularly those with a known risk, I can't help but be fascinated by the mechanism of action of the biguanides, which control blood sugar, while *lowering* the elevated insulin levels. This is what the obese diabetic and prediabetic wants to accomplish. The biguanide metformin has recently become available in the U.S. and Canada under the name Glucophage. Ask your doctor about its pros and cons.

## What About Hypoglycemic Symptoms?

Suppose the symptoms of hypoglycemia, the ones you've been treating all your life with a "fix" of sugar or other carbohydrate, won't respond to abstinence and instead are worse than ever. How do you rectify that?

Fortunately, abstinence almost invariably does work, but there can be a time when the symptoms seem to become a hurdle impossible to scale.

There is a nutrient almost *designed* to get you "over the hump" of symptoms so severe it seems only a direct dose of glucose will make your life bearable. The nutrient is one of our natural amino acids, L-Glutamine, the one amino acid that can directly serve as fuel for the brain. Doses of 500 to 1500 mg, four to five times a day, may be necessary until the cravings and related symptoms abate. Chromium and the other glucose-modulating nutrients I just mentioned are an integral part of the solution, as well.

Another nutrient you can call upon here is glycerol, sold as Glycerine, U.S.P. A tablespoon taken along with glutamine when the cravings are at their worst will surely help. I rarely have to prescribe these remedies beyond a few days when a person remains carbohydrate abstinent. The FMS-induced ketosis/lipolysis will take over in just a few days.

## How Do I Know Your System Works, Dr. Atkins?

I wish I could invite you all to study the case records of the Atkins Center. Here you would see 15,000 examples of people with the combinations of glucose disturbances and overweight. In many ways, it's what the Center treats best. You would see, to cite but one example, that over 50% of the group taking insulin is able to get off insulin completely and 98% on the oral anti-diabetic medications can be successfully weaned from them.

Now, having covered the various manifestations of glycopathy, let's look at DRD from a new perspective.

# 13

## The World of Yeast Infections

What could turn out to produce a metabolic slowdown hazardous to your weight-reduction program, might exacerbate hypoglycemic symptoms, if you have them, and might require you, in the end, to drop cheese, mushrooms, vinegar and other fermented condiments from the Atkins diet? The answer is yeast.

"Yeast? Now I know, Dr. Atkins, that you just get off on being perverse. First you recommend a diet that the AMA criticized, then you find fault with the diet that doctors all agree is good for everyone, then you make sure everyone takes vitamins, which doctors know are all worthless, then you try to get people off their prescribed medications. You go on to tell people that their problem is insulin, when the profession tells us it's cholesterol, then you try to tell us we have hypoglycemia, which the AMA has pronounced to be non-existent, and now you want to tell us we have another non-existent condition—the yeast syndrome."

To this irate and not too hypothetical critic, I can only answer, "When you're right, you're right." And, if you've been on the 14-day Atkins *Induction* diet, you already *know* who's right.

What you are in the process of learning is that the official consensus of the medical establishment, those same folks who brought you a national health-care price tag of $817 billion for 1992 can be that wrong. There are thousands of physicians in this country who treat yeast infections, but there is still an entrenched core of conservative doctors who deny they exist, except in the limited form of vaginal infections.

## Why Yeast in a Diet Book?

This may be the first diet book dealing with yeast, and you may be wondering why it is necessary to do so. One reason is that yeast overgrowth is an integral part of DRD, producing many of the symptoms attributed to hypoglycemia and contributing to much of the food intolerance you'll read about in the next chapter.

Another reason is that a yeast infection affects the metabolism in many often-unpredictable ways, but by and large, those ways tend toward the addition of weight rather than its reduction. The reason for this effect is still highly speculative; the fact that it exists is well known to any physician who treats the disorder.

## So Why is a Yeast Epidemic Denied?

Just as 60% of my patients have abnormal GTTs, so different from the criteria for normalcy that it would make any impartial observer at least wonder whether some truth might be lurking in the figures, so, too, do 30% of my patients have Candida albicans overgrowth diagnosed by direct microscopic visualization or orthodox immunologic blood tests. Yet the prejudice against recognizing this illness is so great that in New Jersey, doctors can lose their license for diagnosing it, and in all states, insurance carriers will delay or avoid payment to patients for whom candidiasis is the primary diagnosis.

Why the intense hatred of what seems to be a legitimate, rather prevalent medical problem?

Just look at the contributing causes of candidiasis and you will see an epidemic actually caused by the actions of health professionals.

Candida outgrows its boundaries (the Candida albicans yeast is a normal inhabitant of our bodies, generally comprising 10% of the microorganism profile of the intestinal tract) when a subject is exposed to:

1. A diet high in sugar and refined carbohydrates.
2. Antibiotics (more than 20 weeks in a lifetime would make Candida overgrowth a probability.)
3. The mercury in silver dental fillings.
4. Birth control pills, prednisone, and other steroids.

Since everything on this list is iatrogenic—meaning caused by the medical care we receive—or diet related and either recommended or condoned by establishment medicine, to admit that yeast is epidemic—which I believe it is—is to admit that medicine and dentistry share guilt in its causation.

First, consider antibiotics, which are capable of destroying or inhibiting the growth of germs such as the pneumococci bacteria, which cause pneumonia. Unfortunately, they will also kill the friendly Lactobacilli that live in your intestines and keep Candida from spreading.[1]

There's nothing wrong with antibiotics when you use them to save your life, but unfortunately, in our pill-popping society, they're taken for a variety of inappropriate reasons. Doctors will prescribe them to snuff out a bad cold, or to treat acne, or to prevent a nearly non-existent complication of mitral valve prolapse.

Antibiotics are probably the main unleasher of yeast infections, but birth control pills have also been implicated, and, finally, there's the poison that almost all of us carry around in our mouths twenty-four hours a day—mercury. The silver/mercury filling that dentists still put in the mouths of their patients is approximately 50% mercury, and mercury just happens to be the most poisonous free element our bodies get exposed to. Dentists have always believed that in amalgams it was stable and would not contaminate its host.

This simply isn't true. Mercury vapor tests in the mouths of real people have made that unambiguously clear.[2]

Mercury figures into this chapter because it's a sure-fire way to weaken your immune system in just such a way that yeast infections flourish. Now let's look at diet.

## What You Eat

I don't believe that your diet necessarily causes candidiasis, but my clinical practice has taught me that the wrong foods will definitely encourage a yeast infection once it has begun and will make it almost impossible to clear up.

The worst offender is sugar. Indeed, nothing is more usual than to find that the victim of a yeast infection has sugar cravings. Sugar is the major growth factor for yeast. Candida patients are warned to stay away from ice-cream, candies, cakes, corn syrup, fructose, maple syrup, molasses, etc. etc. It is no coincidence that Atkins weight-loss dieters won't be eating any of those foods, either. You'll also be avoiding the lactose in milk and all those refined carbo-hydrates like starches, white flour, and white rice that easily turn to sugar in the body.

All of this is very critical for those of you who are going on the Atkins diet to lose weight. A yeast infection can prevent that from happening even though everything else is in your favor.

A good example is Stella Rudman, a 55-year-old woman I first saw in the late 1980s. Stella was 20 pounds over-weight, but that was a minor part of her reason for coming to me. Since menopause, she had had a very hard time with both physical and mental symptoms that were beyond her control. Her weight was going up, she had extreme cravings for sweets, she had numerous gastrointestinal problems from virtually non-stop gas and bloating to extreme rectal itching, and, worst of all, she was frequently and severely depressed. Her doctors initially gave her estrogen to help her get through menopause, but she only got worse. They then turned to the psychotropic drugs to control her de-pression, and when she came to us she was on a formidable anti-depressant cocktail consisting of lithium, pamelor, and imipramine.

Many of you who are not familiar with yeast infections, and indeed many doctors who have never treated them, will be amazed to discover that we were able to pretty easily settle all these problems by treating Stella for her yeast infection, which we confirmed with a blood test. Put on a low-carbohydrate diet, within a week she was over her food cravings. Within two weeks her rectal itching and bloating had subsided almost to vanishing point. As her yeast cleared up, so did her depressions, and we began to wean her off her medication. We suspected that the estrogen she had been given several years before had been one of the major stimulators of her problems, since estrogen stimulates the overgrowth of Candida albicans.

In addition to the diet, we treated Stella by giving her forms of acidophilus to help rebalance the bacterial flora in her gut and then by giving her caprylic acid, a short-chain fatty acid that helps kill yeast in the bowel.

Stella started losing weight, and once off her medications she found herself for the first time in years free of such distressing side effects as mental sluggishness and slurred speech.

Typically, Stella's weight loss was only able to really get moving a month after she came to us, because she first had to get her yeast infection under control. Once that was done, the path was clear, and two months later her weight had dropped to 124. Three years have passed, and it remains in that range. Two or three times over the years, she's given way to temptation and started to binge on carbohydrates. Within days the symptoms of her yeast infection began to return, and she began to gain weight. Once we had to put her back on caprylic acid. But Stella Rudman understands her problem now, and, with her cooperation, these relapses quickly settled down.

She is a very good example of what a yeast infection can do and how essential it is to solve it if one wishes to solve a weight problem too. Slowly but steadily, the medical world is beginning to learn about and accept what we call systemic yeast infections. But they have been slow to do it. Very slow.

## This Disorder is Politically Incorrect

Is this because Candida is rare? Not at all. I'm willing to bet that there have been countless people in your life who had yeast infections—friends, acquaintances, probably relatives. One out of every three of my patients has Candida diagnosable by irrefutable laboratory tests. Yet comparatively little attention has been paid to it. Why? I think because—though the disease exists—it doesn't fit into the solutions that our society wants to deliver to sick people.

Candida albicans infections, though tricky to treat, are treatable. Candida is a yeast, a single cell fungus, and we all have a bit of it in our bodies. Indeed, there are hundreds of species of indigenous biologic forms resident in the human intestinal tract, and Candida albicans is just one of them. It is, therefore, a normal part of us, and, in healthy competition with our other intestinal flora, it serves us well, performing yeasty missions in our gut.

The condition called *candidiasis* begins when, through some disturbance in our body's balance, the bacterial equilibrium is upset, causing an overgrowth of yeast organisms. Most commonly, Candida albicans is the yeast that overgrows, colonizing areas that were formerly alien to it and suppressing less aggressive bacteria. Having, by conquest, acquired this new position in the body, Candida generally shows no inclination to return to its former humble role.

As you only partially saw in Stella Rudman's case, the range of problems that Candida can cause are so wide ranging as to verge on the fantastic—and, of course, that's part of the problem. A short list includes lethargy, fatigue, depression, inability to concentrate, headaches, gastrointestinal disorders including constipation, abdominal pain, diarrhea, gas and bloating, respiratory ailments and disorders of the urinary tract and reproductive organs. The most specific symptom is bloating—gas in the lower abdomen. Candida patients often have a tell-tale lower abdominal pot belly that seems forever filled with gas. If this describes you, and you have had exposure to one of the risk factors, such as oral antibiotics, do yourself a big favor and see a doctor who claims to be proficient at finding and treating Candida.

*There is a very pragmatic reason why a yeast problem should be identified. If you have it, there must be dietary restrictions beyond those involving carbohydrates. If you don't do that, you'll wonder why everybody else got better on the Atkins diet and you didn't.*

One out of three of you will find that it's necessary to avoid "yeasty" foods, some of which you might otherwise be eating on an Atkins diet. These include cheeses, vinegar and other fermented condiments, mushrooms, yeast-containing vitamins, wine, and beer. Bread and baked goods, which are not allowed on pre-maintenance levels, would be totally disallowed. In general, most people with Candida are allergic to yeast and get symptomatic when fermented food items are consumed.

## Will This Cure Candida?

Sometimes it does. However, it is more likely that the elimination of inappropriate foods will be only partly effective. Therefore, when yeast is identified, you'll probably find it necessary to proceed to a more aggressive solution.

The bolder treatment traditionally centers around the anti-

Candida drug nystatin, which is effective taken by mouth. Nystatin has become the gold standard in Candida therapy. However, it is not my first choice of specific therapy.

I am just as interested in strengthening the immune system, cleansing the bowel, which has usually been attacked by protozoal parasites that are found in association with Candida, and treating for the allergy to yeast and molds most of these patients have.

My choice of therapies that do attack the yeast itself include two short chain fatty acids—caprylic and undecenylic acids. I will also use ozone, hydrogen peroxide, or chlorine dioxide, which liberate nascent oxygen. All forms of free oxygen are fungicidal. Garlic is also an effective oral treatment. Like nystatin, all of the above can kill vast quantities of yeast and should be administered carefully because the dead yeast can produce a "die-off" reaction and make the patient feel even worse for a few days than he or she felt before.

Certain treatments to improve the yeast sufferer's condition are employed simultaneously with an attack on the yeast. The care of the bowel is very important and psyllium and bentonite are often prescribed. People with Candida often suffer from constipation, and these agents improve that, as well as help remove the putrefying substances and toxins that have gathered in the bowel.

As you can see, Candida is complicated, and it sometimes requires the sort of complicated attack I've just outlined for you. But the good news for many of you will be that the Atkins diet is, by itself, so effective against Candida that you can have a Candida-complicated case of overweight and clear it up without even knowing you had it.

But that is not necessarily the end of the story, for my experience has been that yeast infections coexist with food intolerances in almost 75% of the patients who have them. Therefore, in the next chapter, we will investigate that problem.

# 14

# Food Intolerances—Why We Each Require a Unique Diet

The third part of DRD is intolerance by specific people to specific foods. This is something that could affect your diet and make further restrictions necessary. Virtually everyone who has difficulty with simple across-the-board carbohydrate restriction will have to consider the possibility of specific food reactions.

This cautionary note to all of you is based on a simple, self-evident truth: *Everybody is different.*

## Everyone Must Be Treated as an Individual

To the heretofore unsuccessful dieter this means: If you get into trouble or you can't achieve the results this book promises you, then recognize your individual food intolerances and eliminate them. The diet may be more stringent, but the success is just about guaranteed.

A good diet can't be bought off the rack; it's custom fitted, made for an individual. Eating a healthy low-carbohydrate diet will do a lot for your body. Finding out what foods you can't handle is what makes the diet a more perfect fit for you.

Happily, the most common sources of food intolerance are generally found in foods I recommend you either avoid entirely or approach very cautiously. The foods to which people most commonly prove intolerant are grains (such as corn, wheat, rye, and oats), soy, milk, cheese, brewers and bakers yeast, and eggs. The only two you might be eating on an Atkins weight-loss regimen are eggs and cheese.

But those foods are hardly the end of the story. There are many other allergy-producing foods. Strictly speaking, you *could* be allergic to *any* food you eat—and a very small number of people seem to be universal reactors, which means, as you may have guessed, reactive to all of them.

## Alas, the Foods You Love

Perhaps the first and most basic principle of food allergy is this: The foods you eat and love the most will usually be part of your problem. In fact, it has been observed that many Orientals are allergic to rice, and many Mexicans are allergic to corn. Consequently, you carbohydrate addicts will often find that on an Atkins diet, you do more than just lose weight and feel more energetic. You may also clear up nagging physical ills, from headaches to diarrhea, that you never did understand the source of.

The trouble with food intolerances is that we actually become addicted to the very foods we're intolerant to. The term you will see often repeated in the writings of special-ists in environmental medicine is allergy/addiction. It works something like this: Those foods that make us ill actually make us feel better for a short time after we eat them. It's a classic addiction pattern, isn't it? The sugar addict, the drug addict, the alcoholic, all feel better when the fix is in. But they all feel worse later.

For each and every addicted person, there's the difficult process of withdrawal. If you're allergic to a food that has become the mainstay of your diet, then you will suffer unpleasant withdrawal symptoms when you quit. The worse these symptoms are, the happier I, as a doctor, am. That's because the greater your addiction is, the greater your physical improvement will be once you scale the withdrawal hurdle. So put up with feeling worse for a few days, because after you give up the food "you can't live without," you're almost certainly going to feel better. The general rule is that after two to five days, the withdrawal symptoms cease.

A few of the other very common allergic foods are the nightshade family (potato, tomato, aubergine, paprika, tobacco), sulfites, coffee, chocolate, citrus fruits, and— among the foods permitted on my diet—shellfish, beef, chicken, onions, mushrooms, pepper and other spices, and artificial sweeteners.

## This Could Happen to You, Too

As you might imagine, going on a low-carbohydrate diet will clear up a large percentage of food intolerance. When we treat for food intolerance using the cytotoxic blood test, we find that the majority test positive for problems with one or more carbohydrates and most often show no reaction to the animal-based, low-carbohydrate foods. The conclusion is warranted that some of the minor physical miseries of your life will clear up on the basis of avoiding food-intolerant items.

But if you've been on the Atkins diet for some weeks and you do not feel considerably better than when you began, then your next move should be to look into possible food intolerances to some items you are still eating.

## What Causes Food Intolerances?

No one knows for sure, but I believe many food intolerances are related to the weakening of the immune system, secondary to problems like yeast infections. It is rare to find a person with a yeast infection who doesn't have some food intolerances.

Food intolerances are implicated in scores of health disorders. One of my favorite medical studies was done in 1983 by five physicians at the Hospital for Sick Children in London.[1] The researchers took 88 children, all of whom had been having migraine headaches at least once a week for the previous six months, and put them on a rotation diet that strictly excluded many varieties of food for weeks at a time. To the doctors' admitted astonishment, 93% of the children became headache-free once their food intolerances were discovered and the foods were taken out of their diet. One child had reacted to 24 foods and was symptom free when all those foods were withdrawn. Cow's milk, eggs, wheat, chocolate, and oranges were all foods to which more than twenty children responded. Of equal importance was the fact that the change of diet corrected such other disorders as abdominal pains, behavior disorder, epileptic fits, asthma, and eczema in a number of the children.

## How Do I Discover My Food Intolerances?

The range of techniques is wide. You'll notice I haven't mentioned conventional allergists, who look for a substance in the body called immunoglobulin E, or IgE, for short. Most practicing allergists have the strange conceit that only "their" allergy—the kind caused by IgE—is a real allergy. That's why I try to use the term food intolerance as much as possible, so as not to get into a battle over language.

Probably less than 50% of food intolerances are related to high levels of IgE produced in the body when the antigen, as any allergy-producing substance is called, is eaten. These can be detected, therefore, by the skin tests that allergists use, though the principal test, called a RAST test, is by no means free of false positives and negatives. For non-IgE food intolerances there are a variety of techniques of discovery. I prefer those systems based on the dissolution of the granules of the white blood cells (granulocytes). This is called cytotoxic testing. In cytotoxic testing, a blood test is performed in which a technician notes the degree to which granules have dissolved. Presumably this correlates with the degree of food intolerance that the patient has at that moment to each of the foods tested. Though not perfectly accurate, it is a very good test when done by skilled hands, and is quite reasonable in price.

But even without lab tests, there is a very successful system of avoiding food intolerances that people have used with great success and that I would like to introduce to you here. The basic principle is to go on a rotational diet in which you avoid the repeated consumption of anything.

Generally, on this sort of diet, all the foods you are to eat are arbitrarily divided into four different but equal groupings. They are assigned to Days 1, 2, 3, and 4. On Day 1 only foods from the Day 1 group are eaten; and then three days must pass before foods from that group are eaten again (i.e. on Day 5). Similarly the Day 2 menu must be avoided until it is repeated on Day 6. And so on. Thus you take advantage of a "loophole" in the production of symptoms from most food intolerances, which is that most people can ingest an "intolerated" food if the time that passes before they repeat the action is at least four days.

With this system, you may never learn what your food intolerances are, but you avoid the symptoms, anyway. The disadvantage is that the choice of foods you may select on any given day is only 25% of what it would be on your already restricted diet. This makes it a tough diet, but to the person with persistent symptoms, it can be worth the extra effort.

Whatever technique is used to determine food intolerances, I employ the following system for reintroducing foods.

The first project is to eradicate the symptoms, even if it means using a diet of total austerity. This is best accomplished by using any and all systems of avoiding intolerances (cytotoxic testing, avoidance of known and suspected food intolerances, yeast restriction, removal of caffeine and, of course, sugars). Once that is accomplished, you may *then* reintroduce the foods that you hope will prove acceptable. These you replace, one food at a time. Those that bring on your symptoms upon being reintroduced are the ones you're going to have to eliminate permanently, because bringing on symptoms is the proof of food intolerance. Those that you tolerate, happily, can be restored to your permanent diet.

# 15

## Good Protection for Your Heart

One of the reasons this book is being written is that I have interviewed hundreds of my old, previously successful patients, and, although most are prospering healthwise, a certain percentage of them are now overweight, not in the best condition, and, although still aware of the need to diet, are no longer using the low-carbohydrate diet they did so well on.

Since recidivism is not a problem one often has to deal with once a person has made a low-carbohydrate lifetime commitment, I went into great detail to find out why they weren't using the Metabolic Advantage techniques I'd taught them.

I asked, "Was the Atkins diet experience a bad one?"

"Not in the least," they would answer, "best diet I've ever been on."

"Did you like the food?"

"Can't recall a diet where I ate so luxuriously."

"Well, how did you feel on the diet?"

"You know, now that you ask, that was the best I've felt in my adult life."

I then proceeded to review the old medical records and noted that their lab values improved considerably on the regimen, as they usually do. Whereupon, I inquired: "OK, then explain to me why you don't eat that way today?"

Then the inevitable answer: "I heard (or read) that the diet isn't good for you."

Think of it! A large group of individuals absolutely turning their backs on common sense, defeating themselves by rejecting the very program which, by their own recollection, suited them best—and all because they were snookered by the prevailing winds of propaganda. Rather than choosing to repeat their previous success, they became enthralled with the naked emperor's clothes.

At first I was angry with my former patients, but now that I've observed this reaction a number of times, I'm angry with the society that creates this No Win Situation.

What I've just told you about is cognitive dissonance— the inability to believe what you've been programmed not to believe, however compelling the evidence. I imagine many of you have it, too, so I must deal with it before it defeats you.

Let us start with the main area of cognitive dissonance. People believe that the Atkins diet is bad for the heart. They believe it with such certainty that any attempt to demonstrate that the facts show otherwise is met with a smile of incredulity.

## And Yet, With a Low-Carbohydrate Diet, I Found the Beginning of an Answer

I'm a cardiologist by training, and I've spent a lot of my life treating cardiac patients. Naturally, it has always been deeply satisfying to me that the Atkins diet is so remarkably heart-healthy. Almost from the first moment that I began using it more than twenty-five years ago, I saw the good effects it had on my patients.

Patients with chest pain found their angina clearing up, often within days of going on the diet. Patients with episodes of cardiac arrhythmias maintained a normal rhythm as long as they kept to the diet. Patients with hypertension lowered their blood pressure—and fast.

I'll bet that's not what you've heard. You've had the opposite message drummed into your head so repetitively that I'm afraid you think I'm lying to you. You know with more certainty than you know the sun rises in the east and sets in the west that a diet allowing cream and butter and red meat *causes* heart attacks and that it'll make your heart symptoms worse.

So let's talk about the preconceptions you may have formed, ideas that could quite possibly lead to your being touted off a diet that may fit you as well as Cinderella's slipper fit her.

I'll start with a rhetorical question: How could the Atkins Center have shown a steady 25-year growth pattern into the significant clinical facility it now is if I had treated my patients with a diet that in any way jeopardized their health?

No, the facts are quite the opposite, and what may come as a surprise to many of you, the rationale and the all-important bottom-line observations are all documented in the doctor's ongoing bible, the widely disseminated medical journals, which we in the field refer to as "peer-reviewed medical literature." As we review it together, you may then see why I have spent much of my career developing and utilizing a diet that superficial observers persist in criticizing for its hypothetical effects on the heart, and why I actually treat *cardiac patients* with as much success on this diet as Dr. Dean Ornish claims (I'm sure truthfully) for the patients who he treats on a wildly different diet, an extreme low-fat, vegetarian diet.

I can only applaud Ornish's approach—he is not an ivory tower, academic theorizer; he's shown the results on his patients. But then, so have I.

## Misled by Words

The faulty preconception that a low-carbohydrate diet should, by rights, be heart hazardous is based on a knee-jerk linguistic reaction to the words fat and cholesterol. There is a fixation on the idea that, if fat and cholesterol are eaten, cholesterol levels will surely go up.

In fact, criticizing my diet, the AMA said they were "deeply concerned about any diet that advocates the unlimited intake of saturated fats and cholesterol-rich foods."[1] Then they scrutinized all the medical literature they could bring to bear and came up with *a single case described in 1929.*\*

Let's look at their language: "Individuals responding to such a diet with a rise in blood fat will have an increased

---

\*This was the study of the Arctic exploror, Vilhjalmur Stefansson, who, impressed with the health of the native Eskimos he observed, volunteered with an associate to be observed for a year on an all animal food diet. In this study, one of the two subjects' cholesterol levels did go up but the other's dropped. The AMA inaccurately reported that both men had cholesterol increases.[2]

risk of coronary artery disease." Absolutely. All I can say is: "I agree, and individuals who jump off a curb with a parachute and are thereupon attacked by an enraged bull will have an increased risk of torn garments."

The AMA's *ad hoc* nutrition panel had to phrase it that way, because they knew, of course, that they could not find any evidence that would have allowed them to make a stronger indictment.

I think it is clear from their circumspect language that the AMA was aware of the difference between the results when fat and cholesterol are added to a high-carbohydrate diet and the results that occur when they are added to a low-carbohydrate lipolytic diet. In the usual scenario, *when carbohydrates are a large part of the diet*, the undesirable lipid readings *may* get worse if there is an increased intake of fat as well; on the Atkins diet, such a result is rare indeed.

What studies were available to the AMA certainly supported my contention.

In 1979, I had occasion to review all of the published literature on the effect of low-carbohydrate diet programs on cholesterol and triglyceride levels. I was able to find ten which showed a lowering of the mean cholesterol level, and a single one covering, on average, only one week of low-carbohydrate dieting, showing an unfavorable result.

## Looking in the Literature

One study was published in 1966 by P. K. Reissell and his Harvard/Massachusetts General Hospital associates.[3] They studied eight patients with both high cholesterol and triglycerides, before and after a 1500 calorie, 26 gram carbohydrate diet. The lowering of lipid elevations was every bit as dramatic for those subjects as what I see in my office today. The average triglyceride level dropped from 1628 to 232, while the cholesterol fell from 470 to 278, with one subject dropping from 610 to 186.

Then there was the study done by Dr. Willard Krehl and his associates at the University of Iowa that I told you about in Chapter 6.[4] Krehl was no friend of low-carbohydrate dieting, yet when he put two older women on the 1200 calorie low-carbohydrate (only 12 grams daily) diet he was testing, he found no change in their cholesterol after two and one half months, and their triglycerides were significantly lower. In addition, the five obese teenage girls he studied dropped their cholesterol levels an average of 20 points.

In Germany, where low-carbohydrate dieting is much more enthusiastically accepted and studied, many confirmations were published. The importance of the German studies is that they were done on sizable groups of patients. Dr. U. Rabast's many studies included a group of 104 clinic patients who followed a diet of 40 grams of carbohydrate for three to four months.[5] The group's cholesterol average fell from 239 to 220, the triglycerides from 159 to 118. A subgroup with higher starting readings did better, their cholesterol dropping from 314 to 259.

Dr. Ewald Riegler confirmed the same phenomenon on a group of 128 patients.[6] The most dramatic improvements once again came when the cholesterol was very high, one group dropping the cholesterol from 465 to 216 after six months.

This painstaking review of the medical literature leaves us with a paradox that may be unequalled in the annals of medicine. That ketogenic levels of carbohydrate restriction will lower a normal cholesterol level slightly, an elevated cholesterol level moderately, a midrange triglyceride level impressively and a high triglyceride level dramatically has been demonstrated, confirmed, and reconfirmed. And with the exception of a brief study of one week's duration, there is not a scintilla of published data to refute it.[7]

By all the usual standards of medical proof, the benefit of carbohydrate-restricted diets on serum lipid levels is an established medical fact.

But the paradox is this. Because American medicine is more responsive to the dogmatic pronouncements of academicians appointed to consensus panels than it is to scientific research, it is not an *accepted* fact.

The irony is further compounded by the fact that the diets recommended by these folks have an inconsistent cholesterol-lowering effect.

In fact, we can just about throw out half a century of research on the effect of diet upon cholesterol levels now that Stephen D. Phinney, M.D., a well-respected researcher from the University of California at Davis, has tracked cholesterol levels over time in a group of patients following an extremely low-fat formula diet.[8]

These obese subjects started with a mean cholesterol reading of 211 and successfully brought it down to 139 after one or two months of austerity dieting. Nice going. But his team continued observing their patients for another six months, *while on the diet*. Their group cholesterol had risen to 234! It wasn't until they went onto their maintenance diet that the cholesterol fell to 189. Since the observation of such a biphasic cholesterol response was reported in 3 other studies, we can only conclude that all studies not measuring cholesterol responses *over time* are of only limited value, and, in fact, the vast majority of studies on cholesterol as it relates to diet are of that nature.

The only published study of the low-carbohydrate diet over time that I could locate was the one by Riegler, who clearly showed that the six-month cholesterol level was as low or lower than the one-month level on a low-carbohydrate diet. This correlates closely with my own clinical findings where my patients' lipid levels stay down as long as they follow the program.

But the good news for cholesterophobics is yet to come. Dr. Jonathan Wright, who practices nutritional medicine and teaches it via seminars to hundreds of physicians, has observed that he has found 28 different nutrients for which there are published scientific studies demonstrating a cholesterol-lowering ability. I use many of them, and, in a few pages, I'll tell you how we do it.

Add the nutritional supplements useful for lipid-lowering to the already potent lipid control effects of the ketogenic/lipolytic diet and you see why we have collected so many examples of patients with dramatic cholesterol/triglyceride lowerings. These lowerings are of the order of magnitude found in patients who demonstrate *reversal of heart disease*.

## Reversal of Heart Disease?

Some of you may not know that heart disease, once thought to pursue an inexorable downhill course, has been shown in recent years to be reversible by serious lifestyle changes. This has great significance for those for whom a coronary bypass or angioplasty has been suggested. Surgeons tend not to inform you that you can improve the circulation to your heart and cheat them out of their day in the operating room, if you are willing to make lifestyle changes.

Since I am not willing to ask my patients to undergo the risk of angiography even once, let alone twice, I have not been able to *prove* reversal of heart disease on our program (as manifest by improved patency of coronary blood vessels). However, we have demonstrated reversal of the *symptoms* of heart disease in over 85% of Atkins Center overweight coronary patients who have diligently followed our program consisting of the lipolytic diet, nutritional supplements and chelation therapy.

The combination of a high-fat, low-carbohydrate diet and nutritional supplements has been reported on in the *Southern Medical Journal* of January 1988 by Dr. H. L. Newbold.[9] During the 3 to 18 months of follow up, his seven patients dropped their mean cholesterol levels from 263 to 189.

At the Atkins Center we tabulate our results every few years. The latest was published in my last book, *Dr. Atkins' Health Revolution*, and we reported a drop in cholesterol from 256.4 to 217.6 and of triglycerides from 166.5 to 97.2. But only half those patients were on the weight-loss diet, which has consistently produced more spectacular results.

So you can clearly see that, if the Atkins diet is a heart-attack diet,

a) It certainly is not mediated by any worsening of the serum lipids.
b) It would contrast sharply with the usual result wherein my heart patients almost always show a dramatic improvement, as manifested by their ability to discontinue medications which were previously necessary.

You certainly should know *why* the ketogenic/lipolytic diet is so beneficial to the heart. The scientific literature of the past ten years goes a long way toward explaining it.

## Gerald Reaven, Norman Kaplan, and Others

What is gradually being unveiled is an association not so much between fat consumption and heart disease (remember the French with their high-fat diets and fifty percent fewer heart attacks than we have), but between cardiovascular risk and four consequences brought about by a single metabolic cause.

Dubbed the "Deadly Quartet" by Dr. Norman Kaplan from the University of Texas' Southwestern Medical Center, these four consequences are upper-body obesity, glucose intolerance, high triglyceride levels, and hypertension.[10] Kaplan asserted that these problems were found together because there was a common causative element in all of them, and that element was our old friend, hyperinsulinism, the very thing that, back in Chapter 4, I showed you was part and parcel of metabolic obesity. What Kaplan's article, published in the *Archives of Internal Medicine*, in fact ended up saying was that high insulin levels might, in truth, be one of the chief determining factors in heart disease. As you'll soon see, he is not alone in this conjecture. The 76 bibliographical references in his article give you some idea of how *many* scientists' research have contributed to his conclusions.

I'll come back to the reasoning behind this, but first let me demonstrate what sort of statistical evidence there is for insulin's role in heart disease. Everyone knows that the famous Framingham study begun in Massachusetts in 1948 found a positive correlation between serum cholesterol levels and heart attacks.* Has anything of this kind been found relative to insulin levels? Just listen.

---

*When considering cholesterol levels and diet, it is important to keep in mind that the Framingham study *did not* show that there was a relation between the cholesterol or the fat *in people's diets* and their rate of heart disease. The study only demonstrated that there was a direct statistical

The three most significant studies were done in Wales, France, and Finland, and were published and widely discussed in the major medical journals of the world.

The Caerphilly, Wales Heart Disease study observed 2,512 men aged 45–59 years and demonstrated a connection between fasting plasma insulin levels and heart disease that existed independently of other confirmed risk factors. In the Finnish study—known as the Helsinki Policeman Study—1,059 men from 30 to 59 years of age were initially followed for five years. The data revealed that fatal (and nonfatal) heart attacks were more common in those who had the highest insulin levels (both fasting and in response to glucose). Finally, the Paris prospective study followed 7,246 men for an average of 63 months. Again coronary heart disease was found proportionate to the insulin levels, and the relationship was greater when the subjects were obese.[11]

And more recently, a study published in *Circulation* by the team in Helsinki showed that those with high triglycerides plus an unfavorable LDL/HDL cholesterol ratio could lower their heart attack risk rate by 71% when these problems were corrected.[12]

These very large studies have set many of our leading medical scientists on a course of rethinking. More and more of them are beginning to question whether the high-carbohydrate diets recommended for heart patients may not be so ideal as has been supposed.

Framingham director William Castelli, M.D. commented: "The findings swing the pendulum and show that high triglycerides can be a significant risk factor for some patients."[13]

---

relation between the level of cholesterol *circulating in the blood* and risk of heart disease.

It has, after all, been consistently shown that triglycerides parallel the insulin level and that the control of insulin levels can be done with supreme effectiveness on a *low*-carbohydrate diet. Grey and Kipnis demonstrated this in the early 70s. In 1979, Dr. Sheldon Reiser did a study with human volunteers demonstrating that a diet providing 18% of its calories from sugar—and this is now less than the U.S. national average—produced significantly higher lipid and insulin concentrations than did a diet with 5% of its calories derived from sugar.[14]

Among the many scientists who have begun to respond to this really formidable array of evidence, I would first like to mention the distinguished Stanford professor, Dr. Gerald Reaven, and his associate, dietetics expert Ann Coulston. Reaven has been pursuing the close connection between hyperinsulinism, hypertension, and cardiovascular risk factors with indefatigable zeal for almost twenty years now.[15]

He was the pioneer, but since 1985, more than a dozen major articles in the leading medical journals have followed in his lead.[16] One piece of the puzzle that Reaven showed was that hypertension—which no serious medical theorist has ever questioned as a risk factor for both stroke and heart disease—is intimately related to hyperinsulinism. In 1989, in a major article in *The American Journal of Medicine* titled "Hypertension as a Disease of Carbohydrate and Lipoprotein Metabolism," he wrote, "Patients with untreated hypertension have been shown to be resistant to insulin-stimulated glucose uptake and both hyperinsulinemic and hypertriglyceridemic . . ."[17]

In 1988, giving the Banting lecture at Stanford, he noted a clustering of risk factors for coronary artery disease, all of which were associated with high insulin levels and increased insulin resistance.[18] These included hypertension, high triglyceride levels, and decreased HDL cholesterol—the kind of cholesterol which has been found to be heart protective.

Other researchers have noted that insulin increases levels of LDL cholesterol—the kind of cholesterol that promotes heart disease. The mechanism by which this takes place was already clear. The Belfast scientist, R. W. Stout, had written in 1985 that "the arterial wall is an insulin sensitive tissue. Insulin promotes proliferation of arterial smooth muscle cells and enhances lipid synthesis and low density lipoprotein (LDL) receptor activity. *Insulin also promotes experimental atherosclerosis in a number of species.*"[19]

The circle has begun to close, and, I must admit, to my great satisfaction, the reasons why a low-carbohydrate diet is so heart-protective are becoming clearly visible. It is no accident that I have been able to use a low-carbohydrate diet to treat cardiovascular disease with ever-mounting success. Why should we be surprised? You remember I remarked that this was the natural diet of the human omnivore. People are well-fitted to eat fresh meat, fish, fowl, berries, nuts, seeds, vegetables, and, in moderation, fruits. Nature is not trifled with, and this was our diet for millions of years, long before the bizarre dietary habits of the 20th century were unleashed to plague us.

Vegetarians have suggested that the natural human diet is based on grain since that is what most civilizations have been growing in the form of wheat, rice or corn for the past 5,000 years. Yes, but what about the hundreds of thousands of years that preceded that? What are all those bones doing around the campfires of primeval man and what were they doing with all those hunting tools we've discovered? Using them for letter openers?

Let's return once again to Norman Kaplan's intriguing article on the "Deadly Quartet." Look at the diagram at the top of the following page.

Kaplan has had the good sense needed to notice the obvious. All these conditions characteristically occur in subjects with high insulin levels, and, moreover, these conditions are very likely to coexist in the same person. Thirty-five million people in the United States are obese (20% over ideal body weight), and 40 million people are hypertensive. Among the obese, hypertension is three times more common than among the non-obese. High triglyceride levels are twice as common among the obese as among the non-obese. The association is even stronger if one measures patients with upper-body obesity. The paunch so characteristic of the middle-aged man is closely related to metabolic factors that put him at risk for a heart attack.

If you still wonder just how strong these associations are, listen to a statement made by Dr. Albert Rocchini, a medical scientist at the University of Minnesota. He writes: "It has been estimated that by the fifth decade of life, 85% of diabetic individuals are hypertensive and obese, 80% of obese subjects have abnormal glucose tolerance and are hypertensive, and 67% of hypertensive subjects are both diabetic and obese."[20]

It is now known that in all these conditions, hyperinsulinism is generally found. In fact, when I first meet an overweight patient, I expect to learn from blood chemistries that the patient has high triglycerides, glucose intolerance, and high insulin levels, and my misgivings are seldom disappointed. Of course, I am more pleased by the fact that these cardiovascular risk factors go down together, once a correct dietary approach is instituted.

And what is that approach? Well, to quote Norman Kaplan one more time: "Weight loss, however it can be accomplished, is then the obvious way to correct obesity and its attendant hyperinsulinism and hypertension. . .However, *the use of a low-fat/high-carbohydrate diet, as usually recommended for weight reduction* [my italics] *has been found to accentuate both the hyperglycemia and hyperinsulinemia . . .*"

The alternative is, of course, a low-carbohydrate diet. And the heart-health advantages of my recommended alternative are correspondingly immense.

## Special Advice for Heart Patients

Most of you are candidates for heart disease; simply having a weight problem puts you in that category. Therefore, all of you are understandably concerned with preventing heart disease, and you are certainly not interested in doing anything that would increase your risk. I hope the preceding discussion convinced you that your heart-disease risk will be considerably lessened on our program.

But for many of you, prevention comes a little late in the game because you may have learned that you already have some cardiovascular problem. Some of you may already be taking prescribed medications.

There is good news for over 90% of those who fall into this latter group, for that is the percentage of our patients who have been able to discontinue, or at least reduce, their medication burden at the Atkins Center. The nutritional pharmacology is part of the reason behind our patients' success, as is chelation therapy. Both are outside the scope of this book, but they were very much in the scope of my last book, *Dr. Atkins' Health Revolution*. You really owe it to yourself to get it and study it as though your life depended on it. The predictable improvement of overweight heart patients on the total regimen is the closest thing to a "sure thing" in my entire medical practice.

But I do want to give some specifics for those who love to see their cholesterol levels plummet to new lows, a quest which has become sort of a national pastime.

First, let's talk about the diet strategy. Bear in mind that a low-carbohydrate diet can be relatively high in fat or low in fat, and that the fats may come in a variety of forms. You've heard the terms saturated, monounsaturated, poly-unsaturated; consider, too, that each individual fat or oil has its effect on your serum lipids, both good and bad. The stearic acid component of red meat just happens to have a good effect, to give but a single example.

To perfect your lipid levels you have to be willing to have the blood tests analyzed frequently; otherwise, you are as guilty as those consensus-formers, always assuming everybody's metabolic response is the same. The strategy is to systematically test out various hypotheses and then look at blood test results to see if they are operative for you.

## Testing for Fat Sensitivity

I admit that there are individuals who are fat-sensitive and will develop a less favorable cholesterol level on a high-fat diet than on a low-fat diet. Intensive study of medical reports strongly suggests that fewer than one person in three falls into this category. But you don't know if you are in that subgroup, so let me show you how to find out if you are.

Stay on the *Induction* diet and the first several levels of the OWL as long as you want, taking the supplements I will be outlining. Then draw a complete lipid profile involving cholesterol, triglycerides, HDL, LDL, etc. *to compare with your baseline levels*. All should show improvement. You should particularly note the ratio of LDL to HDL, which the Helsinki study demonstrated to be so important. If you (and your doctor) are satisfied with your progress, there is, of course, no need to change.

If the results are not to your liking, you may be a person who is fat-sensitive. So for the next interval, eat only the lean proteins—turkey roll, skinless chicken breast, fish, farmer cheese, lean cuts of meat, and so on—but do not increase your carbohydrate intake more than 5 grams. However, if you're not happy on the low-fat version of the diet or get hungry or don't feel as well on it, then don't bother with it; go back to the regular Atkins diet that you enjoyed more. Since there can be so much benefit from the nutritional supplements, it may be better to give them a chance so that you will not have to abandon your successful diet for the sake of a cholesterol reading. But if you are happy with the new lower-fat version of the diet, still losing at a comfortable rate, and feeling just as well, stay with it and have another lipid profile drawn. If the results are better, good, but you still have one more task to perform. Go back to the original free-use-of-fat system long enough to have another profile. If it bounced back up from the previous one *then you are fat-sensitive* and *should follow the fat-restricted variation of the diet*. Our studies have shown that there is generally a steady improvement on the regimen, and therefore a falling cholesterol is expected. A cholesterol elevation runs counter to the anticipated trend and would be significant. Don't ever draw bloods if you have not been faithful to the diet, because carbohydrate deviations can raise the cholesterol much more readily than can high fat intake.

A similar experiment can be done with regard to the kind of fat. Check out the effect of switching from saturated (meat) fat to monounsaturated oils, as in olive oil, canola oil, avocados, and macadamia nuts. The monounsaturates may be your best ally. Another concept is the use of medium chain triglycerides (MCT), shown in research to be an aid to energy metabolism, weight loss, and cholesterol reduction. An appropriate dose of MCT is 2 to 3 tablespoons a day as a substitute for other dietary oil. You can use it in your fying pan. More MCT can be used if you're careful to avoid the diarrhea which can result in sensitive individuals. Finally, if you are curious about the effect of egg yolks (one of nature's most perfect foods), check out that hypothesis; don't assume they're bad without proving it to yourself.

## And Now for Nutrients

All of the above discussion should prove academic if you find the effective nutritional supplements in the right quantity to be effective in lowering your cholesterol and triglycerides. In my private practice, I find that those patients who need still further reductions in their levels can achieve results satisfactory enough that I never have to prescribe cholesterol-lowering medications.

The following is your lipid/nutrient checklist.

• Lecithin granules (much better than the capsules) two to three tablespoons daily. Can and should be sprinkled on the food; goes well on salad or vegetables or mixed in with scrambled eggs.[21]

- Lots of GLA. I frequently use borage oil, 2–3 capsules daily. If you use primrose oil, you have to use more than a dozen to match the GLA content of borage oil.[22]
- Omega-3 oils. Fish oil containing EPA, DHA. I use 1500–2000 mg of the EPA on many patients. It is particularly valuable in those who have triglyceride elevations. Some studies have described a cholesterol elevation in some people taking EPA, but I'm not convinced I see that response. I think it's very valuable. Alternately, flax (linseed) oil contains a different Omega-3 oil and may be of great value to certain individuals.[23]
- Chromium (nicotinate or picolinate). The dieter's best friend. Helps in controlling diabetes, hypoglycemia, and contributes greatly to cholesterol control. As the critics say, a must! Adults use 200–600 mcg.[24]
- Pantethine. A derivative of pantothenic acid, the precursor of coenzyme A, pantethine plays a pivotal role in cholesterol metabolism. Would be the "drug of choice" in cholesterol control if it were a drug. I usually provide 900–1800 mg when the lipid picture is not favorable.[25]
- Niacin. This is the nutrient that most doctors know about. Used as a drug, it can worsen diabetes and cause liver abnormalities. Used as a nutrient (i.e. with the rest of the B complex, and in lower doses) it is simply a contributor to cholesterol and LDL control. I usually prescribe 1000–2000 mg in a timed release form to avoid the rather unpleasant flush (heat wave) that develops at peak absorption time.[26] More recently, the product inositol hexanicotinate has been made available. It, too, avoids the flush.
- Garlic. Well-documented cholesterol-lowering effect, to say nothing of its other cardiovascular and blood

pressure benefits. Also great for knocking out acute infections and controlling Candida. I like it better on rack of lamb or scampi, but, if you like pills, consider 6 to 12 of them a day.[27]

• Carnitine. A nutrient essential for transport of fatty acids, it is valuable to heart patients with angina, cardiomyopathy and heart rhythm disorders. I use it when I want to help lower triglycerides or raise the HDL cholesterol, and I use 500–1500 mg daily.[28]

• Fiber sources. Psyllium, glucomannan, carageenan, pectin, guar gum. All have a documented cholesterol-lowering effect, probably by binding cholesterol in the gut and decreasing its absorption. This may be less desirable than it sounds, because the body very much *needs* cholesterol. I believe it is better to present the body with all the cholesterol it needs and then still the signals in the body demanding that the liver produce more cholesterol by enhancing all nutritional enabling systems in the body.[29]

• Anti-oxidant nutrients. In line with the previous paragraph, you should know that many nutritionally-oriented doctors believe that cholesterol is manufactured in the body because it serves as an anti-oxidant (as does uric acid) and therefore will be synthesized to excess when the body is being bombarded by free radicals.*

Providing the nutritional anti-oxidants seems to help with cholesterol control, and it certainly is a good idea to protect against all degenerative diseases, such as cancer, arthritis, and even aging. Vitamins A, E, C, glutathione, selenium, cysteine, and bioflavonoids are the major nutritional anti-oxidants. 3 to 6 capsules of a

*See *Dr. Atkins' Health Revolution,* page 218, pages 225–228.

good anti-oxidant formula is worth everyone's consideration.

- Vitamin C. Recent research is confirming the long-term lipid benefit of using this nutrient. You may have assumed by now that I concur that vitamin C is a cornerstone of preventive medicine. Dose ranges for my patients begin with 500 mg, and many people thrive on doses 30 times that much.
- Many, but not all, of these nutrients are in the Atkins Center Lipid Formula, plus the Essential Oils Formula.

Cholesterophobia seems to be an American epidemic. I've already met 200 terminal cancer patients who were more concerned with their cholesterol levels than with their immune systems. I don't encourage cholesterophobia; it's as irrational as any other phobia. But it does provide one hidden advantage; it would probably impel you to use a generous assortment of the above mentioned nutritional agents.

Combined with the dramatic lipid-lowering effects of the Atkins diet, these nutrients make you a heavy favorite to improve your cholesterol readings. In fact, with all of the above in proper dose, your chances of getting a bad result is about the same as is mine of being elected president of the United States. It is only fair to point out, however, that I am over 35, and American citizen, and would run if drafted. And I would like to clean up a few things in Washington—especially the FDA.

## Just Another Cardiac Patient

I have so many cardiac patients with good results, and, alas, I only have room to tell you about one of them. But every one makes the same basic point—the Atkins diet and its adjuvant therapies are solid gold when it comes to dealing with cardiovascular disease.

Patrick McCarthy is a 55-year-old teacher who first felt the indications of his heart disease when he was tramping up and down the hills of Ireland during summer vacation four years ago. A tightness in his chest, a pain in his left arm. The alarm bells began to ring. He got back to the States and went to the HMO that handled his health care. An echocardiogram and a thallium stress test were quite clear: he had obstruction in some of his major arteries.

He was reluctant to consider a bypass, and his doctor put him on propranolol. The result was total exhaustion. Climbing a flight of stairs was a challenge, and he found he was too weak to talk to his class. Later he was put on verapamil, and when further testing revealed no improvement in his condition, the medication dose was doubled. Patrick could see in front of him nothing but risky surgery or life as an invalid. In the fall of 1989, he came to the Atkins Center.

We put him on the Atkins diet, gave him the nutrients you've just been reading about, gave him chelation therapy, and within four months he was off his medication because he didn't need it anymore. A recent stress test has shown indications of reversal of the ischemia in his major arteries. His chest pain has not returned, and all of his risk factors for heart disease have turned around.

His cholesterol level had been 199 and is now 174. More significantly, his level of good HDL cholesterol has gone up from 35 to 56. His triglycerides—now increasingly recognized as major risk factors for heart disease—have done what triglycerides always do on low-carbohydrate diets: They've sunk like a leaky rowboat in a tropical hurricane. A triglyceride level that was 341 before the diet is now 58.

His weight (Patrick is 5'9"), which was in the mid-190s

when he started the diet a few weeks before he came to the center, is now 157 and has been in that region for almost two years. Best of all, Patrick McCarthy's energy level for work and play has zoomed back up to better than normal. No more panting at the top of stairs. Patrick now takes a brisk 3–4 mile walk twice a week, and he's just started a course in ballroom dancing with his wife.

Is this man on an austere diet? Listen. Patrick has a two-egg cheese omelet for breakfast each morning, sometimes supplemented by some slices of filet mignon. He has chicken, beef, or fish with a salad or vegetables at lunch, and his portions are large. Patrick has always had a *big* appetite. At our last meeting, he told me he had had 9 pieces of chicken at lunch that day.

At dinner he'll have a large steak or lamb chops or a pot roast, or a beef stew with plenty of vegetables. He likes broccoli with cheese and salads with blue cheese dressing. For dessert he'll have diet jelly or some of the treats you'll find in our recipe section. When snacking, macadamia nuts are his favorite. Such austerity! Such suffering! Although, it's true he *has* had to give up the cakes and donuts he used to nosh on in the bad old days before he went on the Atkins diet.

I suppose his case speaks for itself. It does for me, because I have seen so many thousands of people like Patrick eating the way he eats and reversing their heart disease. And that's why I *know* that cheese omelets and steaks are heart-healthy in the context of a low-carbohydrate diet.

## Those Who Have Tried the Diet Already Know the Answers

The irony is that every working day I encounter two or three others with stories similar to Patrick's. You cannot imagine the incredulity (and occasional hot indignation) these successful dieters express when they go back to visit their previous cardiologists, who had been intent on convincing them that the best treatment they were going to get was the high-carbohydrate, high-pharmaceutical program they had prescribed for them—sometimes with a bypass to follow. Their resentment becomes supercharged when they actually hear criticisms of the diet that relieved their heart symptoms, their high blood pressure, their serum lipids, their excess weight, and allowed them to be free of their need for medicines. And more often than not, they were going to good, dedicated physicians who just didn't know any better.

I don't know whether I have convinced most of you of who's right in this controversy about the heart healthiness of low-carbohydrate diets. In my mind, it's not a legitimate controversy, since the scientific support for carbohydrate restriction is unequivocal, but rather a deliberate attempt by people whose ideology overrides their common sense to push a one-sided and misleading interpretation of the facts.

I do know that virtually all of you who have already completed the 14-day diet are already on the road to conviction. A successful experience is worth a thousand words.

For the remaining doubters—those who won't try the diet until they finish the book—I've written a follow-up chapter on fat. I mean the kind you put in your mouth and that advertisers of nutritionally horrific cereals and other garbage foods boast of excluding. Fat has been getting a bum rap. Let's see what we can do about it.

# 16

# Dietary Fat: Real Offender or Innocent Scapegoat?

Fat is finished, right? The United States government and perhaps a dozen medical societies have sounded the official death knell. Their consensus panels, academic medical authorities all, have unanimously concluded that we as a nation should, each and every one of us, reduce our fat intake to 30% of our total calories. Rich or poor, fat or thin, well or infirm, young or old, there can be no exceptions to this edict. Both Jack Sprat and his pleasingly plump wife must now heed the official dictum. The *real* scientists have spoken and those who feel we should consider biologic individuality and who would tailor diets to an individual's metabolic profile are wrong, because scientists who hold such heretical opinions are simply not worthy of being appointed to consensus panels.

These consensus panels are now in total agreement: All fat, any fat, even essential fatty acids, must not amount to more than 30% of our total intake. If our most eminent scientists appear to be in accord, then we ordinary people must conclude that there is incontrovertible evidence that eating the amount of fat that we as a nation do is proven to be harmful to our health. We cannot but accept the dogma that *low-fat* diet and *healthy* diet are equivalents. But are they? The answers might surprise you.

We know that *low-fat* diet and *satisfying* diet aren't equivalents. Just consider the expression, "He eats like a king." Was the mental picture it produced of a rather dry skinned, austere-looking fellow wearing a crown and munching on a carrot? I doubt it.

Fat has earned its high place in the cuisines of the world because of its luxurious, satisfying taste, its richness, and its capacity to satiate appetite. Fat is *par excellence* the food of feasts. If they were of a tougher material consistency, butter and cream would undoubtedly be referred to as the backbone of fine cuisine. But you know what I mean. And so do the heart-healthy French, who put one or both of those fatty delights into as many dishes as will take them.

Fat is what makes flesh food tender and delectable. The great steak houses, now somewhat diminished by the low-fat craze, have thrived on offering their customers "select" cuts of beef that they couldn't even get in their supermarkets. What that "select" meant was that the beef had a higher percentage of fat. When you eat an absolutely mouthwatering filet mignon, it's the fat that makes the mouth water. (Glance into the recipe section, and you'll see what the master chef, Graham Newbould, who we recruited to do recipes for this book, offers in the way of delicious eating with the liberal use of cream and butter.)

Well now, it's rather sad that we have to give all that up, isn't it. Apparently, if we don't, fat will be our executioner. The evidence is overwhelming, right?

The curious fact, however, is that the evidence is rather

underwhelming! The assertion that eating a significant percentage of fat in your diet will bring you briskly down the road to heart disease and cancer is startlingly simplistic. Major studies in medical literature cast serious doubt upon these claims. Before we look at the evidence, let's see what else fat can contribute to your diet besides sumptuousness.

First, however, let's consider if I'm not beginning to sound like the fat-pusher I have been accused of being. You might think so, yet I always maintained, as the work of Yudkin and Stock illustrated, that, as a rule, people eat considerably less fat on a ketogenic/lipolytic diet than they do on their usual diet.

That's a direct result of one of fat's greatest virtues, namely that, when carbohydrates are restricted, fat causes a profound induction of satiety. Every researcher comparing diets of the same number of calories has noted that the one higher in fat produced less hunger and was considerably easier to follow.

And then there is the matter of your physical appearance. This point is a little more subtle, and no one has yet set out to prove or disprove it; yet, to me, it is as obvious as the head on your shoulders.

Did you ever study the features of one of today's "successful" low-fat dieters? It is true that their bodies look great, especially when they have worked hard at the exercise and physical-fitness aspects of their health. But study well their faces. Do you see the dryness of the skin, the pastiness of the complexion, and most specifically, do you see the deep furrows in the facial lines that extend from the side of the nose to the side of the mouth and below, called the nasolabial folds? Somehow they seem to look older than their age. You may not be as struck with this as I am, since it comes as a visual shock to me, because Atkins dieters don't get that look.

That look, the look that most people just pass off as the look of someone on a diet, is really a characteristic of a low-fat intake, and can also be seen on those who restrict fat but have not lost weight. So those of you who are dieting to enhance your physical beauty may want to prove to yourself *that* one advantage of a fat-containing reducing diet by studying your appearance in a mirror after a stint on both types of diet.

Now why am I, by allowing fats and oils, so much at odds with nearly all consensus panelists, who seem to feel that the inescapable conclusion is that fat restriction is the only acceptable path to fat loss? Upon what cogent arguments do they base their end-of-discussion-victory-is-ours conclusion?

Their arguments have been:

a) Fat contributes too many calories, and we will eat fewer calories if we eat low-calorie foods.
b) High-fat diets must be low in carbohydrates to work, and we will never be willing to live permanently without some carbohydrates.
c) Man is by nature primarily a vegetarian.
d) Animal foods are polluted with hazardous quantities of growth hormones and antibiotics, which we should all wish to avoid.
e) High-fat diets cause or contribute to heart disease.
f) High-fat diets cause or contribute to certain types of cancer.

## A Crop of Refutations

Let's quickly dismiss the first three arguments, all of which seem to me to be rather spurious.

That we eat fewer calories when the fat is removed may be true when carbohydrate intake is high, but it certainly is not true on low-carbohydrate diets. Two recent studies by Angelo Tremblay and his associates at Laval University in Quebec demonstrate that.[1] In these studies, fat was added to a high-carbohydrate diet and it was found that the subjects of the study increased their intake of calories, but when added to a low-carbohydrate there was a decrease in calories because the subjects sharply curtailed their choice of carbohydrate foods. Satiety, after all, is not a matter of fooling your stomach, it is a matter of humoral (blood constituent) factors. You eat *less* on a low-carbohydrate diet than you do on a low-fat diet. If you're not convinced, try them both.

In response to the idea that we won't be happy without carbohydrates, I can only submit that more people are happy on the luxurious butter-and-cream-containing Atkins diet than are happy on less luxurious fare.

That man developed on a low-fat or vegetarian diet is simply not true. It's even more significant that until six generations ago, man's consumption of *refined* carbohydrates was nearly zilch.

To objection d) I readily concede. We have certainly polluted our supply of animal foods with hormones and antibiotics. Unfortunately, critics of fat who mention that don't always go on and mention the next fact: We have also polluted our supply of plant foods with pesticide residues and inorganically treated soil. The situation is something of a stalemate, and it's not an argument for eating one kind of food over another, but for cleaning up our entire act. Ever since the 19th-century German scientist Baron Justus von Liebig invented inorganic chemical fertilizers, we have been doing things to our soil and the food that grows in it, the hazardous consequences of which we hardly yet know.

My recommendation to you is that when you eat animal food, just as when you eat plant food, you should go out of your way and even pay the extra few cents to get un-polluted, organic food if at all possible. Frequent health food stores. Buy free-range chickens and their eggs. Get your hands on some Coleman's beef. Mel Coleman, a rancher in Colorado, is now making major waves in the cattle industry by marketing beef free of any taint of hor-mone or antibiotic, and, if you'll believe me, you can also taste the difference. We can expect more and more com-panies like Coleman's to carve out a niche for themselves. Bother your supermarket, and let them know what you would like. You'll be surprised how responsive they are to the customer's desires. You're their livelihood, after all.

Now let's look at the evidence behind the heart disease and cancer claims, and, as we do, let's keep in mind that there is no good direct evidence to show that a low-carbohydrate diet leads to these health hazards. *What evi-dence there is in population studies showing an association between high fat and heart disease are actually simulta-neously studies showing that diets high in* refined carbo-hydrates *are associated with heart disease. And the same is true for cancer.*

I'd like to talk to you about heart disease first.

## Heart Attacks and Us

The very plausible assertion has been made that the mod-ern diet is responsible for the extraordinary prevalence of heart disease in the 20th-century industrial societies. I'm inclined to think that's true. The further claim has been made that our rich, high-fat diet is the culprit. Long ago, I imagined this was true, too, until I began to look at the historical evidence.

You may wonder what history has to do with it. Actually, quite a lot. You see, the main focus of intellectual attention with regard to the overall prevalence of heart disease has been directed to what medicine calls epidemiological studies. These are studies of the statistical breakdown of illness in various population groups. This is a crude and speculative way of studying illness but also a very intriguing one.

Let's suppose a researcher is struck by the fact that nomadic desert Bedouin don't get any heart disease but that New York City pastrami slicers do. He could scrutinize the differences between the two groups, note that the deli workers ate considerably more corned beef fat and conclude on the basis of this correlation that fat is the cause of their heart disease. Of course, if he did that, he would have overlooked the fact that heart disease *also* correlated with the consumption of rye bread and mustard and the use of subway tokens, TV sets, and meat slicers. Or that the absence of heart disease correlated with riding camelback.

More seriously, for epidemiology really isn't ludicrous, he might have concluded that the pastrami slicers get less exercise than the Bedouin or that they smoke more cigarettes or that they eat more sugar, or that they lead more driven, stressful lives. If he were interested in environmental factors, he might cast an evaluating eye over the quantities of lead, ozone, and other chemicals that the unfortunate counterman daily absorb.

But, for the most part, if our epidemiologist is a typical epidemiologist and wants to be chief of epidemiology one day, he will do what's expected of him and conclude that dietary fat did it. (As Claude Rains put it in *Casablanca*, "Round up the usual suspects.") That he jumps to this conclusion is part of the paradigm conformed to by a medical statistician at a modern American medical school, but it is easy to show that it is not a necessary conclusion from the evidence.

In virtually all the societies in which it is suggested that high fat causes heart disease, the main dietary modification in this century has been an increase in the consumption of sugar, high-fructosc corn syrup, and white flour—all refined carbohydrates. Surgeon Captain T. L. Cleave, who wrote the classic study, *The Saccharine Disease*, argued convincingly that increases in coronary artery disease could be traced to increases in refined carbohydrate intake.[2] He noted that diabetes, hypertension, ulcers, gall-bladder disease, varicose veins, colitis, and heart disease, to name a few, are all virtually non-existent in primitive cultures until refined carbohydrates are introduced into the culture. *And there were no exceptions*. The process took twenty years to develop and so Cleave proposed the Rule of 20 Years— that's how long after sugar or other refined carbohydrates are added to a culture before diabetes and heart disease begin to appear in that group of people.

The epidemiologic truth is that virtually all poor, non-industrial societies have very low rates of heart disease. Most of them also have very low rates of sugar consumption, very low rates of fat consumption, fairly low rates of urbanization, and many other differences from we modern people who live in Europe and North America. How do we tell what causes the heart disease?

A generation ago, the dean of British nutritionists, Dr. John Yudkin, and Dr. Ancel Keys, mentor for a large number of American nutritionists, conducted a running intellectual battle over epidemiology. Keys would study nations and cultures with varying degrees of heart disease and show how profoundly heart disease correlated with fat intake. Yudkin would look at the same statistics and find an almost identical correlation with sugar intake. The fact is that in over 90% of cultures there is a strong correlation between fat intake and sugar intake. Thus to choose between the two theories, we must look at the exceptions. Let's do that.[3]

The first thing we can notice is that in two primitive cultures, the Eskimos of North America and the Masai of East Africa, a high-fat diet correlates not with heart disease but with virtually the complete absence of heart disease.[4]

Let's look at a couple of atypical Western countries. In Iceland, heart disease (and diabetes) was almost unheard of until the 1930s although the Icelanders ate a diet tremendously high in fat. In the early 1920s, however, refined carbohydrates and sugar arrived in the Icelandic diet and true to Cleave's rule of 20 years, the modern degenerative diseases arrived on schedule. Finally in Yugoslavia and Poland, the development of high heart-disease rates in the middle of this century *was concomitant with a quadrupling of the sugar intake and occurred despite a fall in animal-fat intake*.[5]

These studies prove nothing. In general, epidemiological studies never do, but they do cast serious doubt, just as an examination from history does, on the theory that high-fat diets are the main cause of the epidemic of 20th-century heart disease.

## And What About History?

Why didn't they have heart disease in previous centuries? Because they didn't eat our diet, you say. Exactly right: They didn't eat the diet high in sugar and white flour that we eat. Oh, you didn't mean that? You mean you meant they didn't eat a high-fat diet? But they did! Certainly a significant percentage of them did. Everyone who was well

off, and by the late 19th century that included a minimum
of several million people in America alone, ate a diet that
was very high in meat, fish, fowl, eggs, butter, and lard.
There was no margarine—lucky people.

These folks ate, as well-to-do people had always done,
enormous quantities of animal food—their dinners were
feasts, with the roast chicken followed by the fresh trout
and preceded by the pork roast. Read 19th-century novels,
and you'll get the picture. I know you've all seen westerns.
Those giant cattle drives that began in the 1860s were
aimed at getting the herds up to Chicago from whence the
red meat of America was distributed.

Did they suffer from heart disease the way we did? The
truth is they didn't suffer from it at all. All through the
second half of the 19th century, research was being done,
medical journals were being published, and yet coronary
artery disease was so insignificant that the first study of it—
examining four cases—was done in 1912.[6] Those several
million examples of meat-eating, lard-consuming, well-to-
do Americans went merrily along eating like kings and
queens off the *fat* of the land, and they never paid the coronary price, apparently because there was no coronary price
to be paid. In fact, the late 19th century was the great era
of pathologists, and a coronary occlusion, visible even to
the naked eye, was never reported.

Paul Dudley White, later to be Eisenhower's personal
cardiologist, remembered that in a single year (early 1920s)
in his residency training at Massachusetts General Hospital,
he didn't see a single example of a myocardial infarction
(heart attack).

The inescapable conclusion is that coronary artery disease was a rare illness in the 19th century. But why was it
beginning around 1912? Remembering Cleave's rule of
twenty years, I can't help wondering if it didn't date from

the cola revolution of the early 1890s, which coincided with the introduction of flour mills that produced a much more refined flour.

After twenty-five years of treating heart patients who showed consistent improvement from the diet I prescribed for them, just as did Patrick McCarthy—with unrestricted, meat, fish, and fowl—and who had shown every sort of ill effect while on high-carbohydrate diets, I feel there's a very strong case for the *unique* characteristics of the 20th-century diet being precisely what's wrong with people. Those unique characteristics are not fat but refined carbohydrates—the plague of our time.

I rest my case. Now, let's take a quick look at cancer.

## Cancer

The same flawed epidemiology we saw with heart disease applies to cancer. No one really knows what it is in our highly complex environment—including our nutritional environment—that is most directly contributing to our explosive cancer rates. But there is good evidence that it may not be fat.

To understand that, let's first understand case-control studies. In these, we might study only the New York pastrami slicers and observe them over a period of years noting who came down with what condition. If we decide to learn about diet and cancer from them, we collect the names of all of them who developed the disease and painstakingly question them about their diet. We then compare the food and beverage profile of those who got the illness and those who did not. Studies like this are, in fact, done all the time, but some are more important than others. And some are better because they gather the dietary data *in advance* of the illness' development.

Well, the Harvard Nurses Study was one of these, and it could always make headlines. After all, this enormous enterprise had been observing nearly 90,000 American nurses for more than four years and since *most* case-control studies have less than a thousand subjects, you can be sure that the media hung on every word issued by the head of the study, Walter Willett, and his colleagues.

That's why, at the end of 1990, every newspaper carried on its front page the story that animal fat causes colon cancer. In the interviews, Dr. Willett indicated that, if we had any sense at all, we would all restrict our consumption of animal fat. You could bet that the Nurses Study uncovered powerful, conclusive evidence that animal fat is a killer. But who would win that bet?

Let's study their study.[7] They divided every factor they looked at into quintiles, meaning five groups of equal size; thus, the 20% of the nurses with the highest intake of a nutritional element, let's say red meat, would be in the fifth quintile, and the 20% with the lowest intake in the first quintile. This was done for all the nutritional categories the researchers chose to study. In that way they could look at each dietary variable to see whether they could identify elements where the amount of cancer in the fifth quintile was much higher than in the first.

In their study, published in *The New England Journal of Medicine*, they found 150 cases of colon cancer, which conveniently meant that each quintile could expect 30 cases (150 divided by 5). So how many cases occurred in the quintile with the highest intake of animal fat? Thirty-eight cases. Statistically significant, yes, but so minor in magnitude that it's definitely not worth abandoning a diet that controls your blood pressure, your weight, supports your well-being, and keeps down your blood-lipid levels.

Remember, this portion of the Nurses study didn't talk about all kinds of cancer, just colon cancer. Some of you will remember that breast cancer is supposed to be another one that comes from animal fat. Official government agencies say it's so. What did the Nurse's Study say about that?[8]

In the Willett breast cancer study, it was the *low-fat* quintile that stood out from all the rest. Every woman whose total dietary fat intake was 33% or *more* developed breast cancer at a rate of 114 cases per quintile (636 per 100,000), but the one quintile whose total fat intake was below 33% of the diet, just the way official government bodies suggest it should be, had a whopping 145 cases in their quintile, which comes to 813 cases per 100,000.

Willett's team denied that this finding was statistically significant, but my statistical analyst says it certainly is. In fact, there is only 1 chance in 100 that these figures, suggestive of *low*-fat intake as a contributing factor in breast cancer, could have been achieved by chance and what this really adds up to is the most significant diet/cancer connection yet discovered epidemiologically.

To return for a moment to the colon-cancer study, the underwhelming evidence that the Harvard researchers accumulated could have been predicted from some of the smaller yet well-performed case-control studies done before. Studies in Marseilles, Paris, Japan, and Belgium *all failed to show any correlation between fat intake and colon cancer.*[9] The 1989 Belgian study was even able to "finger" what I think is the real criminal—oligosaccharides, better known as the simple sugars.

What if Surgeon-Captain Cleave was right, and Professor John Yudkin was right? I think the evidence is surprisingly strong. After all, people eat more fat, *because* they eat more sugar: That's because sugar leads to increased calorie intake and obesity. And *sugar is the Western world's most frequently consumed carcinogen.*

I'm sure you want to know why. The great Nobel-prize-winning scientist, Otto Warburg, could have told you. Cancer cells feed on glucose, rather than on oxygen as do normal cells. Sugar intake raises the glucose and provides fuel selectively usable by cancer cells.[10]

Internationally acclaimed Russian scientist, Dr. Vladimir M. Dilman, writing in the *Annals of the New York Academy of Science*, provides even more convincing evidence to support the carbohydrate-causes-cancer theory.[11] He was able to show that breast-cancer patients put out 22% more insulin than healthy controls; that colon-cancer patients had 29% more triglycerides in their blood; and that colon-, rectal-, and endometrial-cancer patients had over twice the likelihood of giving birth to high-birth-weight babies. *The latter, plus high insulin and triglyceride levels, are all signs of disturbed sugar metabolism.*

So you plainly see that sugar has been shown epidemiologically and just-plain-logically to be a strong candidate to be the principal dietary cause of cancer, perhaps a much stronger candidate than fat.

But, you say, these Harvard scientists must have been unimpressed with what their data showed them about the correlation between cancer and the intake of sugar.

Fair enough, I asked one of my colleagues to call them and ask, "Doctors, what were your findings regarding breast and colon cancer and sugar intake?"

Answer: "We didn't look at that; we didn't consider it would have any relevance."

Ninety thousand nurses under scrutiny, zillions of taxpayers' dollars being spent via the National Institutes of Health, and they didn't look at sugar! They failed to because they were wearing blinders on which were written in indelible ink, "Faithful followers focus fixedly on fat." This is a good way to prove the conclusion you've already arrived at (although it didn't do them much good in the breast cancer study), but it's a poor way to do science. Are the endocrine mechanisms linking sugar to cancer and described in the medical journals really to be that easily bypassed?

My colleague and I were concerned. Knowing that the *excess* breast cancer cases on *low fat* outnumbered the colon cancer excess on high fat by four to one, and that sugar-linked endometrial cancer was not included in any paper from the Nurses Study, we were legitimately concerned with the *real* bottom line of the Nurses' Study—across-the-board cancer incidence.

So we asked: "What data do you have about dietary fat and *total* cases of cancer?"

Strangely enough, the reply was: "We don't have that data; it's not really useful information."

Can you imagine? I can't help but imagine Peter Falk as Detective Columbo standing in the doorway in his crumpled raincoat, about to exit, and turning back to ask one last question. With fingers touching his furrowed brow, he says, "Just one more thing, Professor. I don't know much about computers, and I know you're going to think me a pest, but I just gotta ask you this. In a study this big, with all that data on 90,000 nurses and what they ate and what diseases they got, and who lived and who died, and all the rest of it, there's just one little thing that puzzles me. How do you program your computer so you *don't* get the total cases of cancer?"

Our self-effacing detective shared with me the suspicion that the overall incidence of cancer data failed to support the fat-fighters' preconceived notion and was simply no longer talked about. Had the data shown a correlation between dietary fat and all cases of cancer, you can bet anything it would have been reported and covered by every wire service in the Western world.

What looks to the paranoid among us to be a coverup is most certainly nothing more than overzealousness, a pervasive quality indeed among dedicated scientists. To stress this point, let us consider a recent hearing on the subject of dietary fat and cancer held by the FDA and printed in the Federal Register.[12] They concluded:

*"All of the publicly available evidence supports the conclusion that diets high in fat increase the risk of cancer, and more importantly that diets low in fat are associated with the reduced risk of cancer."*

There is only one catch. The literature cited in this major federal health publication contained the Harvard Nurses Study on colon cancer but *not* the study about breast cancer I just told you about in which thirty-one *more* cases were found in the 20% of nurses with the lowest consumption of animal fat. Naturally, I checked and doublechecked. Could this really be true? Indeed, it was.

The studies cited in the cancer section contained many very small and necessarily tenuous reports on 200 or 300 subjects but not the largest study on breast cancer ever conducted, a study on *90,000 subjects* by the same investigators in the Harvard Department of Epidemiology, using the same nurses and published by the same *New England Journal of Medicine* as the colon-cancer study that received such headlines. (*Other* studies showing no relation between breast cancer and dietary fat were also missing.) I am more than curious about these omissions; I hope we will soon be given an explanation. I do know that consensus experts diligently study the data offered to them by the consensus panel staff. It's a shame that national-health policy can be so greatly influenced by research assistants so overworked that they miss little details like the most significant study on breast cancer ever reported.

And yet I haven't written this chapter to focus your attention upon possible discrepancies between scientific *findings* and the beliefs of certain scientists but to reassure you that the next time you confront a bacon-and-cheese omelet that you hotly desire but are afraid to approach, you needn't be afraid. The evidence that you're going to get heart disease or cancer from the fat in your diet isn't strong, it's weak; it isn't persuasive, it's remarkably unpersuasive. False accusations are being passed off as scientific gospel simply because those upon whom our political leaders rely for scientific insight have long ago become devotees of the low-fat cause and don't scruple to slant the evidence, although they may imagine that in doing so they perform a public service.

I hope the foregoing discussion has at least awakened you to the realization that there is not scientific unanimity on those points, either. As with so many other considerations involving your health, you can survive best by becoming critical enough to make your own decisions.

# PART FOUR

# How to Do the Diet for Life

*Here you are returning to the diet once again. Some of you, of course, will never have gone off it since the day you began your original 14-day sprint. The rest of you will have taken a reflective pause to consider the significance of your initial results. Clearly you liked them. Now you are about to begin the most important part of the program. You are about to create a diet for yourself— a diet that suits your lifestyle, your taste preferences, your food intolerances, your metabolism, your medical problem areas, and even your ability to deal with temptation. The hunt for health and slimness is on. I dare to say that your prospects for success have never been better.*

# 17

## Ongoing Weight Loss— The Basic Reduction Diet

If you've done the two week *Induction* level of the diet, and you're ready to go on, then you're about to become a serious dieter in the best possible sense. We continue with what I call the *Ongoing Weight-Loss* diet (OWL), and OWL, though more lenient than your original 14-day diet, will certainly show you what being on a fat-mobilizing, fat-dissolving—yet fat-containing—diet can do for you. After OWL, having become almost as wise as that dignified night-roaming bird, you'll move up to the important, though relatively brief stage of *Pre-Maintenance* dieting, and then to your lifetime *Maintenance* diet. You're going to find that every one of those stages is a comfortable fit.

I'm never going to leave you in the lurch, with your pounds lost and nothing to do but gain them back again. And I'm never going to introduce you to a stage that's hard to do, or that makes you feel bad.

What positive changes you have already begun to enjoy!

What a pleasure to lose weight, but I think, even more significantly, what a pleasure to enhance the quality of your life through painless, hungerless, healthy eating.

Let me also say appetizing. Perhaps spareribs or bacon and eggs were among the luxuries that on a low-fat diet you had to do without. Now you're on a diet that's as healthy as the most rigorous low-fat diet could possibly aspire to be, and consequently, these luxuries, as well as many others, can be yours again.

Juicy broiled New York strip sirloin steak? English cut roast prime rib of beef? Poached salmon with bearnaise sauce? Crispy duck in a Chinese restaurant? Pan fried chicken? Dig in.

But I know that you don't forget (and neither will I) that what initially brought you to this book was probably your overweight.

Let's look at the big weight loss picture, and, as the chapter unfolds, you'll see why you need never be fat again.

First of all, consider that it really helps to know how many pounds you want to lose. It focuses you. It keeps you disciplined in a psychologically pleasing way, since week after week you *do* get to see the pounds vanishing. After so many years as an enemy, the bathroom scale is about to become one of your best friends.

I'd like to remind you yet again that there are people who still can't accustom themselves to this diet because they can't get past the primitive, popular notion that a diet is something you get on and then get off, as you would a bus. But a diet is *not* an excursion, and such dieters—the uncommitted ones—are often the very individuals who need to lose forty pounds but lose interest when they reach twenty-eight. Then they go back to eating their old diet and four or five months later they're back where they were to begin with.

You can be sure that such a person will do that on the Atkins diet as well. Any diet will "fail," if you simply misuse it as a tool for some quick and easy weight loss and don't adapt it to your own tastes as a lifetime diet plan.

Your goal—for a large percentage of you, it will be your destiny—of reaching your desired weight and staying there for life is best met by realistically considering which levels of carbohydrate intake apply to you. While you're losing weight, you want to find a level of carbohydrate restriction that sustains ketosis/lipolysis. Thus you will dissolve your fat; you will maintain control of your appetite sufficiently to curb your urge to eat what you're not permitted; and you will eat healthy foods that you enjoy. Take the physical and emotional well-being promoted by ketosis/lipolysis and combine that with the gustatory pleasure of a rich, luxury diet. Result: One healthy, happy human being.

I think this result is much better than the sad recidivism of the bus rider I described just above.

In this chapter, you're going to learn how to do OWL. Let's start by determining your physical goals.

## Take a Pause for Reflection

It's time to take a serious look at your body, and decide what you want to do with it, and how you want it to look. Be realistic. Give some serious considerations to what you want to be physically. In all probability, you no longer expect to be an Olympic athlete or a fashion model. On the other hand, you may be looking to the other extreme, toward goals that are really too modest, like being *less* than fat and *relatively* healthy. I know that many of my patients come to me thinking that such goals would be quite alright—even more than they can hope for.

Frankly, I think you should set your sights higher than that. How about ideal weight, excellent health, and vigor that's surprising for your age and somewhat more than you ever expected to have again? Trust me, that's not overly ambitious. That's realistic. And when you achieve it, it's oh, so satisfying.

The human body responds rather quickly to determined efforts to improve it. Pounds do drop off, blood pressure does drop down, cholesterol and triglyceride levels do begin to retreat from disturbing heights, blood glucose and insulin levels do stabilize speedily on a diet like this, and the whole human person does commence to feel better. This happens in response to a proper diet; it happens to people who stop abusing their bodies with caffeine, alcohol, and drugs; it happens to people who take large, intelligently chosen doses of vitamins and minerals; it happens with a proper, gradual program of exercise. *Your* body will respond just as other people's bodies respond. There's no mystery. Your body is a remarkably resilient, amazingly tough organism, and it will seize upon anything good that is done for it and make the most of it. If most of what you've done to your body is bad, then it has been hunkering down in a defensive position trying to survive the abuse. If you do all of the above things, then in the space of a few weeks, you will notice remarkable improvements in the way you feel. If you do even one or two of them, you're going to notice a positive change.

This book is primarily about diet, and quite frankly, my experience has been that diet matters more than any other single thing. As you know, I also lay out the basis for a sound program of nutritional supplementation in this book, and in Chapter 20, I describe the fundamentals of a good exercise program. So now, let us refocus on our first question.

When in your life did you look and feel your very best? How much did you weigh then? Can you comfortably weigh that again? Don't skip over the question. As I've always said, you're the greatest expert on your body.

Whatever your ideal weight was, you can almost certainly reach it again. 120? 140? 170? Why not go for it?

## Reaching Your Ideal Weight!

It shouldn't sound like climbing Mt. Everest. I know that if you're metabolically similar to the 25,000 overweight patients I've treated during the last quarter century, you have an excellent chance of succeeding.

Once you reach your goal, you can look at yourself in the mirror and feel triumphant.

Do you have a clear conception of your ideal weight— the weight perfect for your frame and muscular development—when you were a young adult? Many people have a pretty good sense of that number. They held that weight for a good part of their life and found that they gained weight only after specific events, such as getting married, having kids, stopping smoking, starting or stopping medication.

Many others have always been "stocky," and if you fall into this second category, you may have to resort to those not-very-accurate insurance tables. I reproduce an insurance table below in Chart 17.1. Far from perfect, it at least gives you a ballpark figure to aim at.

Now, let's get back to sustaining that weight loss, which you've so happily begun.

**CHART 17.1**

**DESIRABLE WEIGHTS FOR MEN AND WOMEN
AGED 25 AND OVER[1]**

in pounds according to height and frame,
in indoor clothing, and shoes

| HEIGHT | | SMALL FRAME | MEDIUM FRAME | LARGE FRAME |
|---|---|---|---|---|
| | | MEN | | |
| Feet | Inches | | | |
| 5 | 2 | 112–120 | 118–129 | 126–141 |
| 5 | 3 | 115–123 | 121–133 | 129–144 |
| 5 | 4 | 118–126 | 124–136 | 132–148 |
| 5 | 5 | 121–129 | 127–139 | 135–152 |
| 5 | 6 | 124–133 | 130–143 | 138–156 |
| 5 | 7 | 128–137 | 134–147 | 142–161 |
| 5 | 8 | 132–141 | 138–152 | 147–166 |
| 5 | 9 | 136–145 | 142–156 | 151–170 |
| 5 | 10 | 140–150 | 146–160 | 155–174 |
| 5 | 11 | 144–154 | 150–165 | 159–179 |
| 6 | 0 | 148–158 | 154–170 | 164–184 |
| 6 | 1 | 152–162 | 158–175 | 168–189 |
| 6 | 2 | 156–167 | 162–180 | 173–194 |
| 6 | 3 | 160–171 | 167–185 | 178–199 |
| 6 | 4 | 164–175 | 172–190 | 182–204 |

[1]*Adapted from Metropolitan Life Insurance Co., New York. New weight standards for men and women. Statistical Bulletin 40.3, Nov.-Dec., 1959.*

|   |   | WOMEN |   |   |
|---|---|---|---|---|
| 4 | 10 | 92–98 | 96–107 | 104–119 |
| 4 | 11 | 94–101 | 98–110 | 106–122 |
| 5 | 0 | 96–104 | 101–113 | 109–125 |
| 5 | 1 | 99–107 | 104–116 | 112–128 |
| 5 | 2 | 102–110 | 107–119 | 115–131 |
| 5 | 3 | 105–113 | 110–122 | 118–134 |
| 5 | 4 | 108–116 | 113–126 | 121–138 |
| 5 | 5 | 111–119 | 116–130 | 125–142 |
| 5 | 6 | 114–123 | 120–135 | 129–146 |
| 5 | 7 | 118–127 | 124–139 | 133–150 |
| 5 | 8 | 122–131 | 128–143 | 137–154 |
| 5 | 9 | 126–135 | 132–147 | 141–158 |
| 5 | 10 | 130–140 | 136–151 | 145–163 |
| 5 | 11 | 134–144 | 140–155 | 149–168 |
| 6 | 0 | 138–148 | 144–159 | 153–173 |

## Learn Your Levels

First, let's review your weight loss during the first 14 days of the diet and the degree of metabolic resistance it indicated. Chart 17.2 will give you a general sense of where you stand in the metabolic resistance framework.

**CHART 17.2**

Weight Loss During the First Two Weeks on Ketogenic Diet for Patients at Three Levels of Obesity

*Degree of Metabolic Resistance for Males*

Pounds Lost in First 14 Days
When Metabolic Resistance is:

| Pounds to Lose | High | Average | Low |
|---|---|---|---|
| Less than 20 | 4 | 6 | 8 |
| 20–50 | 6 | 9 | 12 |
| Over 50 | 8 | 12 | 16 |

*Degree of Metabolic Resistance for Females*

Pounds Lost in First 14 Days
When Metabolic Resistance is:

| Pounds to Lose | High | Average | Low |
|---|---|---|---|
| Less than 20 | 2 | 4 | 6 |
| 20–50 | 3 | 6 | 9 |
| Over 50 | 4 | 8 | 12 |

As I'm sure you've guessed, the degree of resistance to weight loss that your body shows corresponds to your degree of difficulty in getting well into ketosis/lipolysis. By definition, resistance to weight loss *is* resistance to ketosis.

Now, on the *Induction* diet, which you've just gone through, I asked you to go on virtually the strictest level of low-carbohydrate dieting. You were consuming 15 to 20 grams of carbohydrate. A smart strategy. If your body was capable of going into ketosis, it did. The diet was extremely low because I wanted to demonstrate lipolysis for every-body from the person who can really lose weight quite eas-ily on almost any diet to the hardest case—the person who, until going on the Atkins diet, thought that losing weight was just about an impossibility.

And I am sure that better than 95% of you found that you were losing weight. The other 5% of you will have to look at the next chapter and work with the special diet I've devised for patients with extreme metabolic resistance.

But if you're a normal dieter, you're now going onto a somewhat more liberalized version of the Atkins diet, and you're entering a crucial stage for learning the parameters of your lifetime program. You'll find out what's the *most liberal level of carbohydrate consumption that corresponds to your own individual metabolic capacity to continue tak-ing off excess pounds*. This is the carbohydrate maximum for the *Ongoing Weight-Loss* level of the diet—your Crit-ical Carbohydrate Level for Losing (CCLL).

Naturally, you should wish to move into this phase of the diet with proper caution. I emphasize the importance of sticking to *low*-carbohydrate vegetables, nuts, and other meal accompaniments in these early days. The one thing we don't want to do is get you out of ketosis/lipolysis and put an end to the hormone-like elaboration of FMS. If that happened, we would have to resume the *Induction* diet again, or, as I must chide so many of my patients, "It's back to square one."

Remember, some very common foods have amounts of carbohydrate that aren't insignificant. A grapefruit has around 20 grams and an apple only slightly less. Measure that against the fact that approximately 40% of meta-bolically overweight women can't lose unless they're eating less than thirty grams of carbohydrate a day!

Therefore those are foods that you may always have to

eat with great moderation and restraint, so you must save them for a later date. There will be time enough to try them on your *Maintenance* diet.

Remember that most fruits are high in natural sugars and that your tendency to develop glucose and insulin disorders will always make fruit-eating somewhat risky for you.

## A Private Personal Number Just for You

Remember two basic principles:

1. On this diet, your rate of weight loss is generally proportional to your exclusion of carbohydrates.
2. The level of carbohydrate you are consuming can be measured, and thus, *if you wish*, you can attach numerical quantities to the carbohydrate food you're eating and decide just how much of this or that you're consuming. See the Carbohydrate Counter in the back of the book, as well as Chart 17.2 in this chapter.

With that in mind, I'd like to refer to the level of carbohydrate consumption below which you can lose weight as your CCLL. Below this number, you will indeed have *ongoing* weight loss.

There are two ways to determine this CCLL. Which one you choose will depend on your personality. If you're a precise, methodical person, who likes weighing, measuring, and numbering, then you'll find out the actual number. The way you'll do this is by increasing the quantity of carbohydrate you eat beyond that one salad you ate on the *Induction* level. And as you carry out this increase, you'll measure the grams of carbohydrate in each of your additions. Usually, I consider an increase in carbohydrates of five daily grams as representing a "level" of the diet.

You'll go up until eventually you'll reach a number at which you *stop* losing. That's your CCLL. Above it, you lose no more, or you begin to gain. Below it, you're definitely dieting in the popular sense of that word, i.e. you're losing weight. For those among you who are precise, numerically oriented people, the CCLL will be a fairly precise number.

You'll be able to say to another Atkins dieter, "My Critical Carbohydrate Level for Losing is 45 grams," or 32, or maybe only 19.

On the other hand, you may be a rule of thumb person— many of you will be. That's fine too. If you don't like to fuss about with numbers, then your mode of procedure will be even simpler. You'll increase your carbohydrate consumption steadily until your weight loss begins to become imperceptible and then you'll back down from that level. You'll be able to see roughly how much salad and vegetables you're eating and, as long as you have a good eye for constant quantities, you'll be alright.

If you go beyond your CCLL, your scale will herald the mistake, and you'll make adjustments accordingly. You may ask, where do the lipolysis testing strips (LTS) fit in? They generally fade out and do not change to purple at a point a little bit below your CCLL. When that happens, your CCLL will be only a few carbohydrate grams higher.

The only confusion is that everybody hits plateaus (periods where no weight comes off). The first few periods in which you fail to lose weight will most likely be plateaus and almost never represent the reaching of the CCLL. To identify your CCLL, you must ascertain that you are neither losing pounds nor inches for several weeks. If you feel chagrined about the length of time, then you may well begin to learn your first lesson. *Don't be in a hurry to get it over with; this is one weight loss program that doesn't have an ending.*

At a later stage of the diet, when you've lost almost all the weight you want to lose, you pass from the *Ongoing Weight Loss* diet, pass through (usually in the course of a few weeks, though for some people it might take a couple of months) the important *Pre-Maintenance* phase of dieting, and go on to the *Maintenance* diet. At that point, there will be another landmark level: Your Critical Carbohydrate Level for Maintenance (CCLM) will be the highest number of grams of carbohydrate that you can consume *without starting to gain the weight back.* For most of you now-slim Atkins dieters, that number will be somewhere in a wide range from 25 to 90 grams a day. Look at Chart 17.3.

---

**CHART 17.3**
**CARBOHYDRATE GRAM LEVELS**
**AND METABOLIC RESISTANCE**

| Metabolic Resistance | Ongoing Weight-Loss Level (CCLL) | Maintenance Level (CCLM) |
|---|---|---|
| High | 15 or less | 25–40 |
| Average | 15–40 | 40–60 |
| Low | 40–60 | 60–90 |

---

The degree of metabolic resistance is perhaps better estimated from the CCLLs than from data extrapolated from the response to a 14-day test diet. As you continue to do the diet, you will, by glancing at this table, have a more accurate idea of your degree of metabolic resistance.

## Moving Up the Carbohydrate Ladder

If you do wish for a fairly easy and systematic way of increasing the quantity of the healthy carbohydrates that you can consume while still dropping poundage, my suggestion is that you do it by 5 gram increments. For instance, ½ avocado, 6 to 8 stalks of asparagus, and 1 ounce of sunflower seeds are all 5 gram carbohydrate increments. Thirteen average strawberries is a five gram increment, so is five ounces of hard cheese. Look at the chart below for other suggestions, or turn to the Carbohydrate Counter on page 385, where measurements are given in g/oz.

---

**CHART 17.4**

**CARBOHYDRATE INCREMENTS**

| Food | Quantity | Grams of Carbohydrate |
|---|---|---|
| Almonds | 15 | 4 g |
| Brazil nuts | 10 | 4 g |
| Cashews | 11–12 | 5 g |
| Macadamia nuts | 12 | 4 g |
| Pistachio nuts | 50 | 5 g |
| Sunflower seeds | 1 oz | 6 g |
| | | |
| Asparagus | 6 spears | 5 g |
| Brussels sprouts | ½ cup | 5 g |
| Cauliflower | 1 cup | 5 g |
| Celery | 3 five-inch stalks | 4 g |
| Chicory | 1 cup | 2 g |
| Mushrooms | 10 small | 4 g |
| Radishes | 20 medium | 5 g |
| Soybeans | ½ cup | 11 g |
| Spinach | ½ cup | 5 g |

| Food | Quantity | Grams of Carbohydrate |
|------|----------|----------------------|
| Cooked tomato | ½ cup | 5 g |
| Turnip greens | 1 cup | 5 g |
| Cottage cheese | 1 cup | 6 g |
| Hard cheese | 1 oz | 1 g |
| Lemon juice | ½ cup | 8 g |
| Tomato juice | ½ cup | 5 g |
| Blueberries | 21 average size | 5 g |
| Raspberries | 17 average size | 5 g |
| Strawberries | 13 average size | 5 g |

Now that you've moved on from the one-salad simplicity of the *Induction* phase of the Atkins diet, why don't you get yourself a little notebook and keep track of the food you eat daily. Didn't I tell you you could replace your willpower with your brains? Well, now you can feed your brain this information. The more you know about the carbohydrate quantities of foods you eat, or want to, the better equipped you will be to plan an effective diet strategy.

Meanwhile as you keep raising your level of carbohydrate intake (and even if you don't), you'll notice a slowdown in the rate at which you lose weight. How soon you notice those changes is another major tipoff as to how great is your metabolic resistance to weight loss.

On the fifteen grams of the *Induction* diet you may have been losing 5 pounds a week. In the first week to ten days, some of that loss may have been water weight, since the diet has a strongly diuretic effect. Perhaps your real level of weight loss on the strict level of the Atkins diet was 2½ pounds a week of actual fat, or approximately 10 pounds a month.

That isn't an unusual rate at which to lose. When Madge O'Hara came to see me, she weighed 156 on her 5' 2" frame, and she planned to slim down to 115. She actually lost 21 pounds the first month, and my surmise is that six or seven pounds of that was water weight. The next month she lost seven pounds. By that time, she was at a considerably higher level of the diet, and she took off the last 13 pounds to her goal at a leisurely pace. Those pounds took ten full weeks to go, but, by the time they were gone, she knew exactly how she was going to eat for the rest of her life.

Now that you're liberalizing the diet, you too should expect to see a gradual diminishment of the rate of loss. An additional fact, observed on any diet, is that the rate of weight loss will also be slower as you get closer to your ideal weight. A very important rule is to plan to take two or more months to shed the last 10 pounds. This places you on the *Pre-Maintenance* level of the diet—an almost mandatory level if permanent weight loss is to be achieved. I cannot stress enough how advantageous it is to merge into your *Maintenance* diet, rather than have an abrupt transition. This is the point when formula diets fail their followers.

On the other hand, if you still have thirty or more pounds to lose when you complete the *Induction* diet, you certainly will not be happy with a major slowdown. To you, I would urge adding carbohydrate very slowly, staying for weeks at each 5 gram incremental level.

Let's say in your third week on the diet, you add that half cup of broccoli to the salad you were already consuming. You're up to about 20 grams a day. Perhaps your weight loss that week drops from 4 pounds to 2½. The difference may be water weight. In the fourth week, you add another 5 gram increment. You lose 2 pounds. The fifth week you add five more daily grams of carbohydrate. You lose 1½. And so on.

You may find that you can go up to 35 or 40 grams of

carbohydrate a day and still lose a pound a week. This would put you at an average level of metabolic resistance. Your LTS should still be purple, even if only slightly so, and this, together with your continued weight loss, indicates that you're still in ketosis/lipolysis.

Though the rate at which you want to lose is up to you, I think you might well be content with this state of affairs. As long as the pounds are disappearing, and you're heading steadily toward your goal, why worry? Let's suppose, though, that you are rapidly coming to the conclusion that the extra 10 grams of carbohydrate don't mean as much to you as the extra pound per week of weight loss does. You may opt to stay at a lower level of carbohydrate and be satisfied with the knowledge that you *could* have more, if you chose to. Just remember to use a *Pre-Maintenance* phase as you near your ideal weight.

## What If I'm Not Average?

If you can go up to 50 or 60 grams of carbohydrate a day and still be losing a little weight and showing ketosis, then you have a fairly low level of metabolic resistance. In all probability you weren't all that overweight, and staying permanently slim on the Atkins *Maintenance* diet is going to be a breeze for you. You're a person who's going to be able to eat two salads, two helpings of vegetables, and perhaps a fruit daily and still remain at a stable weight. If you're careful, and you find you don't go into a weight-gaining spiral, you may even be able to have an occasional potato and some wild rice. Considering you're already eating one of the world's most luxurious protein diets, I predict a great deal of pleasurable eating ahead. But I do ask this question: If so little of your problem is *metabolic*, how did you become overweight in the first place? You should be on the lookout for a pattern of self-destructive behavior. It could be that that is a component of your weight problem.

Some of you aren't so lucky when it comes to metabolic resistance. Those of you with a very high metabolic resistance to weight loss are most in need of this book. If you *stop* losing weight after you reach 20 or 25 grams of carbohydrate daily, you will have to adapt to eating not much more carbohydrate than is on the *Induction* diet. And you certainly will want to study the next chapter very carefully, even though it is primarily written for that 5% who can't lose at all on the Atkins diet.

If you're going to stay slim and healthy, then a significant increase in the amount of exercise—which I strongly recommend for everyone—is absolutely essential for those of you with high metabolic resistance. Without it, losing weight may actually be hard for you.

Moreover, with a high degree of insulin resistance, you're at serious risk of developing diabetes and heart disease, unless you ruthlessly control your consumption of carbohydrate. Obesity, because of these medical consequences, is your deadly enemy, and you must conquer or control it.

It's quite likely that I'm preaching to the converted, because those of you with a high metabolic resistance to weight loss are already well aware of how serious your problem is, and I've generally found that people with severe obesity problems can be among the most committed of dieters once they're shown a technique of weight loss that actually works and that doesn't force them to undergo the really horrific pain of semi-starvation.

Here is where a low-carbohydrate diet's suppression of appetite reaps its most handsome dividends. As long as you remain at a ketogenic level of the diet, you'll be able to enjoy them.

Now I'd like to look at some possible solutions for those of you whose metabolic resistance is quite extreme.

# 18

## Treating Extreme Metabolic Resistance: The Unique Fat Fast

By the time you got to page three of this book, you noticed the emphasis I placed on obesity being metabolic far more commonly than it is the consequence of any gluttony. I hope that I provided some emotional comfort for those of you who had never been told that was true. It must be very unsettling to be told that the sole reason for your over-weight is your enjoyment of and indulgence in food. It's no fun to think that one's overweight because one's glut-tonous, and it's just darn seldom that that's the case.

Obesity *is* almost always a metabolic problem, and to be specific, the metabolic disturbance is hyperinsulinism. So far, so good. Now what happens when the metabolic ob-stacles are so great that it seems as though you *can't* lose weight?

The inability to lose weight, even on effective diets, does exist. I have seen scores of patients with this problem and thousands more who *tend* to have it. This very real condition doesn't have any official recognition, you can't find it in the diagnostic code index or in textbooks, and many doctors treating obesity have denied its existence, although an increasing number of them are just recently beginning to acknowledge the phenomenon.

So that leaves it up to me to give it a name. We'll call it "metabolic resistance to weight loss," or, for short, "metabolic resistance."

Let's define it. Somewhat arbitrarily, I'll say, "Inability to lose weight or to continue to lose until a reasonable goal weight is reached on either a diet containing 1000 calories or on a 25 gram carbohydrate diet." It is very rare to find someone who can't lose any weight on these dietary regimens, but it is not so rare to find individuals who get "stuck" short of their seemingly realistic weight goal. I would estimate that 4% of obese subjects have metabolic resistance, and this may be 1% of the total population. In the United States, that comes to two and a half million people; quite a crowd for a condition that could benefit from medical intervention and yet is not even an officially recognized condition.

I'll try to provide some consolation by offering you a chapter of your own.

## How Can You Tell If You're Metabolically Resistant?

You can tell by doing. If you seem to be a slow loser and have had a prolonged "plateau" on some official diet, ask for or find a 1000-calorie version of that diet and follow it for long enough (2–3 weeks) to ascertain that you are still not losing. If this happens, you would be judged "metabolically resistant" by most doctors (as long as they believed you) but not necessarily by me.

For I have found that 3 out of 4 people who do not lose on 1000 calories of balanced food intake *will* lose on the *Induction* diet. Your next step, therefore, is to do the *Induction* diet. There is the distinct possibility that you will lose on the 14-day *Induction* diet but will get stuck on it before you reach your weight goal. You then deserve the official diagnosis of metabolic resistance. The rest of you, who are getting there slowly and with difficulty, would carry my diagnosis of *relative metabolic resistance*.

## What Should the Metabolically Resistant Do?

My first reaction would be to say find a doctor who treats metabolic resistance, for you certainly need some expert medical advice. But, alas, I doubt you could find such a person; *I* have never located one.

Yet there are medical questions that have to be answered at the outset, such as: Are you taking any medications? If you are, there's a very good chance they are the cause of your metabolic resistance.

The worst offenders are the psychotropic drugs; phenothiazines, anti-depressants, including prozac, tranquilizers, lithium, and the like. Secondly, hormones such as estrogen, prednisone and other steroids can cause weight gain and prevent weight loss. Many of the anti-arthritic medications, especially the NSAIDs, do it, too. Then there are the diuretics and, to a lesser extent, other cardiovascular medications. Insulin and oral antidiabetics surely have their effect. In fact, it has been said that when a person is metabolically resistant, *any* medications can aggravate the condition.

## You Don't Expect Me to Just Stop My Medications, Do You?

I most certainly don't expect a reader to do that. The risk could be incredible. But for *my* patients that is exactly what we aim for. You cannot stop a medication deemed necessary unless you can provide an equally effective alternative treatment. It may surprise you to know that for each medication grouping I listed, there is an effective *nutritional* alternative. Since that subject is a little far afield of the subject of this book, I would like to refer you to *Dr. Atkins' Health Revolution*.

The technique is the gradual replacement of the suspect drugs with the nutritional protocol (diet and supplements) that can adequately substitute for them. (*N.B. This requires a nutrition-oriented professional with experience; not suitable for a do-it-yourselfer.*)

If you've attended to the medication problem, the next possibility is to look into your hormonal balance. Certainly a significant percentage of the metabolically resistant have underactive thyroid function.

I test for this with a standard battery of thyroid tests including one to test the TSH levels (an elevation of TSH is the most reliable blood test of all), and another to test the thyroid autoantibodies (there is a new technology for detecting these, much more sensitive than previously). But, if the metabolic resistance is associated with specific low thyroid symptoms such as sluggishness, brittle hair, coarse skin, irregular menses, depression, and difficulty keeping warm, I would do one more test—the basal body temperature.*

---

*This is accomplished by holding a glass thermometer under your arm for 10 minutes, before you get out of bed in the AM. If the average of four or more different mornings' readings is 96.8 or less, that is *prima facie* evidence of sluggish thyroid.

If you show any of these manifestations of underactive thyroid, then the administration of your corrective dose of thyroid hormone (by your doctor) is very likely to correct your metabolic resistance. If your doctor balks at this suggestion, please convey to him my experience—that I have never found a supervised therapeutic trial of thyroid in this situation to be risky.

There is a simple at-home test that you must do if the evidence seems inescapable that you are metabolically resistant. Use the lipolysis testing strips after you have done the strict *Induction* diet for several days—nothing but meat, fowl, seafood, eggs, cheese—this time without even the salad. Those who are truly metabolically resistant will be the only ones who do *not* turn the sticks purple.*

There still are those who do get a measurable ketogenic/lipolytic response and yet do not lose weight. In this instance, we are confirming that fat stores do break down, and we do anticipate a loss of inches. Those who can develop lipolysis but no weight loss usually turn up an explanation based on medication or a hormonal problem.

## For The Hardest Of Hard Core Metabolic Resisters

But there will still be some of you who don't lose on the *Induction* diet or even on a low-fat diet of under 900 calories, and some who don't even get into a ketosis/lipolysis

---

*At the Atkins Center, we can quantitate the degree of ketosis/lipolysis much more accurately, using the ketonanalyzer, which measures the amount of ketone excreted through the lungs, a quantity directly proportional to the blood level. In this manner, we can make hour-to-hour determinations of the ketone level in order to study our patient's metabolic responses.

metabolism under any circumstances. The following discussion is for you.

When you are frustrated that things are not going your way, there are two common responses you might make, one destructive and one constructive. You might, and I've seen this response too many times, give in to your frustration and say to yourself, "Dieting is not worth it," and decide, "I'm going off this diet." The consequences are sad but predictable. If you are not losing on an extremely effective diet, you will surely gain—and rapidly—whenever you ease up on that diet. And since the diet was giving you control over your eating behavior (by suppressing your hyperinsulinism response), the loss of control can only accelerate that weight gain.

The constructive response to "getting stuck" involves a dispassionate bit of self-analysis that leads to the conclusion that "whatever I must do, I will do." Going off the diet *is* the correct response, but it can only be for the purpose of going *on* to a more effective diet.

Remember there are two effective techniques for losing weight that we have been utilizing. One is the restriction of carbohydrate; the other, the restriction of the total amount of food, customarily measured (with some degree of metabolic inaccuracy) in calories.

You might study your response to eating less food; smaller portions, fewer calories, less calorically dense foods (i.e. lower fat). Perhaps you were seduced by the concept of "eat all it takes," which you may have interpreted as "eat all you want," and the two means of determining your optimal quantities may be quite different. For you the most effective strategy might be to say to yourself, "I'll eat just enough that I'm physically free of intolerable hunger signals, and no more." No question, for the person who is stuck, that's the first thing to try.

So do that, and come back to this section after you've given your new quantity concept a fair try (several weeks, perhaps).

You now have to answer those questions. Is the newly modified diet working now? If so, am I as happy as I was on my *Induction* diet? Do I feel as well? Can I do this for a lifetime? If the answer is yes, then do it—you've found your answer. If the answer to any of these questions is no, read on.

The second principle of weight loss we work with (and the number one principle, overall) is carbohydrate restriction. I placed it second here merely because, if you are on the *Induction* diet, you are already quite restricted in carbohydrate. Of course, you're not at absolute zero in carbohydrate—there are the veggies, the salad, the lemon juice, and the other low-but-not-zero carbohydrate items that make this diet so livable. What would happen if you cut way down on them? (I shouldn't have to say this, but, if you're cheating occasionally, stop it instantly, and shame on you for entertaining the notion that your metabolism is at fault, when, more likely than not, it's your discipline.)

Well, try retreating to zero carbohydrate, and then ask yourself the same question. Does the diet now work, and do you feel well, and are you happy, and could you spend your life on it?

If you're still not losing, you have hard-core metabolic resistance, and the worst part must be that nobody seems to understand what a prison you're living in. Stick with me, then. I'm probably one of the few people who understands you. What other professional has acknowledged the existence of your problem?

There was a time when I used to say to people, "Well, you can always cut down calories and carbohydrate, and go all the way down until you are on a fast." Not as bad an idea as it might sound to someone who has never tried it. The fasting state, once induced, is full of self-protective devices. A person on a fast liberates more FMS and other lipid mobilizers than on almost any other diet, and the FMS leads to ketosis/lipolysis, loss of hunger, and a variety of other benefits that make the average fasting person comfortable and often exhilarated.

The beautiful fact about fasting and the Atkins diet is that one can use the *Induction* diet to create a maximal outpouring of FMS and then, without an interruption, switch into fasting without going through the hunger/discomfort that characterizes the first two days of a fast. So by doing 2 to 3 days of a "nothing but meat, eggs, fish, and fowl" diet, you can begin your fast already in an effective state of ketosis/lipolysis.

Now, as the Benoit study and other research has shown, fasting is accompanied by a loss of lean body tissue as well as fat, and some of the pounds you lose will not be the ones you want to lose. Plus, loss of essential minerals such as potassium make it dangerous for many people, and dozens of deaths (usually from heart rhythm disturbances secondary to potassium depletion) have been reported.

So I believe, as does most everyone in the field, that fasting should be modified. It should include lots of electrolytes such as potassium, so a diluted juice fast or a vegetable broth fast is preferable. (If I don't go into details don't fret; I've got something better to tell you about presently.)

One of the current "rages" is the protein-sparing modified fast (PSMF) that you've heard of as "formula diets," the type that helped Oprah Winfrey achieve such a spectacular, albeit evanescent, weight loss. These diets maintain most of the efficacy of fasting and share with it many of the risks, but they do minimize these risks. However, because most of them contain carbohydrate, they still allow for a significant amount of weight loss as lean body tissue. That, plus the fact that they do nothing to prepare you for a lifetime *maintenance*, explains the notoriously rapid regain so often seen after such an experience.

## So What's Your Answer, Dr. Atkins?

The best answer to metabolic resistance to date is not new. It has been known for 27 years. Remember the Benoit study that I described on page 61? Well, he studied a diet that outdid the total fast by 88% as far as loss of body fat is concerned. And Benoit, in turn, had simply used one of the experimental diets devised by Kekwick and Pawan.

That remarkable diet that provided results so spectacular that the closed-minded establishment spokesmen couldn't believe their data, contained 1000 calories, 90% of them as fat! The other 100 calories consisted of approximately 15 gms of protein and 10 gms of carbohydrate.*

I hope I'm not telling secrets out of school when I tell you that the subjects on Kekwick and Pawan's and Benoit's studies *didn't enjoy their experimental diets*, even though they did enjoy the way they felt. But you know how very interested in food I am. So as I read and reread their amazing results, I suddenly shouted "That, I can do!" I knew I could make the Kekwick and Pawan diet enjoyable. I've tried it on my metabolically resistant patients, and they did very well. I have not used it on my usual patients, because I believe that the diet could be risky when applied to those

---

*These numbers imply that the diet is deficient in protein and is therefore not suitable for long-term use, unless amino acid supplements are given periodically. Note that there is no essentiality of carbohydrate and, therefore, carbohydrate need not be supplemented.

who are not really metabolically resistant. Those of you who are simply dissatisfied that your rate of loss is too slow should be using the regular Atkins diet and keeping to it strictly. Don't use this one except for brief intervals of less than five days.

## Now for the Fat Fast Diet

The first thing you will learn is that 900 calories of fat (90% of the 1000 calorie allotment) is provided by 100 gms of fat—not a lot of food. It's less than four ounces of butter, for example.

So let's see how that can be translated into foods you will actually enjoy.

Let's start with two foods which are in exactly the correct proportions and fill the 90% fat criterion quite naturally—rich, luxurious cream cheese and sinfully delicious macadamia nuts. Ten ounces of cream cheese would be an entire day's food allotment, as would five ounces of macadamias.

Since a nibbler's diet works better than a gorger's diet—that is, frequent small feedings are preferable—it is better to divide the food allowance into four nibblings of 250 calories each, or five of 200 calories each. In effect, you will be on a fast modified by five handfuls of macadamia nuts (one ounce each), per day, or the equivalent. The fasting is modified by your intake of fatty foods, much as the protein-sparing fast is modified by a protein drink. And remember, this diet is only to be used by people whose body fat is as resistant to being lost as a color-fast fabric is resistant to losing its color.

That's why I call it the Fat Fast for the Fat Fast. It is not designed for those who want to lose fat fast. There. I said it, and I'm not sorry.

This is the way it could work. You might opt for two ounces of cream cheese at 7 AM, 3 PM, and bedtime, interspersed with one ounce of macadamias at 11 AM and 7 PM. Or vice versa. It is worth trying that for two days, directly after the *Induction* diet, just to prove to yourself that you don't get hungry, that your blood sugar is remarkably stable, and you feel quite well. What a wonderful feeling it will be to know how easily you can adapt to the most effective fat-losing diet ever described in a medical journal!

## Is That All You Eat?

Well, there are a great many things you can eat—and here is where the food lover in me can help make your Fat Fast an enjoyable experience. I can show you modifications of the basic diet that are fun for all of you, and, for those of you who have been fat-deprived all these years because you thought it was the right thing to do, this can be an answer to wish-fulfillment dreams.

For each of your five 200-calorie fat feedings, you may have:

- 2 oz of soured cream, containing 1 tablespoon of caviar, served on three or four crisply fried pork rinds.
- 2 deviled egg halves, served not in the whites, but on the pork rinds or on a thin slice of a soya bread recipe.
- Graham Newbould's Pâté for Royalty (2 oz) served on the soya bread.
- 2 oz of chicken salad made with triple the usual amount of mayonnaise (or ham salad, egg salad, prawn salad).
- 1 oz of the above in a half avocado.

- 2 ½ oz of whipping cream, artificially sweetened, and with ground vanilla beans.
- And then there are choices from the recipe section, including chocolate truffles.

The rest of your diet should consist of calorie-free beverages, taken liberally. See page 316 for a list of permissible beverages.

So there we have taken a diet devised for an experiment to learn about why fat is less fattening calorie-for-calorie than protein or carbohydrate, and converted it into something enjoyable, extremely well-tolerated, and useful for overcoming metabolic resistance.

First, we must establish whether this program works for you. Those who go on the Fat Fast *must* study themselves with LTS before, during, and after. If you don't go into ketosis on this program, you should be seeing a doctor who specializes in metabolic disorders, for you surely have one. Since I don't expect more than a few dozen readers of this book to be in such a category, my staff can certainly take the time to talk to people in this elite group and answer your questions. But for most of you, I believe you will have found a tool that will finally allow you to be slim.

Now it remains for me to tell you how to use it.

I do not believe the Fat Fast should be used for more than one week at a time. This is simply a safety measure because the diet has not been tested for long-term use. It should, therefore, be interspersed with the *Induction* diet or some other strict level of the Atkins diet. The most important aspect of the switchdown is not to interpose any carbohydrate that would suppress the FMS production. Your strategy should be to lose on the Fat Fast and to use the regular Atkins diet to maintain that loss. A person with metabolic resistance cannot expect to lose rapidly and must develop the patience of Job. Figure it will take a year or two to reach your goal and be content if you proceed steadily on that schedule.

## My Metabolically Resistant Patients

I have seen hundreds of metabolically resistant patients in my career, perhaps more of them than any other doctor. I wish I could tell you I discovered a cure for it, but I cannot.

What I have discovered are quite a few nutrients that have helped some of these people, but none that have helped all of them. Those of you with this problem should turn to Chapter 22, where I list them as well as discussing other advantages of an intelligent use of nutritional supplementation. If your metabolic resistance to weight loss is so severe that even this book isn't a complete solution to your problem, I hope you'll find a medical or nutritional professional who has some familiarity with supplementation and can help you with questions of dosages, durations, combinations, and risks involved in using them.

## Your Problems Always Will Be More Severe

Just remember, if this chapter has been about you then all the rest of the book is conditioned by that fact. For you, the occasional indulgences I offer to other dieters in the maintenance chapter are going to have to be very occasional indeed.

# 19

## Pre-Maintenance— Your Preparation for Permanent Slimness

If you've reached this stage of the diet, then you don't have a lot of weight still to take off. I tend to advise dieters to advance gradually toward their *Maintenance* diet when they just have five to ten pounds left to lose. Depending on how much your weight loss has slowed as you advance upon your goal weight, it could be two or three weeks, or one or two months before you'd naturally get there on the OWL diet.

Now, I'm telling you to slow down even further. The slower you lose that last five pounds the better. I think you should increase carbohydrates until you're losing less than a pound a week.

In effect, by the time you reach that "perfect" weight, you will already be on the *Maintenance* diet, and your weight loss will be just cruising to a halt. The previous weeks will have:

1. Accustomed you to your lifetime eating plan.
2. Given you a good indication of what it will be like.

## Constructive Deviations

One of the things you'll learn in *Pre-Maintenance* is what exceptions you can make to the diet you learned in the *Induction* and OWL diets and still go on losing weight, albeit slowly. Start with one or two deviations a week, such as a fruit and a starch dish—a plate of wild rice or a baked potato.

By the time you reach your goal weight and your *Maintenance* level, you might be enjoying three such deviations. A glass of wine, a couple of slices of whole wheat bread, a half a cantaloupe for lunch one day. Or, if your metabolic resistance is at the low end, a few things more than that each week.

But be careful. There are a couple of reasons why people sometimes get into trouble on the *Maintenance* diet.

1. They don't recognize just how strict the *Maintenance* diet still must be.
2. They're startled to discover that without ketosis/lipo-lysis the wonderful advantage of appetite suppression has gone away.

That's why *Pre-Maintenance* is important. This is the stage in the diet at which you become acclimated to the rest of your life. As you do *Pre-Maintenance*, the protection of ketosis is beginning to vanish. You'll want to eat a bit more, so do. But try not to stuff yourself heedlessly. You have nothing to make up for. Unlike other diets, this one hasn't caused you any pain or hunger.

Nonetheless, suppression of appetite has made your life easy up to now. Now you'll have to think a little more about what you're adding onto your menu. Add the carbohydrates slowly and glide sweetly and safely into *Maintenance*. As you're about to learn, a proper lifetime *Maintenance* diet really involves using all four of your diets when appropriate. No ideal weight is constant, just as no person is constant.

There will be times in your life when you gain some weight back. Fortunately, you'll have developed the confidence to know that those small weight gains can be easily taken off. Most people find that on this diet, it's easy to control their weight. So let's see how it's done.

# 20

# Maintenance—Slim Forever

The bells should be ringing, the flags should be flying: You're there. You've arrived where millions of overweight people in this country have never been since they were children—at your ideal weight. The psychological uplift must be considerable. I really don't think there's anyone, man, woman, or child, who doesn't like to look good.

Glance in the mirror, try on some newly tailored clothes, or climb into duds you haven't been able to shoehorn yourself into for years, and then—O, luxury—listen to the comments people make. I'll bet you've taken center stage. Losing weight sure attracts attention!

Have you won the battle of the bulge? Or have you only graduated from boot camp, where you got in shape for the battle ahead? As a part-time dieter and full-time gourmand, I can personally attest to the fact that you have only achieved the latter. And recidivism among dieters who have lost considerable weight is such a well-documented fact that many cynical doctors advise not even trying to lose. Which is why you *need* a maintenance diet and a determined approach.

I remember talking to Marjorie Burke, a 41-year-old nurse who first saw me when she weighed 254 pounds and who had never weighed less than 175 since she became an adult. She had tried all the diets, including a famous liquid-protein diet on which she started to go bald. She said that for more than twenty years, she hadn't gotten up in the morning, gone in the bathroom, and looked at herself in the mirror without feeling disappointed and depressed. Now that is all gone, part of a somewhat grim past.

Was she ever going to fall off the diet? The answer was plainly *never, never, never*.

## Protect Your Weight Losses

You, too, have invested a lot of effort and psychic energy in those lessons. Since you and I both know you have a tendency to gain, I want you to keep a sharp eye open for any resumption of weight gain.

If your metabolism can handle it, I'm about to allow you—in moderation—many of the foods you used to enjoy. (The outstanding exception is sugar.)

My experience treating overweight patients involves managing over a thousand patients who have lost to their goal weight four or more times, only to gain it back every time. So I can assure you, you should not rush blindly back toward the way you used to eat, with the intention of getting as close to your former eating patterns as you can without absolutely violating the rules of the diet. That would show you really hadn't learned anything from this diet. (Which is to be expected, because diets are not teachers.) But this diet is an experience, and experience is supposed to be the best teacher. What I *hope* you've learned is how to make a lifetime commitment to a different way of eating.

## The Nitty Gritty Of Maintenance

What you should be asking yourself is, "What level of carbohydrate consumption do I *feel* best on." That's really a more rational goal than to find the most liberalized level of carbohydrate consumption you can manage without weight gain. Many people find they feel better on a quite low level of carbohydrates—perhaps only 25 or 30 grams a day—than they do on the most liberal version of the diet. That might be two salads and a large helping of vegetables. Together with the satisfying portions of protein and fat, that would provide for a very healthy diet.

Other people feel best on twice that carbohydrate consumption and have the metabolism to support it. This is your opportunity to individualize a perfect diet for you. *Remember, your best carbohydrate level is the one you can be happiest on without weight regain.*

## A Delicious Lifetime

As you've seen, the Atkins diet is really four diets: The *Induction* diet, which is the most austere form of a low-carbohydrate ketogenic diet; the *Ongoing Weight Loss* diet (OWL), which is designed to continue weight loss over the long haul; the pivotal *Pre-Maintenance* diet which thoroughly accustoms you to that all-important transition between losing and maintaining; and the *Maintenance* diet, which we are talking about right now, and which is intended to keep you slim and healthy for a long lifetime.

What most of my patients discover by the time they reach the maintenance phase of dieting is how endlessly varied, rich, and satisfying this way of eating is.

Donna Miller who came to see me a couple of years ago drained of all energy, beset with allergies, and thirty pounds overweight, had always been a bread, bagels, and pizza freak. In four months, she went from being a size 12 (almost bursting out of it, as she admitted) to being a size 8. In addition, her energy had returned almost as soon as we had taken her off of wheat, sugar, and milk. But what was she going to eat?

She was a resourceful woman, and I hope her diet sounds as attractive to you as it does to me. For breakfast now, she often eats sliced raw tuna and a little salad. Or two scrambled eggs with tofu. For lunch, she'll stir fry or steam vegetables the way the Japanese do, and with it she'll have corned beef, or a lean hamburger patty, or some fish. For dinner, she likes courgettes, aubergines or asparagus. She often mixes up minced garlic, herbs, and parsley in tomato sauce, and she frequently has chicken, rib steak, or salmon. She also finds she can have lentils, split peas, and kasha without gaining weight. She often has the kasha with cinnamon a few apple slices.

Donna has been expanding her variety of salads since she went on the diet, and she told me recently that what she particularly appreciates about the diet is that it has a lot of alternatives, which she now finds she enjoys more than the rather repetitive high-starch menu she used to be on. What impresses me the most is that every item in her new eating plan is wholesome, fresh, and healthy.

Frankly, I defy anyone to propose a more luxurious diet

on which you can stay trim and healthy than the Atkins program.

Of course, I've been promising you all along that this is a diet that boasts not so much of its instant weight loss—though it achieves that—but of its staying power. Instead of bouncing back into the land of the fat, the Atkins diet welcomes you permanently into the home of the slim.

But what if you get on the *Maintenance* diet, you're eating happily and feeling great, and suddenly you notice those awful pounds and inches have started staging a recovery?

## Dealing with Weight Gain

Well, since you've started the *Maintenance* diet I know that, by definition, you've reached your ideal (or at least desired) weight. Therefore, you're probably no longer practicing a ketogenic diet, since ketosis/lipolysis by definition involves an element of fat loss. Newly slim people are no longer trying to shed pounds and so they don't burn fat. They're above their Critical Carbohydrate Level for Losing (CCLL).

But here's the catch that many dieters *don't* catch. There is very little leeway before you break through the *other* Critical Carbohydrate Level—the CCLM, the one at which you begin to gain. A typical person of average metabolic resistance may find he must stay between 40 and 60 grams of carbohydrate daily. Eating more than the 40 is preventing him from losing more pounds and becoming too thin; eating less than the 60 prevents weight regain.

At this ideal weight, you are, in fact, pretty finely balanced in the amount of your carbohydrate intake. Nothing is exact, of course. Since life is change, your weight will, in fact, be constantly shifting up and down by small increments. The most convenient way to maintain your best weight now is to not let that *up* get too far out of hand. If it does, then you may find yourself sliding down the uphill path, to coin a phrase.

I recommend that you know your weight—after all, it's one aspect of your general health that you can always easily keep track of. Getting on the scale daily (or at least twice a week) is a *must* for successful weight maintenance. *When you find that you've gone five pounds or more over your ideal weight, then you must promptly put things back on their proper course. And you must do it without delay.*

Doing so is as simple as going on the diet in the first place. But, when you discover you're five pounds overweight, don't put off dealing with it. Maybe Thanksgiving is coming up, or Christmas, or your birthday, or your spouse's birthday, or your vacation. By the time you celebrate any one of those with a bout of unrestrained indulgence, you may find that instead of being five pounds overweight you're fifteen pounds overweight and plummeting uphill fast. Instead of waiting, act.

Your action is as simple as BDK. *What you should do is go straight back to the Induction phase of the diet*. Do *not* go back to your *Maintenance* diet without first losing *all* you have regained. It's simple. A salad a day of carbohydrate and *voila!*, you've slashed your weight back to perfect in as little as six to eight days, or two or three weeks, if you have high metabolic resistance.

It is imperative that your baseline weight be something fixed indelibly in your mind as a goal you must always be at or near. It should not drift upwards over the years of weight maintenance. If it does then you're gradually compromising with the metabolic pull which leads most of us to reach equilibrium only when our lifetime high weight is reached.*

Your strategy here should be very much like the base-runner who allows himself to take a lead off first base, but never so far that he cannot scurry back to the safety of touching the base, should the pitcher suddenly turn to pick him off. For you, your goal weight is the base you must touch between deviations. Getting to it provides you with the safety of never straying too far from your lifetime objective. Thus, after each five-pound bulge you notch, you must dust off and use the *Induction* diet again.

My experience has been that dieters who regain weight on the *Maintenance* diet are the ones who, when they put on some poundage, simply return to their maintenance level of carbohydrate consumption, instead of to the *Induction* level.

For consistent success, you simply must interpose the strict *Induction* diet between your weight gain and the eventual return to the *Maintenance* diet. If you don't do that, you're likely to gain the weight back by increments. You gain five pounds, you stop gaining for a time on *Maintenance*, then you gain five pounds more, and so on. If you let this happen, you gradually slip away from your goal weight until it begins to seem out of reach again. Simply put, you gain when you're eating too many carbohydrates—when you've exceeded your CCLM. And as the extra pounds slip on, the nagging metabolic misfortunes

---

*Many obese people seem to have an appestat (or, more accurately, a ponderostat), which causes them to regain on balanced eating, up to a very specific point at which the weight stabilizes and no further gain takes place, even though the weight-regaining diet remains constant. For most people, the ponderostat is set at their previous lifetime peak weight. Medications can certainly elevate this equilibrium point, as can the cessation of cigarettes or diet pills.

that you thought were behind you rise up again. Your energy level declines and the hyperinsulinism symptoms you experienced before start to come again. Those who got off medications may find they require them again. And those with yeast symptoms may find the bloating and brain fog returning. You're on the wrong road, friend.

## Don't Reactivate Your Addictions

Naturally, in this situation, you may find yourself engaged in a real battle for self-control as your defenses crumble. Perhaps you've been indulging too much in the foods that got you into trouble to begin with. You may suddenly fall right back under their spell.

Hyperinsulinism and the resultant low blood sugar levels plus specific food allergy/intolerances truly create an addictive situation. If you go back on sugar, or—for some of you—on bread, fruit, or fermented foods, you suddenly discover that you *must* have these foods, that no day or meal feels right without them. If this should happen, and you observe yourself carefully, you'll notice that the need that develops is genuinely physical. It isn't simply that a jelly donut tastes good to you, and you'd *like* to have it. No, your body absolutely roars with anxiety and passion for that jelly donut. And then you *know*. You've activated an addiction, just like an alcoholic with his bottle.

This isn't shameful; it's physical, it's chemical, it's metabolic, and that's precisely why you must avoid it. Most of you already know that for a significant portion of your life, carbohydrates have been stronger than you. Don't trifle with them.

Nearly all of you will find that, if those carbohydrate cravings return, you can cure them with several days of

*Induction* dieting. But this simple maneuver is, for many hard-core recidivists, more easily said than done. A professional recidivist, for reasons known only to him or herself, will not return to the *Induction* diet, until he or she has regained *all* the weight or is experiencing intolerable symptoms. But I think recidivists are made, not born, and if you catch yourself procrastinating, or worse yet, not even thinking about nipping your regain while it is still a bud, you can avoid this behavior by recognizing that your decision to lose any regained weight *immediately* is the best way to manage this lifetime plague.

## Back to Maintenance

Meanwhile, how's it going to go while you're cruising along at your desired weight?

On the *Maintenance* diet, you can add in most vegetables, nuts, and berries. You can cautiously reintroduce the vegetables containing more than 10% carbohydrate, as well as whole grains such as oats, barley, millet, wild rice, couscous, or buckwheat. You may even be able to handle an occasional potato and a fruit a day. You can begin to use recipes that contain some carbohydrate ingredients (breaded veal chops, etc.). But the last choice for you, the truly hazardous indulgence, is sweets. Frankly, my suggestion to you is that you restrict your consumption of sweets made with real sugars to the occasional slice of birthday or wedding cake. Those of you who have had a sizable chunk of your life made miserable by sugar may even decide, after graciously accepting them, to quietly deposit those pieces on somebody else's plate.*

---

*My other suggestion is to create your own personal world of sweets made with artificial sweeteners or stevia or tagatose. The recipe section at the

## Your Metabolic Tendencies Are Never Cured

You never are, you know. Your fat is one symptom of a lifetime chronic illness. You do have and always will have a metabolic tendency to overweight. The problem of hyperinsulinism that I identified for you will not go away because you have taken a nutritional path that circumvents it. If you go back to eating the way you once did, or even partly so, you will arouse the sleeping demon. In very short order, your body will secrete large quantities of insulin, you'll suffer the symptoms of low blood sugar, and your insulin resistance will lead to the production of more insulin and that, in turn, to weight gain.

If you want to be healthy and free of surplus body fat, then you cannot return to a perfectly random and careless pattern of eating. Thus one of the chief purposes of this book has been to build good habits into your lifestyle.

## But What About My Bad Habits?

Of course, we all have them. Food is so comforting, so delicious, so psychologically essential even at times when it's not physiologically necessary. We all eat for pleasure and for reassurance, as well as nutrition.

It may have been a hard week at work, and when you get to the weekend, one of the things you definitely intend to get into is a little modest pigging out (or perhaps not so modest).

I, too, enjoy binges. The question really is what type of

---

end of the book will introduce you to the concept and give some of our most successful ideas. By using sugar substitutes, you really have the ability to create sugarless versions of your favorite sweets.

binge. *Parade* magazine did a food survey in November 1991, and, when they asked people what foods they usually binged on, the first five answers were chocolates, desserts, cookies, ice-cream, and candy.

I would prefer that you binge on protein/fat foods. I say that not because you can't gain a pound or two if you put away too many two-inch-thick steaks, but because protein foods are fundamentally self-limiting. Everyone has eaten thirty cookies at one sitting at some time in their life, and many carbohydrate addicts have done it hundreds of times, but how many people have eaten ten hard-boiled eggs at one sitting? People just don't do it. Protein and fat foods satiate appetite quite quickly. It really isn't possible to go on munching them endlessly, and hardly anyone desires to. That doesn't mean that a chicken breast doesn't make a delicious snack, and that, combined with a few other things, it doesn't make a delicious minor binge.

The crucial fact about protein foods is that they don't unleash a metabolic tidal wave in your body. Very few people get a protein addiction. Your blood glucose level doesn't sharply rise and fall when you sit down to eat a western omelet. But it does just that when you sit down to eat a slice of pie. That leads to the need for another slice and then another.

I don't want to scare you with the prospect of never eating another piece of grandma's pumpkin pie. If you weren't an uncontrolled carbohydrate addict with severe obesity that only this diet has been able to cure, then you could probably indulge occasionally.

Only you know how *addicted* you are to the sweet stuff—and that's the real test. If you aren't addicted, then you have room to maneuver. The occasional slice of pizza or the ice-cream everyone seems to enjoy just might be permissible. But be careful: When those first five pounds go back on—and they will—take yourself firmly in hand and get back to your ideal weight.

And remember, the way you're eating now is healthful. Junk food isn't, and it isn't going to make you feel good. After you've been off them for a while, the ice cream or the pizza go down nice, but once you've eaten them, you may notice a temporary return of some familiar old symptoms. I don't recommend such compromises, I simply recognize that human nature demands them now and then. And in case you're worried about the fact that *your* personalized, metabolically corrective, heart-healthy diet is quite different from the high carbohydrate, 30% fat diet that the government agencies and their food-industry-supported advisers are recommending, just look back at Part III of this book. The facts should provide some comfort.

## Some Parting Recommendations

For those of you who have been successful, your diet voyage seems to be almost over. In fact, it continues, but you're going to be at the helm, and the boat will be responding to your guidance. So, I want to leave you with a few basic principles for your lifetime on the Atkins diet:

1. Be food aware—remember that fresh meat, fish, fowl, vegetables, nuts, seeds, and occasional fruits and starches are the foods nature designed you to eat. That packaged stuff in the supermarket puts money in somebody's pocket. But try not to put it in your stomach. This is the only body you've got. Notice how good it feels now. Notice how much better it looks. Keep it that way.

2. Be wary—endlessly wary—of sugar and corn syrup, and white flour and corn starch. Look at the labels of whatever packaged foods you find yourself obliged to buy and avoid like the plague the packages that contain sugar, corn syrup, honey, maltose, dextrose, fructose, lactose, sorbitol, and all the other variations and inventions of the modern sugar-refining industry.

3. Individualize your diet. Try new foods. Increase the variety of foods that you like and enjoy. Use the recipes provided in Part 5 of this book. This will help to prevent you from going back to eating foods that you have enjoyed in the past, but which simply aren't good for you. I most strongly recommend that you develop a menu that's appealing, tasty, and satisfying to you. You need to be happy with the food you eat. Once you're happy with eating healthy foods, your dietary future is almost assuredly going to be a healthy one.

4. Continue your already established and effective program of vitamin and mineral supplementation. I've told you some of what you need to know. Chapter 22 provides further details.

5. Use caffeine and alcohol in moderation.

6. Remember that addictions can only be managed through abstinence.

7. Take care of weight regain promptly and effectively by returning to the *Induction* phase of the diet for as long as it takes to get all the way back to the weight you have designated as your goal weight. Swear that you will *never* allow yourself to be more than a two-week diet away from that goal weight.

8. Exercise.

One final word. A National Institutes of Health consensus panel recently reported that in the USA the record of the best low-calorie diet programs suggests that "90 to 95% of dieters regain all or most of their hard-lost pounds within five years."

But when a program changes the *composition* of the diet, not the quantity, and when pre-maintenance teaching and the five-pound rule are consistently applied, recidivism is a rare phenomenon, indeed. Our patient files resoundingly confirm this fact.

# 21

## Exercise—A Pleasant Path to Slimness

Since I thrive on controversy, I haven't mentioned exercise. My stand on exercise (I applaud it and encourage it) is the least controversial part of the book. Which doesn't mean exercise isn't important for you. Not only is it an essential part of the program, but in cases of severe metabolic resistance, it's likely to be the difference between success and spinning your wheels.

Of course, exercise really ought to be a part of any diet program. I've helped many people become slim who didn't want to exercise and therefore, never did, but all of them would have been much better off if they had been willing to incorporate a reasonable amount of healthy exercise into their lives.

When you go on a diet, you're trying to change the shape of your body. It's pretty clear that exercise is complementary to this, for exercise is the only other normal activity that actually alters the size, thickness, contours, etc. of the physical you. In our society, the number of people who want to lose weight so they'll feel better is probably exceeded by the number who want to lose so they'll look better. Exercise is important for both purposes. It's just plain good for you.

## Take Out Some Heart Insurance

I suspect that the modest decline in the rate of heart disease that we saw in the 70s and 80s is directly attributable to the fitness boom. Dr. Kenneth Cooper's *Aerobics* and the many running, jogging, stretching, and jumping books that came after it really touched a nerve in America. People saw that this was something good, something entirely positive in a time of great negativity—the era of Vietnam and Watergate—and they went right after it.

Exercise's time had come, and a good thing too. What a bunch of couch potatoes we were becoming! I was as guilty as the next person. It's so easy to sit down in front of the TV and let gravity have its way with you. But I've discovered like millions of other people that there's a great deal of exhilaration to be gotten out of moving one's limbs. I didn't need to be convinced about the health benefits.

Population studies—what the medical world calls epidemiological studies—can clarify your thinking quite a bit on this point. Coronary artery disease has been shown to be almost three times as likely among Washington, D.C.'s sedentary postal clerks as among its physically active mail carriers. In another study, North Dakota's non-farmers were found to be twice as much at risk as its farmers.

Nor is heart disease the only area in which exercise functions protectively. Obesity, hypertension, adult-onset diabetes, osteoporosis, and even cancer are all significantly less common among the physically active.

## And What If You're Having a Hard Time Losing

Meanwhile, you want to lose weight. If you fell into that category of metabolic resistance that I've just been discussing, then exercise can be tremendously important. You're going to need every edge you can get—not just the dietary edge I've been teaching you but the physical movement edge I'm discussing now.

It has been calculated that you could lose 15 pounds a year just by doing thirty minutes of aerobic exercise three times a week. After all, each mile you walk burns a hundred calories. It doesn't sound like much, but those miles add up.

Moreover, even modest quantities of exercise build muscle mass, especially if you've been sedentary, and the cellular structure of muscle is so constituted that it burns more energy than do your fat cells. That's true even while you're being inactive. Therefore, a person who exercises is slowly but steadily shifting his body toward greater energy consumption and therefore greater slimness. This, too, is a form of metabolic advantage, and I hope you'll seize it.

## What are the Advantages to Exercise?

1. Exercise can be fun.
2. Exercise can make your body look better and help you lose weight.
3. Exercise can (indeed, almost certainly will) make you healthier.

4. Exercise can make you feel good. After the first few days of fatigue, it will give you more energy, and it will make you fitter for any and all of life's challenges.

## What are the Drawbacks to Exercise?

1. There are none.

## What are the Reasons Given for Not Exercising?

1. Laziness. This is usually the real reason, and I can hardly criticize you with a straight face since, for much of my life, I've been guilty myself. The solution for you may be what it was for me: Find an exercise you really like (in my case, tennis) and build your fitness program around that. I still don't like many forms of exercise, but I do some of them, because I tell myself they'll help me to play tennis better.

2. Lack of time. Oh, how often I've heard this one. Please, tell it to the marines. Listen, folks, if you sleep 8 hours a night, that still leaves you with 16 hours a day. Subtract 8 hours for working and 2 for eating and personal hygiene, and there are still 6 hours left. You can find *some* time in those 6 hours for exercise. Your body is one of your most serious responsibilities, since you're going to have an extraordinarily difficult time fulfilling your other responsibilities without it. If you can't squeeze out half an hour a day, you know whose throat you're cutting.

3. Age and/or poor physical conditioning. If you're over a hundred call me for a special consultation to discuss

the possibility of your not exercising; the rest of you won't get away with this lame excuse. As for poor conditioning, that's exactly what we're trying to remedy.

4. Ill health. That's a reason to start slowly and proceed cautiously, not a remission of sentence. An exercise program can be tailored to any condition, and the sickest person can start at a level appropriate to his condition. If you still have the use of your limbs, then you can exercise.

## What are the Types of Exercise?

> Remember, if you're over 35, before you undertake any exercise program more strenuous than brisk walking, have a doctor examine you and conduct a stress test to check for cardiovascular problems.

### *Aerobic Exercise*

Aerobic exercise is exercise that challenges your heart rate and causes increased oxygen consumption. Walking is only very mildly aerobic because the level of exertion is so low. Aerobic dancing, cross country skiing, simulated skiing, running, swimming, speed walking, rowing, and bicycling are all highly aerobic. The benefits of such exercise are immense, quite apart from weight loss. Every cell in your body requires a constant supply of oxygen, and if you've been a couch potato for years, then many of them are being starved of their proper supply. *This means that once you accustom yourself to a regular routine of aerobic exercise, you will positively begin to feel physically better than you did before*. Except for death and taxes, nothing is more certain than this fact.

If you take up some form of vigorous aerobic exercise, then I'd urge you to get some form of professional advice or at least buy a self-help book on the type of exercise you want to do. It's important to learn how to do limbering and stretching exercises, so you can loosen up your muscles, prevent tightness, and reduce the chance of injuring yourself. Running, because of its impact on your knees and ankles, requires care *and* a good pair of running shoes.

Those of you who haven't exercised in a long time, or who want to prevent osteoporosis, might want to try an exercise trampoline. The purpose here is to increase the vertical stress on the weight-bearing skeleton such that the vertebra respond to a signal that more calcium must be laid down along the stress-bearing planes. The springs in the trampoline allow you to absorb a cushioned major impact. The more calcium you accumulate pre-menopausally, the better you will withstand the involutional calcium loss.

### Anaerobic Exercise

This term refers to any type of exercise that isn't significantly aerobic. This includes many types of exercise that build muscle mass, like weight lifting and indeed many forms of physical work. Such exercise is not nearly as healthy and heart protective as aerobic exercise, but it can have two benefits: It will help to shape your body and make you more attractive, and because it builds muscle, it will make it easier for you to maintain an ideal weight. If you increase your musculature by a considerable degree, then you will find that that ideal weight is somewhat higher than an insurance table would lead you to expect, since muscle weighs more than fat.

### *Mildly Aerobic Exercise*

Exercise such as walking, golf, tennis, horseback riding, Ping-Pong, and dancing may only mildly increase the pumping action of your heart and the activity of your lungs, but they are still tremendous improvements on the lifestyle of a non-exerciser. If you want to feel good and live a long life, then I think the least you should do is accustom yourself to taking a half-hour walk each day, preferably at a brisk pace.

For the lifelong non-exerciser, walking is just simply the best way to begin. I know that many of my readers will be people who for years haven't traveled further than two blocks except in an automobile. Great! Tremendous improvements in your well-being lie just ahead of you. Walk five blocks. Then try six. If a ten-minute walk is hard on you today, after three or four days, it won't be. Your muscles will loosen up, stiffness will ease, breathing will improve, and relaxing endorphins will be released into your body. Before you know it, you'll be walking a mile. All you need do is break through the initial crust of bad habits. Feeling good when you move is natural. Not feeling good is a highly artificial state. Remember that Mother Nature would certainly consider today's "modern" lifestyle an abberation.

## What Do You Do to Get Started?

1. Work with your own schedule and figure out what part of the day you're going to reserve for exercise. Many people who have busy lives find that the only way they can consistently get in their exercise is to do it first thing in the morning. If that's the case with you, then why don't you lay out your clothes and your

walking or running shoes before you go to bed at night, and when you get up in the morning simply step into them and get going. You can always wash and eat after you've put in your half hour.

2. Start your exercise plan slowly for the first few weeks. Begin by doing less than you think you can do. If a ten-block walk seems hard, then do eight. You'll find that progress is rapid. Each successive day, you can do a little more. Lots of people start too aggressively. The purpose of an exercise plan is not to exhaust yourself. If you do vigorous aerobic exercise, then you should not do it seven days a week; five should be the maximum. If you start a weight lifting program, *never* do it two days in a row.

3. If you're very overweight, you should start with walking. That will be challenge enough. After all, until you get that weight off, your chance of injuring your joints with some form of highly active exertion is *much* greater.

## A Few Final Comments

When you exercise, there should be a normal elevation of your pulse rate. If you feel dizzy or have chest pain, *STOP*. It is obviously time for you to check things out with your personal physician.

If everything goes normally, you will probably find that you can increase your exercise by 10 to 20% each week.

Many people will discover after just a couple of weeks of exercise that they're pleasantly addicted. This is one of the few addictions in this life of ours that you need never fear.

Even the most confirmed non-exercisers among you will

find that after two or three months, you've formed a habit that can remain pleasantly and easily part of your life forever.

Go to it. The only things you have to lose are the chains of inactivity.

# 22

## Nutritional Supplements— The Secrets of the Atkins Center

The essential fact you must know for this chapter is that the best doctors I know actually *treat* their patients with vitamins. By that I mean they use what I call a "nutritional pharmacology" and they prescribe what Dr. Stephen de Felice calls "nutraceuticals."

These terms may lead you to ask, "Is there a system of treating illness with nutrients and natural substances, instead of the drugs and pharmaceuticals that nearly every doctor prescribes?"

Well, I'm glad you asked; I was afraid you never would. There indeed is such a system. It is rapidly growing in popularity and has been embraced by over a thousand physicians and a hundred times that many non-physician health practitioners. I call it Complementary Medicine, because the basic tenet is that all healing arts can and should be made to complement one another. Another basic tenet is that the practitioner of Complementary Medicine should select the safest therapies first. That's why the Complementarist is so likely to use nutritional therapies; their safety, when compared to the drugs they replace, approaches infinity.

Now I certainly am a Complementary physician. In fact, there are a few plaques on my wall suggesting that there are those who think I'm one of the leaders of this movement. And so I have a confession to make. Mary Anne Evans, Harry Kronberg, and all the other patients of mine whose case histories help personalize this book were all given something more than the Atkins diet.

All my patients—and my case examples were no exceptions—receive a fairly significant amount of vitamins, minerals, essential fatty acids, and other nutritional agents called intermediary metabolites. I prescribe them because I have learned from my clinical experience, my reading, and my attendance at medical meetings, to say nothing of interviewing around one hundred of the world's greatest health science leaders every year for my weeknightly radio broadcasts, that nutrients can impact anyone's health.

I have found so many nutrients to be valuable, conferring health advantages *even for healthy people*, that I no longer consider that a person following a theoretically optimal, even "perfect," diet could live as long or as healthfully as he could were he also to take nutritional supplements.

I'll cite just one example to prove my point. The antioxidant group of nutrients, when tested scientifically, are consistently shown to confer significant protection against damage caused by free radicals, violently active environmentally-engendered electrons implicated in the causation of cancer, heart disease, and aging. Even a person with a perfect diet is not living in a perfect environment and so he can maintain his good health longer if he takes the effective doses of vitamins A, C, E, plus selenium, glutathione, cysteine, and bioflavonoids.

Studies have been done seeking to find the maximal effective doses of nutrients. Two-time Nobelist Linus Pauling concluded that most of us should be taking ten gms of vitamin C daily. In fact, when all the useful nutrients are considered and we ask the question what is the optimal dose for each, the best scientific answer might lead us to take over 100 vitamin pills per day.

Since that clearly isn't practical, I was led, of necessity, to devise a system of nutritional prescribing I called Targeted Nutrition. This allows me to prescribe (and individuals to select for themselves) a variety of formulations targeted to the nutritional needs appropriate to certain clinical problems. For instance, if a person is subject to frequent colds and viruses, and wants to make sure that he has the nutritional support to help prevent one, he might opt for an acute infection formula such as the one we at the Atkins Center call AI#6. Such a formula contains the vitamins C and A, plus zinc, bioflavonoids and the B-complex constituents that published studies have shown to make a nutritional difference in our ability to fight off such invaders.

Unlike drugs, the nutritional agents are not directed against the disease. Rather, they are in support of the host's ability to mount a defense against the disease, which he can do so much better when his nutrition is provided for. The world has been programmed to believe that one fights illness by attacking it with a combination of killer drugs, but, since I have been using nutrition, my patients get well much faster and much more thoroughly when their own resistance is supported nutritionally.

The application of Targeted Nutrition certainly extends to those whose chief concern is the loss of weight, and, for this purpose, I have devised a dieter's formula, a sort of companion piece to the Atkins diet. I'll tell you about it, so you won't have to get it from the Atkins Center (in the sale of whose vitamins, I, of course, have a personal financial involvement) but can simply provide yourself with a collection of vitamins providing the equivalent nutritional support.

Our Dieter's Formula (Basic 3) contains all the ingredients in our basic multiple vitamin, although in somewhat different dosages. It was designed to be taken in a dose of six to nine a day (the larger dose for 200 + pounders), but even double that would present virtually no risk of overdosing. It differs from the usual basic formula in that it contains greater amounts of chromium picolinate, pantethine, selenium, and biotin. This group of nutrients is emphasized because of scientific reports suggesting that they all play nutritional roles in glucose, insulin, and lipid metabolism. Our Dieter's Formula (Basic 3) follows.

---

### Dieter's Formula
### Basic #3

| | |
|---|---|
| Vitamin A | 200 IU |
| Beta-Carotene | 500 IU |
| Vitamin D-2 | 15 IU |
| Thiamine (HCl) ($B_1$) | 5 mg |
| Riboflavin ($B_2$) | 4 mg |
| Vitamin C (Calcium Ascorbate) | 120 mg (150 mg) |
| Niacin ($B_3$) | 2 mg |
| Niacinamide | 5 mg |
| Pantetheine (80%) | 25 mg (30 mg) |
| Calcium Pantothenate ($B_5$) | 25 mg |
| Pyridoxal-5-Phosphate | 2 mg |
| Pyridoxine (HCl) ($B_6$) | 20 mg |

| | | |
|---|---|---|
| Folic Acid | 100 | mcg |
| Biotin | 75 | mcg |
| Cyanocobalamin (B$_{12}$) | 30 | mcg |
| Vitamin E (D alpha tocopherol) | 20 | IU |
| Copper (Sulfate) | 200 | mcg |
| Magnesium (Oxide) | 8 | mg |
| Choline (Bitartrate) | 100 | mg |
| Inositol | 80 | mg |
| PABA | 100 | mg |
| Manganese (Chelate) | 4 | mg |
| Zinc (Chelate) | 10 | mg |
| Citrus Bioflavonoids | 150 | mg |
| Chromium (Picolinate) | 50 | mcg |
| Molybdenum (Sodium) | 10 | mcg |
| Vanadyl Sulfate | 15 | mcg |
| Selenium | 40 | mcg |
| Octacosanol | 150 | mcg |
| N-Acetyl-1-cysteine | 20 | mg |
| L-Glutathione (reduced) | 5 | mg |

In a base of lactobacillus, bulgaris and bifidus acidophilus, B Complex and growth factors.

Suggested Dosage: One to three tablets three times a day after meals.

---

Chromium deserves the most attention. First discovered as the unique mineral constituent of the Glucose Tolerance Factor (GTF), a molecule which serves as a sort of catalyst for the action of insulin at its receptor sites, chromium was beginning to be thought of as an essential nutrient, and GTF was being considered for recognition as a true vitamin. In many ways this was a frustrating state of affairs, because finding a food source for chromium is actually quite difficult. Only brewer's yeast seemed to qualify, and, as you learned in Chapter 13, the 30% of the population deemed to be overstocked with Candida albicans would not do well on such a food. However, it has recently been discovered that the picolinate of chromium is well assimilated, and a spate of studies have shown that chromium will build muscle (an anabolic effect) and decrease body fat, plus lower the cholesterol levels.[1]

You are probably best served by taking in chromium picolinate in dosages of 300–600 mcg per day.

Pantetheine is the intermediary between the B vitamin pantothenic acid and the important coenzyme A. It plays a pivotal role in many metabolic pathways and is a remarkable cholesterol-control nutrient. It is valuable in allergy, colitis, stress, and in yeast infections. I use 100 to 400 mg daily.*[2]

Selenium is valuable as an antioxidant and its deficiency seems to provide an increased cancer risk. In addition, a recent animal study by McNeill suggested that it plays a beneficial nutritional role in diabetes prevention. I think 200 mcg is a proper adult daily dose.[3]

Biotin is one of those unsung B vitamins whose nutritional role was recently emphasized when J. C. Coggeshall and his associates noted a significant drop in diabetics' blood-sugar levels when biotin was given.[4]

And just another good word about vitamin C supplementation. G. J. Naylor and his associates did a double blind placebo-controlled study on 41 extremely overweight women who had failed at previous weight-loss efforts. After six weeks, the control group had lost an average of 2.1 pounds, but the group receiving 3 gms of C daily lost 5.7 pounds.[5] Not earth-shattering to be sure, but when com-

---

*Pantetheine poses problems for the vitamin manufacturer since it exists as a liquid form. We have seen products where pantetheine was listed on the label but, on assay, contained none. Make certain that the product you use contains adequate pantetheine.

bined with vitamin C's advantages in shoring up our resistance to infections, I want to make sure you are all adequately provided with ascorbic acid.

After you decide on an appropriate multiple vitamin and mineral preparation, the next most important nutritional group for long-range supplementation is the essential fatty acids. You won't find these in a multiple vitamin because they exist physically as oils. Oils and dry powders mix very poorly, and so they must be taken separately. There are two types of essential fatty acids that most of us really do need. One type is the omega-3 series which occurs in animal sources (fish and marine mammals primarily) and vegetable source (linseed or flax oil) providing the essential oil, alpha-linolenic acid. Another type is a special omega-6 subdivision called gamma linolenic acid, found useful in atopic eczema, PMS, cholesterol elevation and many other deficiency situations and contained in EPA, borage oil, and black-currant oil.

Essential-oil administration is best done individually by a nutrition counselor, but, for general purposes, I might suggest 2 capsules of borage oil, 2 of super-EPA, and 2 of flaxseed oil. Convenience lovers may opt for 6 of the Essential Oils Formula, which contains all of the above and which I prescribe to my patients.

Then there are nutrients whose deficient supply sometimes causes a nutritional log jam. Occasionally metabolic resistance can be explained in part as a nutritional shortcoming. I would like to mention three such nutrients. You may want to study the effect of these upon your dietary responsiveness.

The first of these is L-carnitine. Carnitine is involved in fat transport, and, when it is deficient, overweight people have difficulty getting into ketosis/lipolysis. Carnitine's primary use is in heart disease, where it corrects a common type of cardiomyopathy, helps stabilize heart rhythm, lower triglyceride levels, and increase HDL cholesterol. For these conditions, the dosage ranges between 1000 and 2000 mg daily.[6]

Coenzyme $Q_{10}$ is another nutrient essential to heart function. It is also essential to proper working of the immune system and is a specific nutritional correction for periodontal (gum) disease. But overweight readers might be interested in a Belgian study, headed by Dr. Luc Van Gall, which showed that over half of a group of obese patients had *deficiency* levels of $CoQ_{10}$ and compared them with a similar group without deficiency.[7] After nine weeks, the formerly deficient group lost 29.7 pounds on a standard diet, compared to the non-deficient ones who lost 12.7 pounds on the same diet. If this work mirrors the incidence of $CoQ_{10}$ deficiency in all overweight subjects, then one out of two of you will benefit considerably from this single nutrient. Van Gall used 100 mg daily in his research.

Pyridoxine alpha-ketoglutarate (PAK) is less well-studied, but it does seem to have a favorable effect on diabetes. Any nutrient capable of facilitating the action of insulin should quite logically be helpful for those who are struggling to lose weight. I use between 500 and 1500 mg daily.

So the basic supplementation consists of:

Basic formula for dieters—6 times a day.

Chromium picolinate—300 mcg daily or slightly more, unless it is in your basic formula.

Essential oils—3 to 6 a day, or individual GLA, EPA, and flax.

Carnitine, $CoQ_{10}$, and PAK—if you determine that they help.

## Additional Advantages

Now that I've laid out the basic framework of supplementation for all of you, here are specific nutritional answers to common dieters' problems:

- For constipation: You may use magnesium oxide, extra vitamin C, or a variety of vegetable laxatives and bulking agents. My favorite choice is psyllium husks. Start with 1 tablespoon in one full glass of water and increase or decrease the dose until the optimal bowel movement is obtained.
- For sugar craving: L-glutamine, 500–1000 mg before meals and perhaps right at the point in time when craving is greatest.[8] Extra chromium is valuable here, too.
- For hunger not assuaged by being in ketosis: L-phenylalanine or acetyl L-tyrosine, 500 mg of the former, or 300 mg of the latter, before meals.[9]
- For fluid retention: Pyridoxal 5 phosphate, 50–100 mg, plus L-taurine 1500–3000 mg daily.[10] Asparagus tablets work very well here, too.
- For fatigue: Octacosanol, 5–10 mg, PABA, 600–2000 mg, dimethylglycine, 3 to 6 sublingual tablets per day, sublingual $B_{12}$ tablets, 1–3 daily, or 1–3 B complex tablets daily (50 mg strength).[11]
- For nervousness: Inositol, 500 to 2000 mg daily, and herbal teas such as camomile, valerian, and passion flower.[12]
- For insomnia: The above taken at night, plus melatonin 3–6 mg before bed (ties your sleep cycle into day/night cycle; counterproductive for night workers). Calcium, magnesium, niacinamide, pantothenic acid, and 5-hydroxy tryptophan may all be useful here as well.[13]

## Nutrition and Health Problems

Now let's talk about a supplement program for common medical problems that affect a significant portion of my dieting patients.

Let me simply list what I prescribe. I make no claims that the nutrients below have a direct therapeutic effect on the conditions for which they are used. The effects they have are accomplished through nutritional pathways. Since I have been prescribing in this manner, my patients show clinical improvements four or five times more frequently than they did when I practiced a very competent brand of orthodox internal medicine. This fact can only be attributed to the high percentage of my patients who have specific nutritional deficiencies.

- For hypoglycemics, I use the basic formula, plus chromium, L-glutamine, zinc, selenium, magnesium, all of the B complex, PAK, extra biotin, L-alanine; or else I use Atkins Formula HF-12.[14]
- For diabetes, I use the basic formula, plus extra chromium, zinc, selenium, inositol, $CoQ_{10}$, PAK, biotin, vanadyl sulfate, magnesium; or else I use Atkins formula DM-19.[15]
- For the lowering or prevention of cholesterol elevations, I use lecithin granules, chromium, pantetheine, niacin and other B complex factors, garlic, vitamin C, GLA (borage, primrose, or black currant oils), EPA (fish oil), sitosterol, glucomannan, guar gum, pectin, psyllium husks, dimethyl glycine, $CoQ_{10}$, phosphatidyl choline, or I use the Atkins Lipid Formula* plus the Essential Oils Formula.[16]

*Read labels here. The lipid formula itself should be supplemented with chromium, pantetheine and the essential fatty acids.

- For elevated triglycerides, the slate is similar to the list for cholesterol, except that L-carnitine and EPA are emphasized. Also because of the correlation of triglycerides and hyperinsulinism, the nutrients helpful in diabetes will prove to be helpful here.[17]
- For hypertension, I use magnesium (preferably as orotate, taurate, arginate, or aspartate), L-taurine, pyridoxal 5 phosphate or pyridoxine, garlic, essential fatty acids (GLA and EPA), $CoQ_{10}$, potassium, or I use the Atkins formula AH-3, plus the Essential Oils Formula.[18]
- For coronary heart disease, I use one of the above mentioned magnesium compounds, L-carnitine, vitamin E, $CoQ_{10}$, serrapeptase and/or bromelain, garlic, chromium picolinate, or I use formula CV-4.[19]
- For arthritis, I use shark cartilage, superoxide dismutase, calcium EAP, pantetheine, niacinamide, pyridoxine, PABA, vitamin C, bioflavonoids, vitamin E, SOD/catalase, copper sebacate, or I use Atkins formula AA-5, plus the Essential Oils Formula.[20]

The roster of nutrients which have been studied favorably in these conditions should provide a glimmer of insight into how much published work there is on nutraceuticals. Consider at the same time the almost obscene profit margins consistently reported by the pharmaceutical industry and you may get a flash of recognition as to why all these bona fide medical studies supporting a competing therapy are not widely disseminated. When your doctor doesn't tell you about them, it's only because nobody told him about them.

The restriction of carbohydrate gives you an edge and, similarly, the targeted use of nutritional supplements gives you another kind of edge. Learn about them, learn how to use them, and use them properly. When you do, the Edge will surely be with you.

# 23

**Eating Your Way to Permanent Slimness in the Real World**

I have thoroughly explained the glorious experience of discovering the Metabolic Advantage, inducing a hunger-free state by the unrestricted eating of protein food, advancing level by level into more and more interesting meal plans, merging happily, yet imperceptibly, into a lifetime of eating luxuriously and healthfully while keeping at your goal weight. But does it really happen this way?

You can be sure it does, but ask me how often the scenario unfolds in precisely this sequence, and I would have to estimate about once in ten times. On the other hand, how often is that goal of slimness reached and kept through a more circuitous course involving starts and stops, and recoveries and snafus and thrills and disappointments and surprises and frustrations and the need to resort to willpower and discipline, *and* the cleverness and wisdom to use the metabolic edge to your own advantage? Put another way: How often is the trip to slimness more like something planned by a very inept travel agent? My patient records indicate this happens more like six times out of ten.

We don't all get there the way it was worked out on the drawing board because we are confronted with a gigantic obstacle called the Real World. In the Real World, there can be sad events that can upset us so that we turn for solace to our old reliable friends, the foods that have always comforted us. There can be happy events—vacations, holiday times, let's-bring-out-the-champagne celebrations, family weddings and unrestrained dinner parties. There can be business traveling, unexpected illnesses or surgery, or financial squeezes. In all of these situations, that chain of events I outlined will be broken and we determined dieters will have to find ways to right ourselves and get back on course. And, with the tools I'll give you, you will.

Please note that the Real World problems I just mentioned are not intrinsic built-in obstacles to our program, as they are when you use diet centers that provide you with food or formulas. At such establishments, trying to maintain weight loss *without* the pre-packaged food or protein drinks requires an entirely new technique of adapting to rearranged hunger signals. That transition must be thoroughly provided for in the program; when it is not, it is truly appropriate to call such a program a scam.

Our program starts in the Real World, continues in the Real World, and endures in the Real World. Once you learn to apply the basic principle of staying at or below your CCLs, you never have to change. You make your adjustment at the beginning, and that's that. If the connotation of the word "diet" is "something with a beginning and an end," then this is not a diet, it's simply a new and better way to adapt your eating to your metabolism for the rest of your life.

I, for example, have perfected dieting down to the point

where there is only one thing I cannot resist. That one thing is temptation.

I hope that last line got a chuckle, because it contains so much of the truth. The real obstacle in the real world is, for most of us, temptation.

## Dealing with Temptation

So let's overcome temptation, not with our willpower, which is so often in short supply, but with our brains, a potentially unlimited resource.

Imagine that you're doing great, losing weight, feeling better than ever, thrilled with yourself, hearing compliments from friends and semi-strangers alike, and *you want something you're not supposed to have*. What to do?

There are three long-range strategies you can employ:

1. You can talk yourself out of your momentary passion and stay the course.
2. You can bend the diet, but not break it.
3. You can fall into the non-strategy strategy and break the diet, in which case you'll have to act quickly to get yourself out of trouble. Or alternatively, you can break the diet *as a strategy*, which occasionally can be quite a useful technique.

## The First Strategy

Staying on the diet is your first line of defense. But what if you want something to eat, and it isn't just any food you want and certainly not more of the same, but quite specifically, something *you're not allowed to have*. Worse yet, it may even be something you were allowed to have on all those other diets. You remember, the ones you gained on or couldn't stay on. What now?

My advice is: Never ignore a craving; it may pass, but it is likely to reappear momentarily when your resolve is weak. And then you break the diet. Since craving is part and parcel of addiction, that could trigger a cycle of addictive eating behavior. If this has ever happened to you, then you yourself may actually be an addict.

The correct response, I've learned from experience, is to *change your physiology*. Let me elaborate, because this point might save your diet—and your life. Your craving appeared, most likely, in a relatively fasting state; it was triggered by a fall in blood glucose and your body perceived a need to brake the falling glucose level and gave a signal that sweets were needed. (This theory only applies when you crave some form of quick-fix carbohydrate.)

Your strategy will be to change your physiology from a fasting to a fed state. In layman's language that means *eat something*. In Atkins diet language, food, rich food, and plenty of it, but, of course, fat and protein food with very little or no carbohydrate. This will stabilize your blood glucose and all the other constituents that give rise to the craving signal. Presto! No more craving.

The best foods to do this with are macadamia nuts, the dieter's best friend. Other nut choices are walnuts, pecans, or brazils. Other foods for stopping cravings are cream cheese or rich dessert cheeses like St. Andre's or Explorateur. You can also do this with something sweet—artificially so, I must emphasize—and with whipping cream. Put three or four tablespoons of whipping cream into a glass and make an instant farmers soda by topping it with your favorite diet soda, or you may opt for diet gelatin dessert slathered generously with whipping cream (not the pre-made, sugar-added type, of course).

I'm sure you already understand the basic principle of this kind of eating. Macadamia nuts, for instance, may be on every conventional diet's no-no list because they are so calorically dense, but what counts is the effect they have upon your body chemistry. Macadamia nuts, by having such a high ketogenic ratio (fat divided by carbohydrate) suppress the appetite and tend to result in your eating fewer calories per day. Moreover, let's not forget convenience—all nuts are extremely portable; they can easily be kept in your purse or shirt or coat pocket. If your business or travel schedule forces you to miss meals or be frequently exposed to unacceptable meals, you've got a meal substitute at hand, a perfect tide-me-over.

Another favorite of mine now that we're beyond the level of *Induction* dieting is the avocado. As the only fat-containing fruit in common usage, most of it in the beneficial monounsaturate category, this unique vegetable product provides a welcome taste departure for those who crave something fresh, natural, and filling. A half avocado, with the big hollow where its giant seed resided, can serve as an edible cup in which to place prawns or crabmeat or tuna salad and thus provide that elegant lunch that makes the time between your filling breakfast and your satisfying dinner pass so happily. A California avocado contains about 12 grams of carbohydrate, about the same as ⅓ of an apple. And then there's guacamole; you'll find my favorite recipe on page 371.

At the other end of the spectrum is a convenience food that sounds terribly fatty but, in fact, contains nearly none. Those are the maximizers of crispness, fried pork rinds—the zero carbohydrate consolation prize for corn or potato chip addicts. Virtually all the fat has been rendered off, leaving you with the protein matrix that held the pork fat together. Your pâté, soured-cream-based dips and guacamole find an exceedingly crisp and comfortable home atop a fried pork rind.

But what if we're not talking about an addictive craving or a simple impulse that can be satisfied by a change in body chemistry? What if we're talking about long-term desire? Something you always knew was one of your favorite foods and now is on your no-no list. You know, things like french fries, pizza, bagels, tacos, eggrolls, pancakes, linguini, and. . .well, why torture you any more.

## Finding Food Passion Substitutes

One of the best don't-fall-off-the-diet techniques is to eat foods that substitute for a desired food. If your not-so-secret desire is for any of the above, or for blintzes, lasagne, Yorkshire pudding, or even sweets, from chocolate truffles to ice cream, cheesecake, or strawberry shortcake, then the answer is in using the ingeniously developed substitutes for these foods I've provided in the recipe section. Learn to use them. They are just as much a part of your diet as is a grilled chicken and tossed salad.

Spend as many months as you can integrating these recipes into your new diet and lifestyle and keep absolutely clear in your mind that *our* cheesecake is not *their* cheesecake, and *our* pizza is not *their* pizza, because their foods can be ten times more dense in carbohydrate content. Calorie restricted foods may be legally called low calorie if the caloric level is reduced by 33%, but our carbohydrate alternatives are down a whopping 90% in carbohydrate. Great, isn't it? It is unless you deviate. There is enough carbohydrate in the real thing that it will change your body's chemistry around completely. One full portion of real pizza or ice-cream will send your fat mobilizers, ketones, and lipolysis to a screeching halt.

But there are also carbohydrate-containing foods that are among my favorites. They break the steak-and-salad prototype quite dramatically and yet don't contain enough carbohydrate to do more damage than raise your carbohydrate count a five gram level or two.

Among these discoveries are the crisp breads. My dieting life improved considerably when I found something crunchy and toasted to pile my cream cheese or cold cuts upon or to serve as finger size appetizers at parties. One brand, GG Bran Crispbread, claims only five grams of carbohydrate per slice. And its strong wheat-bran flavor makes you think you never had to give up bread. Another brand is Kavli, containing slightly more carbohydrate but very usable once you're past the *Induction* level of the diet. I won't repeat this again, but every food idea I mention could be off limits for those of you who demonstrate food intolerance to one of its ingredients, and wheat is one of those foods that turns up rather frequently as a food intolerance item.

## The Second Strategy

Bending the diet? How can one bend a diet as clearly defined as this one, Dr. Atkins? Well, you can.

By now, you're into the *Ongoing Weight Loss* diet or perhaps the *Maintenance* diet, and you're personalizing your food strategy. You should be using the Carbohydrate Gram Counter at the end of the book to help you decide what foods you can add.

Study the list with regard to a) how much you would enjoy the food item, and b) how many grams of carbohydrate it would contain in the portion size you would be content with. You might even want to make a mathematical ratio—enjoyment value/carbohydrate grams—to help you select candidates for your next diet level. Although, I would hope that your response would be a little more spontaneous, such as, "Hey, that sounds good to me, and only $x$ grams of carbohydrate!"

At any rate, select those candidates for addition to your diet that to you have a high enjoyment-per-gram ratio—and don't forget our recipes! Write the selected items down on some note paper and list the gram counts beside them. If you are doing well, and you have found some five or six gram items, you will immediately recognize that adding one of those items per day simply means that you will have moved up one full level on your OWL diet. You're still on track.

But suppose your favorite diet fantasy has ten grams—or twenty. An alternative system for advancing a level is to add forty grams a week. So you might opt for a ten-gram "extra" on Tuesday and Thursday and twenty-gram diet bender on the weekend. If your CCLL is fairly high, you may even, a few weeks or a month later, add another forty grams per week, or even another after that.

What you are doing is creating your own personal diet plan, based on your demonstrated degree of metabolic resistance and your favorite foods, perhaps the very items you thought would never get on a diet. You are not on the Atkins diet; there never was an Atkins diet; you're on the "Atkins and I" diet. I contributed the principles; you contribute the personalization and execution.

## But Sometimes Bending Becomes Breaking

Sometimes, of course, one does more than just bend the diet's carbohydrate quantities, one eats something one is supposed to be avoiding. Every time a dieter does that I am concerned that the food in question may turn out to be the trigger mechanism for an addiction. Then, look out! A full blown binge usually begins right then and there.

Binges come in all shapes and sizes, and can prove so disastrous they can turn a seemingly sure-fire diet success story into an instant failure. The weight regain is usually so profound it can be measured in pounds-per-day, and sometimes in pounds-per-hour. And the time that you're on the binge is certainly an essential question. Don't let it run its course, because all too often that course is not run until you are at your lifetime high point.

To stop a binge, your first responsibility is to know you're in trouble and immediately apply an effective technique. The best way I have found to stop a binge is to take certain nutrients: chromium nicotinate 400 mcg, 3 times daily for 2 days; plus L-glutamine 500-1000 mg, 3 times daily; plus B complex, 50 mg strength. At the same time, overwhelm the cravings by instituting a high-fat, zero-carbohydrate diet. Fatty red meats, cream cheese, diet gelatin with whipping cream—and nothing with carbohydrate. Two days after you induce ketosis/lipolysis the cravings should be gone, you should be once again in control, and the weight gained so rapidly during the binge should already be falling to its previous level. And congratulations, you just dodged a bullet.

Back in control again, you had better be figuring out what food or food combination was the binge trigger. You certainly won't want to play with that again.

But there is a hardcore problem that arises when you

discover there's something about dieting you don't like. Or more specifically, that there's something you like too much, and you're not getting it. Naturally, you're thinking, "Why did I promise that I would never have that food again? I'm no longer willing to keep that promise." Must always be *always* and never be *never*?

This important question has several answers. In one answer, I ask you to consider the plight of a recovering alcoholic. Most of us realize that when an addiction such as alcoholism is the problem, it is far far better that never really be *never*. So if your proposed carbohydrate deviation involves something you're addicted to, I sadly must give you that never-never advice. But most of us feel deep down that when we enjoy a lifetime favorite food we're doing it for the sake of pleasure and not out of addiction.

So I guess I must allow you to try it and find out.

## Breaking With Intent: You Might Try a Reversal Diet

And there is yet another answer—a strategy that will allow you to break away from the constriction of your own successful diet. This strategy is simple, and, I'm sure, to the careful readers of this book, startling. Suppose your favorite missing foods are on *another* diet, but not on this one. You merely have to announce to yourself, "I'm ready to go on the XYZ diet right now." Then do it.

Suppose you develop a longing for a specific food category such as fruit or pasta? You may want to go on an all-fruit diet for three or four days, or an all-pasta diet. This radical departure from what you've been doing so successfully for quite a stretch may seem counterproductive, but it serves a few purposes. It allows you not to have to say to yourself, "I can never eat my favorite food again," and it acts as a metabolic reversal technique, which can sometimes jumpstart the low-carbohydrate diet, if it has shown any signs of slowing down. Let me explain.

After many months on a diet which works by virtue of forcing the body to take inefficient metabolic pathways, and thus dissipating hundreds of calories as heat (which presumably is what happens on a strict low-carbohydrate diet) the body may begin to adapt by becoming more efficient, thereby slowing the rate of weight loss. Don't panic as you read this, this adaptation to the lipolytic pathway has never been scientifically demonstrated. Most of you will be able to reach your goal weight and stay there without ever noticing the adaptation phenomenon. But some of you will get the sense that the rate of weight loss has slowed inordinately. You should consider a period of time on a reversal diet.

On the other hand, those of you who cleared up a variety of symptoms on the Atkins diet may have to think twice before embarking on diet reversal, because it's highly probable all (or most of) your symptoms will return on the reintroduction of high-carbohydrate items.

But I think all of you should know the principle of a reversal diet, and many of you should try it somewhere along the line. In reversal dieting, you should go on a regimen very low in fat and protein and high in complex carbohydrates. The aforementioned all-pasta diet, if not mixed with an oily/creamy sauce, qualifies; the all-fruit diet, because its carbohydrates are not complex, does not. (But for three days, why not?) And there are more serious diets that make for ideal reversal techniques. The extreme low-fat version of Dr. Julian Whitaker's diet is an example.

The main purpose of reversal dieting is to reestablish the dramatic effect that you must have noticed when you first went on the *Induction* diet, namely, rapid, sustained weight loss. You do it to break up a log jam. Please note that the reversal diet itself is an austere program; it is not a balanced diet, and it most certainly is not taking a break from dieting for a while. When you try to interpose a period of balanced dieting, the result is all too often a rapid regain of weight. The lesson you must learn is that if you "go off the diet," you don't go off into a vacuum, you go *onto* another diet. Make sure that other diet is also one on which *you are in control*.

## The Mini-Binge

There is another technique for breaking the diet deliberately, yet remaining in control. It is the 60-minute mini-binge popularized by Drs. Rachael and Richard Heller, and designed for carbohydrate addicts. The Hellers called this carbohydrate binge a reward meal and allowed it every single day. In their program, an austere low-carbohydrate diet could be interrupted by an hour of unrestricted eating, as long as the food was nourishing and well-balanced. The operative principle behind that technique is that insulin is released in two phases when carbohydrates are consumed, and the second and greater amount begins about 75 minutes after your first contact with carbohydrate. You must be sated before that and must have stopped eating within an hour.

If the Hellers' system can be made to work for you, its advantages would be obvious. The disadvantages are: no emptying of glycogen reserves, therefore no fat mobilization, therefore no ketosis/lipolysis, therefore no metabolic advantage. Those whose overweight is metabolic, in contrast to addiction-based, would not do well. I would suggest, then, that you not do any Hellering until you are close to your goal weight and then to do it little by little, so that you will have familiarized yourself with the effect it has upon your subsequent diet control, your appetite level and your weight. But you should be aware of the principle because, in case carbohydrate happens to jump into your mouth uninvited, you can do considerable damage control by finishing before an hour is up. And whatever you do, don't do it in a dining establishment with slow service.

## You, Your Diet, and Your Environment

You will note that I have given you a series of strategies for bending the diet or reestablishing it, but that one common denominator can be found in all of them: You are the master strategist. You are in control. Believe me, I've seen a lot of potentially successful dieting experiences fall apart, and almost all of them do so for the same reason—the dieter's loss of control of himself or his environment.

We've just run through some strategies teaching you how to control yourself, so now what's needed is an awareness of what you must do to control your environment.

There can be no doubt that your immediate external environment is much less hospitable to low-carbohydrate dieting than it was at the time the first Diet Revolution was proclaimed 20 years ago. The combined counterrevolution of fat phobia and pharmacophilia has made it difficult for the person who recognizes his own individual differences from the masses and who demands his freedom of choice in matters involving his own health. Instead of being swept up in the hysteria, you now have to fight for the privilege of being different, enlightened and effective at self-preservation.

## Training Those Special People

Your first obstacle is people. People whom you normally rely upon for advice—spouses, family members, well-meaning friends, even health professionals with expertise in other areas—are likely to share the all-too-human trait of being "knee-jerk reactors"—people influenced by buzzwords they've heard so often that they cease to question how the conclusions came about. "Oh, that's a high-fat diet; that can't be good for you," is their reflex response, but you can bet they've never heard of Yudkin or Kekwick or Reaven or Benoit, nor have they ever made an in-depth study of my life's work.

So how do you take charge and teach them? Because, valuable as these persons' advice has been to you in the past, you must remind them that you don't *know* something until you look into it. If your naysayer is someone you live with or must deal with every day, then you know you need their total cooperation as much as you need your own singleness of purpose. If I were you, I would start by insisting that they read this book. "I'm impressed that Dr. Atkins has used his program on so many thousands of people and that he still stands by it," you might suggest, "and I want to know if I can make it work for me. Since I need your support, why don't you study his arguments and his backup carefully and see if you can poke holes in his argument."

You must gain the cooperation of everyone in your immediate environment; resisting temptation is a lot easier if you don't see and smell your favorite carbohydrates. I've mentioned the problem with non-believers, but what about those who feel, "Dieting is *your* problem; eating is *my* privilege?" Here you must use the pragmatic take-charge person's motto: "If you can't lick 'em, get 'em to join you."

My recommendation is to get your significant others to join you in dieting. If that person in your life is also overweight, you will have a very good selling point—the prospect of *painless* weight loss. But, if he's locked into the low-fat-will-do-it fairy tale, you may suggest: "Why don't we try both diets and see what is best suited to our metabolisms?"

Now suppose you're in the situation where you're the only one who has to lose weight. You should suggest our "meat and millet" diet for normal weight people whose objective is to become healthier. You can get the instructions in *Dr. Atkins' Health Revolution*. It's a diet allowing unlimited complex carbohydrates, but because meat is allowed and sugar is not, it makes for dieting compatibility with the "Atkins and I" diet.

One more very important message. Suppose the temptation takes the form of the sugar-laden junk food that's in the house "for the kids." Kids like that stuff, you know." If you think that the most dangerous food additive on the planet is proper nourishment for growing members of the human race who happen also to be your loved ones, then perhaps you should rethink your position. Who, more than someone with virtually their whole lives ahead of them, stands to be damaged the most by a substance that helps create diabetes, hypertension, and heart disease? Allowing kids to eat according to the pleasure principle and not according to the principle of health maintenance is probably not the kind of parenting you wish to do. So, make the resolution now: *Sugar is not going to enter my home.*

## Dieting in the Big World Outside Your Home

But how do you control your work environment? With common sense. The coffee and danish cart at 11 and 3 smells so good! Not if you've had scrambled eggs and bacon for breakfast and a satiating lunch as well. Your sales-resistance is at its greatest when you're sated. Does the cafeteria or luncheonette nearby serve suitable food? Check it out, because if they don't, you start packing your lunch.

Low-carbohydrate dieters will find restaurants to be much more friend than foe. They stay in business because of their ability to make food taste better than most of you manage to achieve in your kitchens. So most of their main courses qualify. The trick is not to be seduced by all the extras. If it's at all possible, know what you're going to order before you walk in. And don't go for the carbohydrate extras just because you're "entitled."

The fun comes when you discover restaurants that do great things with the diet automatically. It shouldn't be too difficult to find a good cut of meat, fish, or fowl with the right seasonings, prepared well, and still having no carbohydrate. I've had well over 5000 wonderful restaurant meals—100% on the diet. I know where to get the best steaks, roast beef, rack of lamb, crispy duck, and poached salmon in my hometown. But I also know the best trout with a macadamia nut crust, the best veal a la triestina, saltimbocca a la romana, Chinese shrimp and lobster, Mexican fajitas, guacamole, and chiles rellenos. Ladies and gentlemen, this is the true gourmet's diet. I always say, "If you're going to lose a hundred pounds anyway, you might as well do it with generous quantities of luxurious food."

The trick in restaurants is not to start eating until the appetizer or main course that *you ordered correctly* arrives. If you can get a celery and olive tray instead of bread and butter, you do have an alternative. Remember, too, never save room for dessert.

Dinner parties can be real obstacle courses. This is the first decade of the century when hostesses are not embarrassed to have an all-pasta dinner party, and so there is the possibility that you may find nothing desirable to eat. Let me warn you about going off the diet for just one meal. That figures to set back your dieting for nearly a week in regard to weight loss. The better policy is to let the host(ess) know you're on a doctor's diet, so that you may ask what is being served. If the meal simply does not qualify, either ask for a raincheck or for permission to bring your own food. If you fear that there won't be enough protein food to last you the duration of your stay at the party, make sure you bring something portable along—those macadamia nuts, for example.

Airline travel can be another diet-breaker. Whenever possible, call in advance and ask for a special diet meal. Tell them you're on a diet that is all protein and no carbohydrate. Their response will probably be, until this book gets its first million followers, that they don't have such a diet. Often it is the kosher meal that is the lowest in carbohydrates of those they offer, so, O'Shaughnessy, order the kosher meal.

## Master Your Strategies and Be Slim for Life

Remember, you have more tools at your disposal than you think. Besides the four diets, there are a variety of levels of each diet, there are combinations of intense dieting on weekdays, with liberal eating on weekends, diets for holding the line and for getting a job done, high-fat and low-fat variations, high- and low-calorie variations. There is even the Fat Fast for short bursts of accomplishment. (See Chapter 18.)

With these tools, you become a master strategist. You are

like a star quarterback, grinding it out for a while, going for a big gain (or loss in this case) when the time is right but always keeping your eye on the goal line—and ultimately the victory.

# 24

## The Self You Serve Will Be Yourself

The low-carbohydrate diet has not been one of the standard diets for a number of years, and, in many ways, that's a bit of a mystery.

If a doctor has to decide whether or not to use a drug—let's say prednisone—to treat his patient's rheumatoid arthritis, he legitimately has a conflict in his mind. He knows the drug will have a positive effect on the arthritic symptoms; he also knows it might have damaging side effects. There's no mystery there. The choice is difficult, the evidence divided.

A low-carbohydrate diet is a very different matter. The scientific evidence is *not* evenly divided. It is quite one-sidedly in support of the effectiveness and the health enhancement potentialities of such dieting. So what could possibly explain the reluctance to give this diet its place in the sun? I'm afraid I don't have an answer. Cynics or economists might point to the influence of the giant food com-panies, for not only are they deeply committed to selling junk carbohydrates, they are also among the chief funders of nutritional research. The Germans, on the other hand, might call it the *zeitgeist*, or, as we would say, the spirit of the age.

Certainly high-carbohydrate diets have had it all their own way for the last decade. During that time, people have not gotten slimmer, but rather we have seen a jump of 32% in clinical obesity. Frankly, I think there's room for more than one point of view, and I hope you'll help promote that.

## What the Success of This Book Will Mean to You

I can't think of anything more gauche than an author encouraging his readers to talk up his book and mention its merits to others. How utterly self-serving it sounds, but, in point of fact, the self you will be serving is yourself.

If enough of you talk about the Atkins diet and the effect it has had on your life, then all that you need to make your diet a breeze will begin to appear. Airlines will begin to serve low-carbohydrate meals, restaurants will instantly understand what you're asking for, hostesses will no longer offer you a choice between various forms of pasta, and hand-held ketone analyzers giving you an instant digital readout will be on the market—I've seen the prototype. Most importantly of all, low-carbohydrate foods will appear in the supermarket. Instead of low-fat ice-cream filled with sugar, you'll find, in the same freezers, low-carbohydrate ice-cream filled with cream. Prepackaged, low-carbohydrate meals-in-a-box will be there, too.

Twenty years ago, when the original *Diet Revolution* was in full stride, this was exactly what did occur. The temporary triumph of the low-fat dogma in the 1980s did away with many of these conveniences, but it only takes a push to see them all return.

And now that this book, in its many editions, is approaching the one-million-copies-in-print mark, and now that newpapers, magazines, and other authors are heralding the failure of the low-fat diet, the tide is beginning to turn. Thanks to word of mouth and word-of-comupter surfers, the low-carbohydrate-diet movement is reaching a critical mass. The time is right to convert that hostile Real World into a friendly environment where the 74% who are overweight but misinformed become transformed into the 74% who are enlightened, cooperative, and controlling weight through carbohydrate restriction.

In fact, it has already begun to happen. In April 1996, the first of a series of Atkins' diet cruises through the Caribbean and Mediterranean set sail, and passengers were enthused with the combination of low-carbohydrate cuisine provided by Costa Cruises, under the tutelage of my wife, Veronica, the luxury of the ship itself, the exciting stops along the way, the daily meeting and workouts with me and my staff, and by the fact that nearly every participant ate luxuriously and lost weight.

If you want to know more about other events going on at the Atkins Center, you may want to subscribe to "Dr. Atkins' Health Revelations" newsletter. You will find it invaluable for being kept up to the minute on the kind of information that people concerned with health alternatives need to avoid the pitfalls of pharmaceutical and interventive medicine. It is also my way of helping my readers stay up to date on information Atkins' dieters will need.

I am constantly updating nutritional formulas to help prevent or relieve the many medical problems that respond to nutritional therapy. Or you may want to know how best to acquire hard-to-find dieters' aids such as pure Stevia, Bioketone strips to test for ketosis, organically raised meats, protein powder without carbohydrates, MCT oil, low-carbohydrate vegetable replacement, or Atkins Diet meal replacements.

Contact the Atkins Center:

The Atkins Center for Complementary Medicine
152 East 55th Street
New York, New York 10022
(001) 212-758-2100

or Atkins Nutritionals on
(001) 516-563-9280

or visit our web site at
www.atkinscenter.com

# PART FIVE

# Menus and Recipes

# The "Dr. Atkins and I"

# Menu

I've looked at many diets, and I've seldom seen one so dedicated to involving the dieter in his own eating as this one. That's because no diet works better than the one that you've helped create.

I thought of presenting you with a meal plan to help you in making your daily selections, but instead I decided to do something different. I've often been struck by the fact that some of my diet failures were people who, when confronted with a meal plan, were excessively literal-minded about it and felt that if the plan said pork chops on Tuesday, they had to have pork chops on Tuesday—even if they *hated* pork chops.

The truth is you don't have to eat any one thing, but you can and should eat everything that's on the menu below and that you love—and everything that's not on the menu but that's permissible (i.e. that doesn't contain inappropriate levels of carbohydrate).

I've divided these menus according to whether they apply to your time on the *Induction, OWL,* or *Maintenance* diets. Once you start doing your lifetime eating on this diet, some of you will find that you do best on the *Maintenance* diet, some of you will get best results on *OWL*, and, of course, there are a few of you whose metabolic resistance requires a lifetime on a diet almost as strict as the *Induction*. Nonetheless, I'm willing to bet that the following menus will light a warm culinary fire in the pit of your stomach, no matter what diet you plan to be on.

Let me remind you that any foods on the *Induction* menus are included on the *OWL* and *Maintenance* menus, and any foods on the *OWL* are included on the *Maintenance*.

My general advice about doing the "Atkins and I" diet for a lifetime is that you stick with basics most of the time and go to the recipes when you want a special treat. As you'll instantly see, many of the recipes are loaded with butter, cream, and egg yolks. This might give the misleading impression that that's what I want you to eat all the time, which is not the case. Unless you're on the special Fat Fast, eating lean foods is quite appropriate. The recipes are high in fat so that they'll be especially delicious on special occasions. As a general rule, however, only a small percentage of dieters should be on a high-fat diet, and that's limited to people who don't do well when the diet is lean.

There's also one general principle I'd like to recommend to you because it may save you a fair amount of physical discomfort, and that's the principle of meal rotation. There's a tendency for dieters to stick to a pattern of eating that they feel comfortable with and to repeat the foods that consistently please. But I think that the habit of eating certain foods every day is one you should take pains to avoid. In fact, I would recommend that you never have the same food on successive days. This is a technique of avoiding the ill consequences of food allergies and food intolerances, and it's well worth the effort. Therefore, I suggest you rotate your food choices. Among other things, have meat, fish, fowl, and shellfish on successive days but always according to your taste, seeking out the foods most convenient and enjoyable for you.

After all, the principal lesson of the book is that good food can be both enjoyable and healthy. Make it your goal.

## The "Atkins and I" Meal Prototypes

The nine meals below give you the prototypical combinations of foods on each of the three main diets—*Induction, OWL*, and *Maintenance*. These foods are not fancy; they're intentionally typical and basic. If you don't like some of these meals, that's fine; after all, what you'll be doing in your actual daily eating is choosing meals that you do like from the extensive meal lists or adding appropriate meals that are your own choice or your own creation. You don't have to eat anything that's listed here.

I hope, however, that the prototypes will give you a quick illustrative sense of what the scope of your eating can be at each stage of the diet.

## Typical Induction Menu

*Breakfast*:
Eggs, scrambled or fried, with streaky or back bacon, ham or
  sugarless sausage
Decaffeinated coffee or tea

*Lunch*:
Bacon cheeseburger, no bun
Small tossed salad
Sparkling mineral water

*Dinner*:
Prawn cocktail with mustard and mayonnaise
Clear consommé
Steak, roast, chops, fish, or fowl
Tossed salad (choice of dressings)
Sugar-free jelly with a spoonful of whipped, artificially
  sweetened whipping cream

## Typical Ongoing Weight Loss (OWL) Menu

*Breakfast*:
Ham omelet
85 ml (3 fl oz) of tomato juice or V-8 juice
Approx one-half slice of thin crispbread
Decaffeinated coffee or tea

*Lunch*:
Chef's salad with ham, cheese, chicken and egg—zero
  carbohydrate or oil-and-vinegar type salad dressing
Herbal tea

*Dinner*:

Seafood salad

Poached salmon

90 g (3 oz) of vegetables from permitted vegetable list

80 g (2½ oz) of strawberries in single cream

---

**Typical Maintenance Menu**

*Breakfast*:

Gruyère and spinach omelet

½ cantaloupe melon

Approx one slice of thin crispbread with butter

Decaffeinated coffee or tea

*Lunch*:

Roast chicken

90 g (3 oz) of vegetables

Green salad, creamy garlic dressing

Soda water

*Dinner*:

French onion soup

Salad with tomatoes, onions, and carrots, any sugarless dressing

110 g (4 oz) permitted vegetables

½ small baked potato with soured cream and chives

Lightly breaded veal chops

Generous cup of fresh fruit salad

Glass of dry wine or two wine spritzers

# Typical Breakfast, Lunch and Dinner Selections

## Snacks and Breads

### Induction

All snacks that are made exclusively from meat, fish, fowl and eggs.

From the Recipe Section of *New Diet Revolution*:

Basic protein bread

Sweet cheese snack

Basic pancakes—These deserve special mention because they are so versatile. The recipe will work for crêpes as well as pancakes and can be used as the basis for blintzes, tacos, all sorts of other savory crêpes and, of course, dessert crêpes too. Pancakes are an enormously adaptable snack ingredient.

## Ongoing Weight Loss (OWL)

*All foods on the Induction diet are also included on the OWL diet*

From the Recipe Section of *New Diet Revolution*:
  Bran-Soy muffins
  Swiss snack

## Maintenance

*All foods on the Induction and the OWL diet are also included on the Maintenance diet*

From the Recipe Section of *New Diet Revolution*:
  Pizza
  Walnut butter cookies

# Breakfast

## Induction

*Main Dishes:*
Eggs, scrambled or fried in butter with streaky or back
  bacon, ham or sugarless sausage
Smoked salmon or sturgeon or whitefish or mixed

smoked fishes and 60 g (2 oz) of cream cheese

Pancakes (see recipe section) and 55 ml (2 oz) soured cream

Leftovers from properly prepared dinner

Snacks from snack list

Basic omelet:

a) Gruyère and spinach
b) Goat cheese and chives
c) Western omelet
d) Spanish omelet
e) Corned beef or pastrami omelet (pancake style)
   Or any other low-carbohydrate omelet of your invention

From the Recipe section in New Diet Revolution:

Cheese Omelet

Scrambled eggs in cheese sauce with sausages

## Ongoing Weight Loss (OWL)

*All foods on the Induction diet are also included on the OWL diet*

### Main Dishes:

Eggs Benedict, using diet bread instead of an English muffin

Welsh rarebit on diet bread

Breakfast on the *OWL* diet may also include:

90 ml (3 fl oz) of V-8 juice or tomato juice, freshly prepared, when possible.

60 g (2 oz) cup onion rings, pan-fried to a crisp (onions only, no breading)

1 slice of a 4–5 g crispbread

1 slice of fresh orange (sliced to 5 mm [¼ in] thickness) as a garnish

2 slices of diet bread recipe, toasted and buttered

Decaf cappuccino

From the Recipe Section in *New Diet Revolution*:
   Cheese pancakes

## Maintenance

*All foods on the Induction diet and the OWL diet are also included on the Maintenance diet*

½ grapefruit, may be baked with artificial sweeteners

135 g (4½ oz) of honeydew, cantaloupe, Spanish, Persian, casaba melon

90 g (3 oz) of berries, any or all kinds, with a dollop of soured cream or whipped whipping cream (not pre-sweetened); may add almond, lemon, orange, vanilla flavours, as presented by Natureland.

120 g (4 oz) unflavored yoghurt

Corned beef hash, using diet bread in the recipe, instead of the standard recipe

Blintzes, using crêpe recipe

From the Recipe Section in *New Diet Revolution*:
   Eggs Florentine
   Mushrooms, onions, and eggs
   Broccoli frittata

# Lunch

## Induction

Cheeseburger or bacon cheeseburger, no bun

Gherkin spear

Clear chicken consommé (read label)

30–60 g (1–2 oz) of tossed salad with a selection of the salad greens and with oil and vinegar dressing, blue cheese dressing or creamy garlic dressing—make sure all salad dressings are sugar-free; better yet, ascertain that carbohydrate counts are below one gram per serving.

Assorted cold meats—ham, cheese, tongue, salami, roast beef, chicken, turkey, and salad as above.

Chef's salad

Cucumbers in soured cream (see recipe section)

Chicken parts, grilled

Tuna, chicken, egg, ham, crabmeat or lobster mayonnaise (made with the named ingredients plus pure mayonnaise, not imitation mayonnaise or salad dressing cream, plus chopped celery, onions, spring onions, capers, etc., and hard-boiled egg, if desired)

## Ongoing Weight Loss (OWL)

*All foods on the Induction diet are also included on the OWL diet*

Prawn or crabmeat or tuna mayonnaise stuffed into a fresh tomato or into ½ avocado

Pizza (see recipe section)
Guacamole
Chicken salad (see recipes, also in dinner section)
Leftover meatloaf
Baked spinach

## Maintenance

*All foods on the Induction and OWL diets are also included on the Maintenance diet*

Spinach egg pie

# Dinner

## Induction

*Appetizers and soups:*
Seafood salad (Frutta di mare)
Prosciutto

### Starters and soups:
Prawns in garlic sauce
Cold prawns in mayonnaise and mustard or mayonnaise and horseradish
Beef tartare
Caviar and soured cream
Pâté (see recipe section)
Soft-shell clams
Mussels Provençale
Smoked trout
Smoked salmon
Quick bouillon

### Salads (and dressings):
Tricolore
Arugula, or rocket, and deep-fried goat cheese
Country salad—mixed greens with bacon chunks and crumbled blue cheese
Caesar salad (no croutons)

From the Recipe Section of *New Diet Revolution*:
   Salmon salad
   Bacon and egg salad
   Mushroom salad
   Avocado dressing
   Russian dressing
   Basic French dressing

### Main Courses:
Steaks, roasts, chops—all kinds
Roast chicken, turkey, duck—in natural gravy
Spareribs—no glazing
Rack of lamb
Grilled, poached, pan-fried, baked fish—
   all varieties

Prawns in garlic sauce
Lobster in clarified butter

From the Recipe Section of *New Diet Revolution*:
Roast leg of lamb
Chicken salad
Meat loaf
Warm beef, mushroom and watercress salad flavored with
  horseradish

**Side Dishes:**
110 g (4 oz) of steamed vegetables, assorted or individual
  from permissible vegetable list
Giant mushrooms (porcini, morels, portobello, etc.) sautéed
  in olive oil

**Desserts:**
Sugar-free jelly (plus a dollop of whipped, artificially
  sweetened whipping cream)

## Ongoing Weight Loss (OWL)

*All foods on the Induction diet are also included on the
OWL diet*

**Starters and soups:**
Avocado cream soup
Lobster soup

*Salads:*
Guacamole
Celeriac salad (see recipe section)

*Main Courses:*
From the Recipe Section of *New Diet Revolution*:
    Poached salmon
    Blackened beef with a basil and parsley cream
    Fried filet of sea bass with leeks and tomatoes
    Sauerkraut with variety of cooked meats
    Beef Stroganoff
    Coq au vin

*Side Dishes:*
From the Recipe Section of *New Diet Revolution*:
    Broccoli frittata
    Aubergine balls
    Brussels sprouts, crisped

*Desserts:*
From the Recipe Section in *New Diet Revolution*:
    Fruit jelly
    Italian sponge cake
    Blueberry ice-cream
    Vanilla ice-cream
    Lemon mousse

## Maintenance

*All foods on the Induction and OWL diets are also included
on the Maintenance diet*

**Starters and soups:**
Chilled marinated oysters
Stuffed fried mushrooms
Cream of onion soup

**Salads:**
From the Recipe Section of *New Diet Revolution*:
    Cold salad of scrambled egg and cottage cheese with
        asparagus
    Baked spinach flavored with basil and ricotta cheese
    Stuffed fried mushrooms with goat cheese

**Main courses:**
From the recipe section of *New Diet Revolution*:
    Chicken cacciatore
    Chicken paprika
    Cassoulet of prawns flavored with vegetables and bay
        leaves
    Chicken curry
    Chicken with okra and peanuts
    Veal stew
    Warm avocado pears and lobster glazed with béarnaise
        sauce
    Stuffed veal chops with wild mushrooms
    Warm lobster salad with tarragon butter dressing
    Escalopes of veal stuffed with a purée of mushrooms
    Mousseline of queen scallops with saffron sauce
    Medallions of lamb with green lentils and bacon

**Side dishes:**
From the Recipe Section of *New Diet Revolution*:
    French beans with walnut sauce
    Stuffed peppers

---

**The Atkins Psychological Advantage Meal**

Take advantage of your newfound liberty to eat all you want by going to someplace where you can do just that. How about going to a buffet-type restaurant and filling up on the protein and salad food? Fill your plate and then go back for seconds. Maybe even thirds. Make sure there's no sweet taste in any of the food you eat. Experienced dieters will recognize that taste instantly.

---

*Desserts:*
From the Recipe Section of *New Diet Revolution*:
    Chocolate truffles
    Rum truffles
    Strawberry torte
    Zabaglione
    Italian sponge cake

# Beverages

## For all diets

Water (especially spring water, mineral water)
Soda water and sparkling mineral water
Flavored sparkling mineral waters (black cherry, raspberry, etc.; must specify no calories)
Hot or iced herbal tea (no barley, figs, dates, honey, etc.)
Decaffeinated coffee or tea

On *Induction* or *Maintenance* diets:
Artificially sweetened fizzy orange drink containing some natural juice.

# Recipes

Ah, you must all have noticed the number of times I said the Atkins diet is fit for a king. I am convinced that this is one slimming regimen on which you'll think you're royalty.

One of the reasons low-carbohydrate dieting did not sweep through the planet like a brushfire is that its early proponents, although agog with excitement over its capacity to melt down body fat stores, were very disparaging about the palatability of the diet. They described their experimental subjects as being unhappy with the monotony of the diet, and they suggested it would never be suitable for long-term use.

That's where the then-young Dr. Atkins entered the picture some 30 years ago. All my life I have been a cross between a gourmet and a gourmand. I loved and still do love to eat. I have read magazine articles entitled "How the Diet Doctors Eat," and I came to the conclusion that the world has never known a diet doctor who loves food as much as I do. This is bad news for me, but wonderful news for you. It caused me to create an Eater's Diet, a Hungry Man's Diet. If *Dr. Atkins' Diet Revolution* was an international success, it must have been in part because I succeeded in communicating my own excitement over food.

Well I couldn't allow this book to achieve any less in the food line, so I had to find a chef to match the royal pleasures I was planning for you. While I was holidaying in Barbados, fortune smiled upon me. I sampled the cuisine of Graham Newbould, master of the kitchen at the famous Treasure Beach Hotel. For six years, Newbould had been one of the chefs for Prince Charles and Princess Diana, and I soon understood why. Once you sample his recipes, so will you. Chef Newbould's recipes are distinguished, appropriately enough by a crown, ◣◢. Compared to our standard recipes, they are admittedly more elegant, more spectacular when served, and they are basically not meant to be daily fare. As you can see by the gram count, most are appropriate on the *Maintenance* diet—at those dinner parties where you simply want to show off how luxurious dieting can be. The other recipes were devised by my wife, by the dieticians at the Atkins Center, or come from *Dr. Atkins' Diet Cookbook*.

If Newbould is the jewel in this section's culinary crown, I can't pretend I'm anything but proud of our other recipes, loosely grouped according to meal and purpose. I haven't attempted to include everything. After all, most of you have been preparing protein main courses all your life, and it would be superfluous to tell you how to grill a steak or cook bacon and eggs for breakfast.

I have, however, included the sort of rich recipes that dietary committees have been leading you away from but that will certainly produce a direct and immediate effect on your salivary glands. Since the Atkins diet is mainly a main course and salad diet, make those dishes as scrumptious as possible. If that extra touch of richness is what makes the dish a success, then don't feel constrained against using these rich things—the rule is: if dieting is inevitable, you might as well enjoy it.

Meanwhile, we all know there are certain things you aren't going to get on this diet. The most frequently dreamt of include sweet desserts, pasta, chips, and bread.

And yet, over the years, we have learned substitutes for those much-desired starches and sweets. I am able, because of my wife Veronica's imagination and the contributions of many of the culinarily-inclined patients I've known, to have desserts that are better than the real thing. I've eaten chocolate nut bars of an excellence that could not be equaled by all the cooks in the entire city of Hershey, PA, even if they had the assistance of a special panel sent over from Switzerland. I've been able, in moments of need, to enjoy coconut custard pie or piña coladas—and all without indulging in an ounce of sugar.

I simply don't feel deprived. These are the things I want to share with you.

Let me now deal with a few specific ideas, so that you will know how to use this section. Turn your attention to the basic pancake recipe. This can make it possible for you to enjoy your own variations of pizza, blintzes, and tortillas, or you can roll them up with pork packed inside, as the Chinese do.

And then there's our bread, an exceptionally tasty, low-carbohydrate creation that can be used for sandwiches, croutons, toast, finger foods, garlic bread, or even pseudo-matzoh balls in chicken soup. Or how about, with the proper additives, creating ginger bread, banana bread, or Boston brown bread; not to mention the bread's most elegant use of all—as something that can mop up the exquisite juices of your fried eggs.

As you taste these recipes and taste Graham Newbould's gourmet delights, I believe you'll become convinced you're not going to go on any other diet. Where would you find a diet that allows you to be a gourmet while you still go on dieting?

# Soups

## Avocado Cream Soup Barbara

8 servings (115 ml [4 oz] each)

*1 medium avocado*
*470 ml (17 fl oz) whipping cream*
*230 ml (8 fl oz) water*
*½ teaspoon celery salt*
*¼ teaspoon seasoning salt*
*½ small clove garlic, minced*
*8 slices streaky bacon, cooked crisp*

Peel avocado and remove pit. Place avocado in liquidizer with cream, water, celery salt, salt, and garlic. Liquidize at medium speed for 15 seconds.

Pour into saucepan. Cook over medium heat for 5 minutes, stirring constantly. Do not boil.

Serve warm or cold garnished with crumbled bacon.

TOTAL GRAMS 24.0
GRAMS PER SERVING 3.0

## Lobster Soup

6 servings

*450 g (16 oz) fresh or tinned lobster meat*
*40 g (1½ oz) butter*
*700 ml (1¼ pints) whipping cream*
*¼ teaspoon onion powder*
*230 ml (8 fl oz) water*
*½ teaspoon seasoning salt*
*60 ml (2 fl oz) sherry*

Cut lobster meat into bite-sized pieces. Melt butter in frying pan and add lobster. Cook for 5 minutes over low heat.

Separately mix cream with water. Add to frying pan, stirring constantly. Do not boil. Add salt and onion powder. Refrigerate overnight.

Reheat. Add sherry. Serve in soup bowls.

TOTAL GRAMS 22.2
GRAMS PER SERVING 3.8

## Quick Bouillon Pickup

1 serving

*230 ml (8 fl oz) hot bouillon*
*1 egg*
*dash of Tabasco sauce*
*dash of salt*

Liquidize egg in food processor until light and foamy. Add bouillon slowly. Blend in Tabasco sauce and salt.

Serve hot in mug.

TOTAL GRAMS 1.6

## Cream of Onion Soup
## Lightly Perfumed with Curry

4 servings

*4 medium-sized onions, sliced*
*15 g (½ oz) butter*
*2 cloves garlic, peeled*
*2 bay leaves*
*470 ml (17 fl oz) whipping cream*
*230 ml (8 fl oz) chicken stock*
*1 tablespoon curry powder*
*1 tablespoon chives, chopped*
*salt and pepper (optional)*

Melt the butter in a warm saucepan. Add the onions, garlic and bay leaves. Sauté until golden brown.

Add the curry powder and cook for 1 minute, stirring so that the curry powder cannot burn.

Add the chicken stock and boil until the liquid has reduced by half, then add the cream and simmer for approximately 15 minutes. Remove bay leaves.

Allow the mixture to cool, then place in a liquidizer or food processor. Pass the soup through a fine sieve and season with salt and pepper according to taste.

When serving, reheat the soup (do not boil) and sprinkle the snipped chives and a little whipping cream on top.

TOTAL GRAMS 57.6
GRAMS PER SERVING 14.4

# Egg Dishes

## Basic Omelet

1 serving

*2 eggs*
*1 tablespoon chives*
*1 tablespoon fresh parsley, chopped*
*⅛ teaspoon salt*
*1 tablespoon whipping cream*
*15 g (½ oz) butter*
*1 pinch freshly ground pepper*

Combine all ingredients and beat lightly.

Melt butter in non-stick omelet pan.

After foam subsides, pour egg mixture into pan. Cook without stirring for about 1 to 2 minutes until sides and bottom are set but center is still wet. Carefully flip one side of omelet on top of other side to form a half moon.

Slide onto plate and serve.

TOTAL GRAMS 1.5

## Cheese Omelet

2 servings

*4 eggs*
*60 g (2 oz) grated Cheddar cheese*
*1 tablespoon chopped parsley*

Follow recipe for Basic Omelet (see page 323). Before folding omelet over, add grated Cheddar cheese and chopped parsley.

After folding omelet over, continue cooking for 2 minutes to be sure cheese is melted.

Serve hot.

TOTAL GRAMS 2.4
GRAMS PER SERVING 1.2

## Scrambled Eggs in Cheese Sauce with Sausages

6 servings

*12 chipolata sausages (be sure they contain no sugar)*
*90 g (3 oz) cream cheese*
*15 g (½ oz) butter*
*170 ml (6 fl oz) single cream*
*60 ml (2 fl oz) water*
*1 teaspoon seasoning salt*
*2 teaspoons parsley*
*8 eggs, beaten*

Sauté sausages in frying pan until brown. Drain.

In double boiler or pan over saucepan of simmering (not boiling) water, heat cream cheese and butter. Add cream, water, salt and parsley.

Stir in beaten eggs with fork. Cook until eggs have thickened.

TOTAL GRAMS 9.6
GRAMS PER SERVING 1.6

## Cheese Pancakes

6 servings

*170 g (6 oz) cottage cheese*
*6 eggs*
*3 tablespoons soya flour*
*40 g (1½ oz) butter, melted*
*1 teaspoon seasoning salt*
*oil*

Put all ingredients except oil in food processor. Blend until smooth. Heat oiled frying pan until very hot. Drop batter by tablespoonfuls onto frying pan. Brown on both sides.

TOTAL GRAMS 15.6
GRAMS PER SERVING 2.6

## Mushrooms, Onions, and Eggs

3 servings

*230 g (½ lb) mushrooms, sliced*
*1 small onion, chopped*
*60 g (2 oz) butter*
*seasoning salt to taste*
*6 eggs*
*2 tablespoons whipping cream*

Sauté mushrooms and onion in butter until well browned. Add salt.

Beat eggs with whipping cream. Pour over mushroom mixture and stir until eggs are cooked (about 4 stirs). Serve immediately.

TOTAL GRAMS 18.0
GRAMS PER SERVING 6.0

## Eggs Florentine

6 servings

*430 g (15 oz) cooked fresh or frozen spinach*
*6 eggs*
*salt to taste*
*1 recipe Cheese Sauce (see below)*

Preheat oven to 180°C (350°F/gas mark 4).

Drain cooked spinach well. Chop fine.

Place hot spinach in shallow baking dish.

Make hole for each egg in spinach. Break egg into each hole. Sprinkle with salt.

Prepare cheese sauce. Pour over eggs and spinach.

Bake in oven for 25 minutes.

TOTAL GRAMS 36.0
GRAMS PER SERVINGS 6.0

## Cheese Sauce

18 tablespoons

*170 ml (6 fl oz) single cream*
*75 ml (2½ fl oz) water*
*340 g (12 oz) Cheddar cheese, diced*
*1 teaspoon prepared mustard*
*1 teaspoon salt*
*½ teaspoon paprika*

In double boiler or pan over a saucepan of simmering water, combine ingredients for cheese sauce and stir constantly until smooth.

TOTAL GRAMS 10.8
GRAMS PER SERVING .6

## Bacon and Egg Salad

6 servings

*9 hard-boiled eggs*
*9 slices streaky bacon, cooked crisp*
*½ teaspoon seasoning salt*
*¼ teaspoon dry mustard*
*80 g (2½ oz) mayonnaise (sugar-free)*

Chop eggs and bacon together in wooden chopping bowl. Add salt and mustard.

Fold in mayonnaise and mix well.

TOTAL GRAMS 9.0
GRAMS PER SERVING 1.5

## Broccoli* Frittata

6 servings

*4 eggs*
*110 g (4 oz) cooked broccoli florets*
*1 large onion, thinly sliced*
*230 g (½ lb) mushroom caps, thinly sliced*
*½ teaspoon salt*
*½ teaspoon freshly ground pepper*
*55 g (2 oz) butter*
*30 g (1 oz) grated Parmesan cheese*
*1 teaspoon bicarbonate of soda*
*minced parsley for garnish*

Put about two-thirds of butter in frying pan. Sauté onion and mushrooms until golden. Remove from hob.

*You can use any non-starchy leftover vegetable instead of broccoli.

Put eggs, bicarbonate of soda, salt, and pepper in a bowl and beat thoroughly. Add onions and mushrooms and broccoli. Mix well.

Add remaining butter to pan and pour in egg mixture. Tilt pan to cover bottom with mixture. Fry until eggs start setting. Sprinkle Parmesan cheese on top and place under medium-hot grill until golden.

Cut into wedges and serve garnished with minced parsley.

TOTAL GRAMS 31.2
GRAMS PER SERVING 5.2

# Poultry, Beef, Seafood

## Coq Au Vin

6 servings

*1.8 kg (4 lb) chicken parts*
*110 g (4 oz) streaky bacon, diced*
*60 g (2 oz) butter*
*230 ml (8 fl oz) red wine*
*230 ml (8 fl oz) chicken stock*
*3 cloves garlic*
*1 bay leaf*
*2 large onions, chopped*
*450 g (1 lb) mushroom caps, sliced*
*salt to taste*

Sauté diced bacon in butter until golden. Remove from frying pan and reserve.

Thoroughly wash and dry chicken. Brown in bacon fat. Remove and set aside.

Sauté onions and mushrooms. Return chicken and bacon to pan. Add chicken stock, garlic, wine and bay leaf. Simmer gently 40 minutes to 1 hour in uncovered frying pan. Add salt to taste.

TOTAL GRAMS 49.8
GRAMS PER SERVING 8.3

## Chicken Curry

4 servings

*1 chicken, cut into 8–10 pieces*
*2 onions, minced*
*3 cloves garlic, minced*
*1 tablespoon turmeric*
*1 tablespoon ground cumin*
*1 tablespoon ground ginger*
*1 tablespoon chilli powder*
*55 g (2 oz) butter*
*230 ml (8 fl oz) whipping cream*
*230 ml (8 fl oz) hot water*
*salt to taste*

Sauté chicken pieces in butter until golden. Remove.

Gently sauté onions, garlic and all remaining condiments 2–3 minutes, stirring constantly.

Place chicken parts into sauce. Add the hot water and whipping cream. Simmer until chicken is tender and sauce reduced to about half original amount.

For variety, you can substitute lamb for the chicken.

TOTAL GRAMS 32.8
GRAMS PER SERVING 8.2

## Chicken with Okra and Peanuts

4 servings

*1 large chicken*
*3 carrots*
*2 leeks*
*1 whole onion*
*salt to taste*
*230 g (8 oz) small okra*
*230 g (8 oz) peanuts*
*1 tablespoon unsweetened tomato purée*
*110 g (4 oz) butter*
*1 tablespoon fresh parsley, chopped*

Combine first 5 ingredients. Cover with water and simmer 45 minutes. Remove chicken from stock and let cool. When cool, de-bone chicken completely and shred.

In ovenproof casserole, heat butter until foam subsides. Lower flame. Put in the shredded chicken, okra, tomato purée and peanuts and sauté gently until golden. Stir often.

Sprinkle with parsley and serve.

TOTAL GRAMS 80.0
GRAMS PER SERVING 20.0

## Chicken Paprika

8 servings

*1.4 kg (3 lb) chicken parts*
*60 g (2 oz) butter*
*60 ml (2 fl oz) vegetable oil*
*3 large onions, chopped*
*4 cloves garlic, chopped*
*6 tablespoons good Hungarian paprika*
*120 ml (4 fl oz) chicken stock*
*230 ml (8 fl oz) white wine*
*450 ml (17 fl oz) soured cream*

Preheat oven to 190-205°C (375-400°F/gas mark 5 or 6).

In a large casserole sauté chicken parts in oil-butter mixture on all sides until golden. Remove to plate.

Add onions and garlic to casserole and sauté until golden. Add paprika, chicken stock, wine and soured cream and simmer gently about 10 minutes.

Replace chicken parts in casserole and coat with sauce. Bake covered in oven about 45 minutes or until chicken is well done.

TOTAL GRAMS 48.0
GRAMS PER SERVING 6.0

## Chicken Cacciatore

8 servings

*2.3 kg (5 lb) mixed chicken parts*
*120 ml (4 fl oz) olive oil*
*110 g (4 oz) butter*
*1 large onion, chopped*
*450 g (1 lb) mushroom caps, thinly sliced*
*4 cloves garlic*
*230 ml (8 fl oz) white wine*
*2 bay leaves*
*2 teaspoons oregano*
*1 teaspoon freshly ground pepper*
*3 tablespoons brandy*
*280 g (10 oz) sun-dried tomatoes*
*salt to taste*

Soak tomatoes in hot water and set aside.

Sauté chicken in half olive oil, half butter, on all sides until golden. Set aside.

Heat remaining oil and butter in frying pan and sauté onions until light golden. Add mushrooms and garlic. Continue sautéeing until soft.

Place chicken parts in a large casserole and pour onion-mushroom mixture on top of chicken. Pour in wine and add drained tomatoes and remaining ingredients. Cover lightly and simmer 30 minutes or until chicken is thoroughly cooked through.

Total Grams 49.6
Grams per serving 6.2

## Meat Loaf

6 servings

*1.4 kg (3 lb) chopped mixed meats (lamb, veal, beef,*
   *pork)*
*2 tablespoons chilli powder*
*3 eggs*
*3 cloves garlic, mashed*
*3 tablespoons fresh coriander or flat-leaf parsley*
*170 g (6 oz) mature Cheddar cheese, grated*
*2 tablespoons Worcestershire sauce*
*salt to taste*

Preheat over to 190°C (375°F/gas mark 5)

   In large bowl, thoroughly mix all ingredients. Place meat
in oiled loaf pan and bake 45 minutes to 1 hour.

TOTAL GRAMS  15.0
GRAMS PER SERVING  2.5

# Parfait of Chicken Livers with Braised Sultanas*

◆◆

4 servings

CHICKEN LIVERS:
*15 g (½ oz) butter*
*230 g (8 oz) warm clarified butter*
*230 g (8 oz) chicken livers*
*1 whole head peeled garlic*
*(approx 8 cloves)*
*1 sliced onion*
*230 ml (8 fl oz) ruby port*
*230 ml (8 fl oz) brandy or cognac*
*10 thin slices streaky bacon*
*1 pinch grated nutmeg*
*1 pinch ground cinnamon*
*1 bay leaf*
*1 sprig thyme*

BRAISED SULTANAS:
*110 g (4 oz) sultanas*
*2 tea bags*
*1 tablespoon Grand Marnier*
*½ teaspoon grated orange peel*

*To Prepare Chicken Livers*:
Place the raw chicken livers and peeled garlic into a bowl and cover with clingfilm. Warm gently on the side of the stove.

Meanwhile, take a terrine or a 480 ml (17 fl oz) casserole and line it with thin slices of bacon.

---

*Braised sultanas can be replaced with 30 g (1 oz) of finely grated leeks sautéed in butter seasoned with black pepper, thereby lowering the carbohydrates grams to 3.9 per serving.

Place the tablespoon of butter into a warm saucepan. Add the sliced onions and steam them until cooked. Add the port, brandy, bay leaf and thyme, and simmer uncovered to reduce the liquid by two-thirds. Strain the liquid onto the warm chicken livers and garlic.

Place the mixture into a food processor and purée it.

While the mixture is being processed, add the warm clarified butter slowly. It is important to add it slowly, otherwise the mixture will curdle. Add the nutmeg and cinnamon. Pass the mixture through a fine sieve.

Then place the mixture into the lined terrine/casserole. Cover the top with bacon and then cover the whole dish with aluminium foil. Place the terrine into a basin/bain-marie and cook in a slow oven for 1 hour.

When cooked, remove from oven and allow the parfait to cool for 24 hours. When cool, slice the parfait and serve with a mixture of lettuce leaves and braised sultanas.

*To Prepare Braised Sultanas:*
Simmer the sultanas in 480 ml (17 fl oz) of water with the tea bags and orange peel. Allow to cool in the tea mixture then add a tablespoon of Grand Marnier. The sultanas can be served warm or cold as an accompaniment to the parfait.

TOTAL GRAMS 32.4
GRAMS PER SERVING 8.1

## Stuffed Peppers

8 servings

*8 medium green peppers*
*2 large onions, finely chopped*
*900 g (2 lb) meat loaf mixture (veal, beef, pork)*
*1 teaspoon dried dill*
*3 tablespoons vegetable oil*
*1 teaspoon salt*
*1 teaspoon white pepper*
*1 large carrot, grated*
*120 ml (4 fl oz) chicken stock*
*3 tablespoons unsweetened tomato purée*
*230 ml (8 fl oz) soured cream*

Sauté onions in frying pan until golden.

Add meat mixture, pepper, salt and dill. Brown and mix about 5 minutes. Let cool.

Wash and core peppers. Fill peppers with meat mixture and place open side up in a large casserole.

Combine chicken stock and tomato purée and pour over peppers. Sprinkle grated carrot on top of peppers.

Cover and cook in oven at 190°C (375°F/gas mark 5) until peppers are done.

When serving add generous amounts of soured cream.

Total Grams 61.6
Grams per serving 7.7

## Beef Stroganoff

4 servings

*2 tablespoons chopped parsley*
*2 large onions, finely chopped*
*450 g (1 lb) mushroom caps, sliced*
*900 g (2 lb) sirloin, cut into strips*
*1½ tablespoons dry mustard*
*120 ml (4 fl oz) soured cream*
*3 tablespoons unsweetened ketchup*
*3 tablespoons oil*
*freshly ground white pepper*
*salt to taste*

Combine mustard, ketchup and enough hot water to form thick paste.

Sauté onions and mushrooms in 2 tablespoons of oil until golden and soft. Remove with slotted spoon to preheated large casserole.

Add remaining oil to frying pan and sauté meat strips in batches (quickly, as in stir-frying). Transfer meat to casserole.

Put mustard paste and soured cream in frying pan with any remaining juices. Stir gently until all ingredients are smoothly mixed.

Pour over meat and onions and mix well. Gently simmer until hot. Sprinkle with parsley, salt, and freshly ground white pepper and serve immediately.

TOTAL GRAMS 40.0
GRAMS PER SERVING 10.0

## Blackened Beef with a Basil and Parsley Cream

6 servings

*700 g (1½ lb) of beef tenderloin, trimmed*

MARINADE:
*110 g (4 oz) butter, clarified*
*4 cloves garlic, crushed*
*1 tablespoon ground black pepper*
*1 tablespoon paprika*
*1 teaspoon grated horseradish or cold horseradish
    sauce*
*1 tablespoon soy sauce*
*1 tablespoon mixed herbs (basil, thyme, parsley,
    marjoram), chopped*

SAUCE:
*470 ml (17 fl oz) whipping cream*
*1 tablespoon parsley, chopped*
*1 tablespoon basil, chopped*
*2 cloves garlic, crushed*
*230 ml (8 fl oz) white wine*
*15 g (½ oz) butter*

Blend together the ingredients for the marinade in a food processor.

Cut the beef into 8 medallions.

Cover the beef with the marinade and allow it to rest overnight in the refrigerator.

*Next day*:

To make the sauce, melt the butter in a warm saucepan. Gently sauté the garlic, parsley and basil, occasionally stirring.

Add the white wine and then simmer uncovered to reduce by one half.

Add the whipping cream and simmer for 5 minutes until the cream thickens. Season according to taste.

To cook the beef, place a frying pan on the heat until it is very hot, then place the marinated beef medallions into the pan (the mixture must remain on the beef). Cook for 1 minute. Then turn the medallions and cook for 1 more minute.

TOTAL GRAMS 26.4
GRAMS PER SERVING 4.4

## Sauerkraut with Variety of Cooked Meats

6 servings

*1.4 kg (3 lb) sauerkraut*
*450 g (1 lb) cooked chicken*
*450 g (1 lb) roast pork*
*1 lb sausages*
*60 g (2 oz) lard*
*60 ml (2 fl oz) beef stock*
*3 tablespoons unsweetened tomato purée*
*2 medium onions, chopped*
*230 ml (8 fl oz) vodka*
*115 ml (4 fl oz) white wine*
*bouquet garni of peppercorns, allspice, laurel leaf,*
    *juniper berries*

Preheat oven to 180°C (350°F/gas mark 4).

Wash sauerkraut. Blanch and drain.

Heat lard in heavy frying pan. Add chopped onions, sauté until golden. Add beef stock, vodka, wine and tomato purée. Mix well and simmer for 5 minutes.

Put layer of sauerkraut in heavy casserole. Place some meats on top. Repeat this until all sauerkraut and meats have been used. Pour beef stock, vodka, etc., mixture on top of sauerkraut and meat. Insert bouquet garni. Cover and bake for about 2 hours.

TOTAL GRAMS 62.4
GRAMS PER SERVING 10.4

## Stuffed Veal Chops with Wild Mushrooms

4 servings

*4 double veal chops (have butcher cut a pocket into*
  *chops)*
*5 shallots, minced*
*900 g (2 lb) fresh tender spinach*
*450 g (1 lb) mushroom caps, thinly sliced*
*30–60 g (1–2 oz) dried Porcini mushrooms*
*120 ml (4 fl oz) chicken stock*
*40 g (1½ oz) butter*
*120 ml (4 fl oz) white wine*
*2 tablespoons cognac*
*1 tablespoon ground white pepper*
*1 teaspoon salt*
*120 ml (4 fl oz) whipping cream*
*2 tablespoons oil*

Preheat oven to 200°C (400°F/gas mark 6).

Sauté shallots and mushroom caps in 15 g (½ oz) butter
and 1 tablespoon oil until golden. Add chopped spinach,
white pepper and salt, and cook until spinach is wilted. Set
aside. Let cool.

Soak Porcini mushrooms in hot chicken stock while preparing stuffing.

Stuff each chop with mixture. Close opening with tooth-
picks.

Heat remaining butter and oil in frying pan and
thoroughly brown stuffed chops on both sides. Place into
casserole.

Mix chicken stock and Porcini mushrooms with cognac, white wine and whipping cream. Pour over chops and bake for 45 minutes to 1 hour. Turn chops once after 30 minutes. Remove chops, sprinkle with fresh pepper and serve.

Total Grams 65.2
Grams per serving 16.3

## Veal Stew

6 servings

*1 stalk celery, diced*
*1 carrot, diced*
*1 bay leaf*
*1.4 kg (3 lb) stewing veal*
*170 ml (6 fl oz) white wine*
*450 g (1 lb) pickling onions*
*700 g (1½ lb) mushroom caps, sliced*
*5 egg yolks*
*230 ml (8 fl oz) whipping cream*
*salt to taste*

In a casserole, bring first seven ingredients to a slow boil. Cover and simmer an additional 30 minutes.

In bowl, stir egg yolks and cream. Dribble in cup of broth, stirring continuously. Stir egg-cream mixture into veal until sauce thickens.

Total Grams 75.0
Grams per serving 12.5

## Escalopes of Veal Stuffed with a Purée of Mushrooms*

4 servings

*4 thin slices loin or tenderloin veal*

Filling:
*230 g (8 oz) mushrooms*
*1 onion, chopped*
*230 ml (8 fl oz) ruby port*

Coating:
*110 g (4 oz) Parmesan cheese, grated*
*2 eggs, beaten*

*40 g (1½ oz) butter*
*1 aubergine, peeled and diced*
*1.4 l (2½ pints) good veal stock*
*230 ml (8 fl oz) red wine*
*minced parsley*

*Purée:*
Melt the butter in a warm saucepan. Sauté the onions until tender, then add the mushrooms and cook for a further 5 minutes. Add the ruby port and simmer the mixture until most of the moisture has evaporated. Occasionally stir to prevent burning. Remove from heat and allow to cool.

Purée the mixture in a food processor.

Flatten veal until very thin. Place a spoonful of the mixture on top of each veal escalope, then fold it in half, sealing the edges.

*The carbohydrate content can be made much lower by using 30 ml (1 fl oz) of port and 200 ml (7 fl oz) of a dry white wine.

Dip each escalope into the beaten egg and then into the Parmesan cheese. Repeat this procedure once more.

*Sauce*:
Reduce the veal stock and red wine together by simmering uncovered until you are left with about 170 ml (6 fl oz). Season with salt and pepper. If the reduction is thin it can be thickened with a little arrowroot and water mixture.

*Garnish*:
Fry the aubergine in a little butter until golden brown.

*To serve*:
Melt a little butter in a frying pan and fry the veal escalopes on both sides until golden brown. Place onto a warm plate and surround with a little sauce. Sprinkle the fried aubergine around and garnish with minced parsley.

Total Grams 70.4
Grams per serving 17.6

## Roast Leg of Lamb

10 servings

*4.5–5.5 kg (10–12 lb) leg of lamb*
*5 cloves garlic*
*2 tablespoons rosemary*
*1 teaspoon salt*

Preheat oven to 260°C (500°F/gas mark 10).
Make slits all over lamb and insert slivers of garlic. Rub salt and rosemary over lamb.

Place lamb fat side up on rack in open roasting pan. Roast in hot oven for 15 minutes. Reduce heat to 180°C (350°F/gas mark 4) and roast for 2 to 2½ hours more.

Total Grams 5.0
Grams per serving 0.5

## Medallions of Lamb with Green Lentils and Bacon

2 servings

*2 medallions lamb, noisettes from the best end of
   neck*
*110 g (4 oz) small French green lentils*
*6 slices of smoked streaky bacon*
*Lamb Sauce with Garlic*
*vegetables to garnish (onion, celery, leek)—30 g
   (1 oz) of each*
*clarified butter*
*2 cloves garlic, minced*

To cook the lentils, finely chop onion, celery, leek and garlic. Steam in clarified butter. Add the lentils, then lamb stock, and cook until the lentils are tender.

Sear the medallions of lamb, place some cooked lentils on top of each piece and wrap in smoked bacon. Skewer the bacon to hold it in place. While this is cooking, cook the noisettes in a hot frying pan.

Place a bed of lentils onto the plate. Place the lamb on top of the lentils and coat with garlic-flavored lamb sauce. Arrange vegetables around the lamb.

Choice vegetables would be fine French beans.

TOTAL GRAMS 35.0
GRAMS PER SERVING 17.5

## Lamb Sauce with Garlic

2 servings

*lamb trimmings, no fat*
*6 shallots, sliced*
*4 cloves garlic, crushed*
*60 g (2 oz) smoked streaky bacon*
*470 ml (17 fl oz) lamb stock*
*¼ bottle dry white wine*

Sauté the lamb trimmings until brown, pour off any excess fat. Add the shallots and crushed garlic and smoked bacon. Sauté for a further 2 minutes. Add the white wine and simmer uncovered to reduce. Then add the lamb stock and reduce. When the sauce has reduced by one half, strain it through a fine sieve. Correct the seasoning and finish with a little unsalted butter.

TOTAL GRAMS 10.0
GRAMS PER SERVING 5.0

## Cassoulet of Prawns Flavored with Vegetables and Bay Leaves

4 servings

> 16 good-sized prawns, peeled and deveined
> 1 medium parsnip, finely chopped
> 1 medium leek, finely chopped
> 2 sticks of celery, finely chopped
> 470 ml (17 fl oz) dry white wine
> 230 ml (8 fl oz) cream
> 2 bay leaves
> 1 tomato, skinned, pipped and diced
> 1 tablespoon chives, snipped
> 15 g (½ oz) butter
> salt and pepper (optional)

Melt the butter in a warm saucepan. Sauté the vegetables and bay leaves in the butter for 2 minutes. Add the prawns and cook for 1 more minute.

Add the white wine and reduce the liquid by half. Then add the cream and simmer for approximately 3 minutes.

Season according to taste with salt and pepper.

Divide into 4 soup bowls and garnish with the chopped tomato and snipped chives.

TOTAL GRAMS 26.8
GRAMS PER SERVING 6.7

## Warm Avocados and Lobster Glazed with Béarnaise Sauce

4 servings

*2 medium-sized ripe avocados*
*230 g (8 oz) cooked lobster meat, cut into chunks*
*110 g (4 oz) mushrooms, sliced*
*1 onion, finely chopped*
*115 ml (4 fl oz) dry white wine*
*230 ml (8 fl oz) béarnaise sauce (see recipe, page 350)*
*15 g (½ oz) butter*

Cut the avocados in half and remove the stones. Scoop out the pulp, leaving the outer shell intact. Cut the pulp into bite-sized chunks.

Melt the butter in a warm saucepan. Sauté the chopped onions and sliced mushrooms for approximately 1 minute. Add the lobster and avocado chunks and give the mixture a stir. Add the white wine. Simmer for 3–4 minutes.

Place the mixture into the empty avocado shells. Coat each one with the béarnaise sauce.

Glaze under a hot grill until golden brown.

Serve immediately.

TOTAL GRAMS 44.0
GRAMS PER SERVING 11.0

## Poached Salmon with Béarnaise Sauce

4 servings

*4 thick salmon steaks*
*230 ml (8 fl oz) chicken stock*
*230 ml (8 fl oz) white wine*
*1 bay leaf*
*Béarnaise sauce (see recipe below)*
*fresh dill*

Put salmon into deep frying pan. Combine remaining ingredients and pour over salmon. Cover and simmer gently 10–15 minutes. Sprinkle with dill and sauce.

TOTAL GRAMS 8.0
GRAMS PER SERVING 2.0

## Béarnaise Sauce

4 servings

*3 egg yolks*
*230 ml (8 fl oz) warm clarified butter*
*1 tablespoon fresh tarragon, chopped*
*3 tablespoons dry white wine*
*1 tablespoon tarragon vinegar*
*6 black peppercorns*
*1 shallot, chopped*

Place the last four ingredients in a pan and simmer uncovered until only 1 tablespoon of liquid remains. Allow it to cool, then strain the liquid.

Place the egg yolks in a bowl with strained liquid and beat them over a gentle heat (bain-marie) until they acquire a ribbon texture. Add the melted butter slowly. Keep beating the mixture until all the butter has been incorporated.

Remove the pan from the heat and mix in the chopped tarragon.

Serve with fish or meat.

TOTAL GRAMS 4.4
GRAMS PER SERVING 1.4

# Chilled Marinated Oysters with a Dressing of Soured Cream and Cucumber

*For a Main Course you will need 12 oysters per person*
*For an Appetizer you will need 6 oysters per person*
*230 g (8 oz) spinach*
*½ cucumber*
*470 ml (17 fl oz) soured cream*
*freshly chopped dill*
*lime juice, freshly squeezed*
*Tabasco sauce*
*cayenne pepper*
*salt and pepper*
*black caviar (optional)*

*Oysters*
Open and clean the oysters. Retain the juice and the shells.

Place the oysters in a bowl with the juice and add a dash of Tabasco, the juice of 1 lime and a little freshly chopped dill. Allow them to marinate for 1 hour.

Cook spinach in boiling water, then refresh it in iced water. Squeeze out any excess water. Season the spinach with a little salt and pepper and place a little of the spinach in each oyster shell.

*Dressing:*

Peel and de-seed half a cucumber, then dice.

Add to the cucumber the soured cream, 1 teaspoon freshly chopped dill and a pinch of cayenne pepper.

To serve, place the oysters on top of the spinach in the shells. Coat each oyster with a little dressing and sprinkle a little cayenne pepper on top.

Garnish the top with black caviar (optional).

Serve the oysters on a bed of crushed ice.

GRAMS PER SERVING (appetizer) 14.0
GRAMS PER SERVING (main course) 28.0

# Fried Fillet of Sea Bass with Leeks and Tomatoes in an Olive Oil Dressing

4 servings

*4 nice size fillets of sea bass*
*2 medium leeks, cut into small strips*
*2 large firm tomatoes, skinned, pipped and chopped*
*1 tablespoon shredded basil*
*1 tablespoon balsamic vinegar*
*4 tablespoons virgin olive oil*
*15 g (½ oz) butter*
*freshly milled black pepper*

Fry the fish in a tablespoon of olive oil in a frying pan until golden brown on each side. Then remove from the pan and keep warm.

Add the butter to the same pan and gently sauté the leeks until tender. Add the balsamic vinegar, shaking the pan. Slowly add the 3 tablespoons of olive oil to make a sauce. Remove from the heat and add the chopped tomatoes, the shredded basil and the black pepper.

Place the mixture on a plate and sit the fillets of fish on top.

TOTAL GRAMS 26.0
GRAMS PER SERVING 6.5

## Mousseline of Queen Scallops
## with Saffron Sauce

4 servings

MOUSSE:
*15 g (½ oz) chives, chopped*
*170 g (6 oz) queen scallops*
*60 g (2 oz) Dover sole fillet*
*230 ml (8 fl oz) whipping cream*
*1 egg white*
*cayenne pepper*
*salt and pepper*

GARNISH:
*4 large spinach leaves, blanched*
*4 queen scallops per person*

SAUCE:
*120 ml (4 fl oz) dry white wine*
*bones of 3 Dover sole*
*30 g (2 oz) shallots, sliced*
*30 g (2 oz) mushroom parings*
*pinch saffron stamens*
*230 ml (8 fl oz) double cream*
*30 g (1 oz) butter*

Line 4 buttered single serving-sized baking dishes with the blanched spinach leaves.

Blend the scallops and Dover sole fillet in a food processor with the egg white. Pass the fish purée through a fine sieve and place the bowl on ice to allow it to cool.

Slowly beat in the cream. Season with salt and pepper and cayenne pepper and add the finely chopped chives. Place the mousseline in the lined baking dishes and cover them with buttered foil.

Place in a bain-marie and cook in a slow oven at 180°C (350°F/gas mark 4) for 10 minutes.

Place all ingredients except the cream in a saucepan.

Reduce the ingredients for the sauce by simmering uncovered to approximately 1 tablespoon with a syrupy consistency and add the cream. Bring to a boil.

Whisk in butter and correct seasoning.

*To serve*:
Place the baking dishes on a warm plate turned over. Around it place a little sauce, on top of which you sprinkle the warm blanched saffron and garnish with 4 slightly steamed queen scallops.

TOTAL GRAMS 39.2
GRAMS PER SERVING 9.8

# Salads & Dressings

### Warm Lobster Salad with a Tarragon Butter Dressing

4 servings

*450 g (1 lb) cooked lobster, chopped into large pieces*
*1 raw onion, chopped*
*1 head cos or iceberg lettuce*
*1 bunch fresh tarragon, ½ chopped, ½ for garnish*
*120 ml (4 fl oz) whipping cream*
*110 g (4 oz) unsalted butter*
*1 tablespoon tarragon vinegar*
*1 pinch cayenne pepper*

*Dressing*:
Place the chopped tarragon and vinegar in a saucepan and bring to a boil. Add the cream. Simmer for approximately 2 minutes. Remove the pan from heat and whisk the butter into the cream. Add a pinch of cayenne pepper.

*To serve*:
Wash and dry the lettuce thoroughly. Break it into bite-sized pieces and arrange on a plate.

Place the lobster and chopped onion in the warm dressing until the lobster has become lukewarm. Place the lobster mixture on top of the lettuce and decorate with leaves of fresh tarragon.

TOTAL GRAMS 40.0
GRAMS PER SERVING 10.0

## Salmon Salad in a Hurry

1 serving

*1 x 213 g (7½ oz) tin salmon*
*2 chopped spring onions*
*½ stalk celery, diced*
*3 tablespoons Roquefort dressing (see below)*

Remove bone and skin of salmon. Break in chunks in bowl. Mix onions and celery with salmon. Turn into salad bowl and pour dressing over. This can also be served on lettuce leaves.

TOTAL GRAMS 2.6

## Our Favorite Roquefort Dressing

240 ml (8 fl oz)

*60 ml (2 fl oz) tarragon vinegar*
*¼ teaspoon seasoning salt*
*3 turns of pepper mill*
*6 tablespoons olive oil*
*2 tablespoons whipping cream*
*½ teaspoon lemon juice*
*30 g (1 oz) crumbled Roquefort cheese*

Beat all ingredients together except cheese. Stir in cheese.

TOTAL GRAMS 6.7

## Mushroom Salad

6 servings

*8 slices streaky bacon, diced*
*1 small onion, minced*
*30 g (1 oz) butter, melted*
*3 tablespoons lemon juice*
*2 tablespoons parsley, chopped*
*450 g (1 lb) white mushrooms, thinly sliced*
*grated Parmesan cheese*

Fry bacon until transparent. Add minced onion; continue frying until bacon is crisp and onion is golden. Pour off bacon fat.

Add butter, lemon juice, and parsley. Bring to boil.

Pour over mushrooms, and garnish with Parmesan cheese to taste.

TOTAL GRAMS 29.4
GRAMS PER SERVING 4.9

## Basic French Dressing

120 ml (4 fl oz)

*3 tablespoons tarragon vinegar*
*1 tablespoon lemon juice*
*½ teaspoon seasoning salt*
*3 turns of pepper mill*
*6 tablespoons olive oil*
*2 tablespoons vegetable oil*
*½ teaspoon Dijon mustard*
*¼ teaspoon dry mustard*

Beat all ingredients together until well blended.

TOTAL GRAMS 2.5

## Avocado Dressing

24 tablespoons

*1 ripe medium avocado, cubed*
*120 ml (4 fl oz) lemon juice*
*60 ml (2 fl oz) mayonnaise*
*1 teaspoon-equivalent sugar substitute\**
*¼ teaspoon salt*
*¼ teaspoon paprika*

Blend all ingredients at high speed until smooth.

TOTAL GRAMS 24.0
GRAMS PER TABLESPOON 1.0

*See note on page 378.

## Russian Dressing

20 tablespoons

*120 ml (4 fl oz) mayonnaise*
*120 ml (4 fl oz) soured cream*
*1 tablespoon Dijon mustard*
*1 tablespoon Worcestershire sauce*
*2 tablespoons tomato sauce*
*½ teaspoon grated onion*
*⅛ teaspoon garlic powder*

Combine ingredients. Mix well.

TOTAL GRAMS 10.0
GRAMS PER TABLESPOON .5

## Cucumbers in Soured Cream

4 servings

*1 cucumber, thinly sliced*
*½ teaspoon salt*
*120 ml (4 fl oz) soured cream*
*½ teaspoon-equivalent sugar substitute\**
*1 tablespoon vinegar*
*½ teaspoon dill seed*

In shallow bowl place cucumber and sprinkle with salt.
Allow to set for ½ hour. Drain.
Add remaining ingredients. Mix well. Chill.

TOTAL GRAMS 13.2
GRAMS PER SERVING 3.3

*See note on page 378.

## Warm Beef, Mushroom and Watercress Salad Flavored with Horseradish

4 servings

> 450 g (1 lb) cooked beef, shredded
> 230 g (8 oz) raw mushrooms, sliced
> 2 bunches fresh watercress
> 1 tablespoon freshly grated horseradish
> 2 egg yolks
> 1 tablespoon wine vinegar
> 4 tablespoons sesame oil
> 1 tablespoon toasted sesame seeds

Wash the watercress and dry thoroughly.

Mix the vinegar and sesame oil. Pour over the watercress and toss. Arrange the watercress on a cold plate.

Mix the shredded beef, mushrooms and grated horseradish and egg yolks together. Place the mixture on top of the watercress and sprinkle with the toasted sesame seeds.

TOTAL GRAMS 13.6
GRAMS PER SERVING 3.4

## Cold Salad of Scrambled Egg and Cottage Cheese with Asparagus

4 servings

*6 eggs, lightly scrambled and allowed to cool*
*230 g (8 oz) cottage cheese*
*1 tablespoon chives, chopped*
*12 asparagus spears, peeled*
*230 g (8 oz) iceberg lettuce, endive, radicchio, baby*
*   spinach leaves; washed and picked over*
*1 tablespoon wine vinegar*
*4 tablespoons olive oil*
*salt and pepper*

Scramble the eggs until quite soft. Allow them to cool. Mix them together with the cottage cheese and chives. Add the salt and pepper to taste.

Cook the asparagus spears by plunging them into boiling water and cooking them for 5 minutes. Cool the spears by placing them in iced water.

Mix the vinegar and olive oil together. Pour this over the lettuce and toss.

Place the lettuce on a cold plate. Arrange the egg and cheese mixture on top and decorate with the asparagus spears.

TOTAL GRAMS 36.0
GRAMS PER SERVING 9.0

## Chicken Salad

6 servings

*2 large chicken breasts, cooked*
*2 large dill pickles, chopped*
*3 hard-boiled eggs, chopped*
*3 spring onions, trimmed, washed and chopped*
*½ teaspoon freshly ground pepper*
*70 ml (2½ fl oz) sugar-free mayonnaise*
*70 ml (2½ fl oz) soured cream*
*2 tablespoons drained capers*
*3 tablespoons fresh dill, chopped*
*60 g (2 oz) pecan halves*

Cut chicken meat into strips. Combine all other ingredients. Add chicken and toss well.

Total Grams 30.6
Grams per serving 5.1

# Vegetarian Dishes

## French Beans with Walnut Sauce

6 servings

*450 g (1 lb) fresh French beans, trimmed*
*120 ml (4 fl oz) chicken stock*
*2 cloves garlic, minced*
*1 medium onion, finely chopped*
*30 ml (2 fl oz) balsamic vinegar*
*3 tablespoons fresh dill, finely chopped*
*70 ml (2½ fl oz) walnut oil*
*110 g (4 oz) walnuts, coarsely chopped*

Bring 3 liters (5 pints) of salted water to a rapid boil. Add beans and boil uncovered for about 10 minutes or until they are *al dente*. Drain beans.

Combine all the remaining ingredients. Add cooked beans and toss until beans are well covered.

Serve hot or cold.

TOTAL GRAMS 58.8
GRAMS PER SERVING 9.6

## Celeriac Salad

2 servings

*1 celeriac*
*2 tablespoons soured cream*
*2 tablespoons sugar-free mayonnaise*
*1 teaspoon soy sauce*

Grate celeriac. Combine with the rest of the ingredients. Mix well and serve.

TOTAL GRAMS 10.6
GRAMS PER SERVING 5.3

## Spinach Egg Pie

4 servings

*560 g (1¼ lb) frozen spinach or equivalent amount*
 *fresh spinach*
*1 large onion, grated*
*3 cloves garlic, crushed*
*110 g (4 oz) butter*
*½ teaspoon salt*
*freshly ground pepper to taste*
*½ teaspoon nutmeg*
*6 eggs*
*1 teaspoon bicarbonate of soda*

Preheat oven to 180°C (350°F/gas mark 4).

   Defrost spinach and sauté in 40 g (1½ oz) butter for 5 minutes.

Put eggs into large bowl. Add pepper, salt and bicarbonate of soda and beat until fluffy. Add cooled sautéed spinach, grated onion, nutmeg and crushed garlic and mix thoroughly.

Grease baking pan thoroughly with remaining butter and place in oven. When butter is melted, remove from oven and pour in egg-spinach mixture. Return dish to oven and bake about 45 minutes or until golden on top.

TOTAL GRAMS 31.2
GRAMS PER SERVING 7.8

## Baked Spinach Flavored with Basil and Ricotta Cheese

4 servings

*900 g (2 lb) tender spinach leaves*
*1 tablespoon fresh basil, chopped*
*2 tablespoons ricotta cheese*
*2 egg yolks*
*450 ml (16 fl oz) whipping cream*
*1 tablespoon grated Parmesan cheese*
*salt, pepper and grated nutmeg*

Preheat oven to 230°C (450°F/gas mark 8).

Cook the spinach by placing in boiling water for 1 minute. Cool the spinach in iced water. Squeeze out any excess water from the cooked spinach and place into a food processor with the basil, ricotta cheese, egg yolks, cream, a pinch of salt, a little ground pepper and grated nutmeg.

Purée the whole mixture. Place the mixture in an ovenproof dish.

Simmer uncovered to reduce the cream by half and pour it over the purée mixture. Sprinkle with Parmesan cheese and bake until golden brown.

TOTAL GRAMS 54.4
GRAMS PER SERVING 13.6

### Brussels Sprouts Crisps

2 servings

*100 g (3½ oz) Brussels sprouts*
*3 tablespoons olive oil*
*¼ teaspoon salt*

Preheat oven to 190°C (375°F/gas mark 5).
Cut end of each floret and separate all leaves.

Put leaves into roasting pan, sprinkle with olive oil and salt and roast for 40 minutes. Stir occasionally.

TOTAL GRAMS 7.0
GRAMS PER SERVING 3.5

## Aubergine Balls

8 servings

4 medium aubergines
2 tablespoons flour
1 large egg
½ teaspoon white pepper
1 small red or green pepper
230 ml (8 fl oz) vegetable oil
salt to taste

Peel aubergines, quarter and boil in salted water until tender.

Combine all ingredients except vegetable oil in food processor until smooth paste is formed.

Heat vegetable oil in heavy pot and drop in aubergine paste a spoonful at a time. Fry until golden. Salt to taste. Drain on kitchen paper.

TOTAL GRAMS 66.4
GRAMS PER SERVING 8.3

## Stuffed Fried Mushrooms
## with Goat Cheese

4 servings

*16 medium-sized fresh mushroom caps*
*230 g (8 oz) goat cheese*
*1 clove garlic*
*1 teaspoon oregano*
*1 egg, beaten*
*110 g (4 oz) ground almonds*
*salt and pepper*

Clean mushroom caps with a clean cloth.
Place the goat cheese, garlic and oregano in a food processor and purée. Add salt and pepper to taste.

Place the mixture in the mushroom caps, then roll the caps in beaten egg and then into the ground almonds. Repeat this process and then fry the mushrooms in hot fat until crisp.

Drain on kitchen paper and serve immediately.

TOTAL GRAMS 33.2
GRAMS PER SERVING 8.3

# Snacks

## Swiss Snack

1 serving

*110 g (4 oz) Emmenthal cheese, cut into cubes*
*4 slices streaky bacon*
*oil*

Wrap each cube of cheese in ½ slice bacon. Deep-fry in very hot oil for 30 seconds.

TOTAL GRAMS 4.1

## Sweet Cheese Snack

18 snacks

*110 g (4 oz) cream cheese at room temperature*
*2 eggs, separated*
*3 teaspoon-equivalents sugar substitute**

Preheat oven to 180°C (350°F/gas mark 4).

Cream the cheese with egg yolks until smooth. Add sugar substitute.

Beat egg whites until stiff, but not dry. Fold cheese mixture into stiff whites. Be careful not to break down egg whites.

*See note on page 378.

Grease baking sheet with butter or ghee. Drop mixture by teaspoonfuls onto baking sheet and bake in oven for 10 minutes.

Total Grams 5.4
Grams per serving .3

## Guacamole

4 servings

1 ripe avocado, cubed
2 medium tomatoes, cubed
1 medium onion, minced
2–3 tablespoons chopped fresh coriander
1 teaspoon sea salt
1 teaspoon fresh lemon

Chop all ingredients together. Chill and serve.

Total Grams 34.8
Grams per serving 8.7

# Breads, Pancakes, Muffins

## Basic Protein Bread

1 loaf

*3 eggs, separated, at room temperature*
*2 tablespoons soured cream*
*30 g (1 oz) butter, melted*
*40 g (1½ oz) soya flour*
*1 tablespoon baking powder*

Preheat oven to 180°C (350°F/gas mark 4).

Combine egg yolks with all other ingredients. Mix well. Beat egg whites until stiff and fold into mixture. Put into buttered bread pan and bake for 50 minutes or until golden.

Store in refrigerator.

TOTAL GRAMS 18.0

## Bran-Soy Muffins

6 servings

*3 eggs, separated, room temperature*
*3 tablespoons sour cream*
*40 g (1½ oz) soya flour*
*12.5 g (½ oz) wheat bran*
*30 g (1⅛ oz) walnuts*
*1½ teaspoons baking powder*

Preheat oven to 350 degrees.

Mix egg yolks with the rest of ingredients. Beat egg whites until stiff. Fold in carefully. Place in buttered muffin tins and bake at 350 degrees until done.

TOTAL GRAMS 31.2
GRAMS PER SERVING 5.2

## French Toast

*15 g (¹/₂ oz) butter*
*1 tablespoon cooking oil*
*60 ml (2 fl oz) single cream*
*1 egg*
*¹/₂ teaspoon vanilla essence*
*powdered cinnamon sweetened with 4 teaspoon-*
*equivalents sugar substitute\**
*dash of salt*
*6 slices Basic Protein Bread*

Heat butter and oil in frying pan. Place egg, cream, and vanilla essence in small bowl and beat gently with fork. Dip bread in bowl and drop in frying pan until golden brown. Sprinkle powdered cinnamon to taste.

3–4 GRAMS PER SLICE

## Basic Pancakes

6 servings

*40 g (1¹/₂ oz) soya flour*
*3 eggs*
*120 ml (4 fl oz) water*
*¹/₄ teaspoon salt*
*cooking oil*

Combine first 4 ingredients in a liquidizer.

Heat 20-cm (8-inch) omelet pan or frying pan covered with oil. When oil is piping hot, add 3 tablespoons of

*See note on page 378.

batter. Spread evenly in pan. Cook quickly one side, then the other. Put pancake on platter and finish batter.

These pancakes can be used as a base for canneloni, lasagne, blintzes, even pizza.

TOTAL GRAMS 12.0
GRAMS PER SERVING 2.0

## Pizza

2 servings

*4 pancakes (see preceding recipe)*
*2 tablespoons unsweetened tomato sauce*
*2 medium tomatoes*
*90 g (3 oz) grated mozzarella*
*60 g (2 oz) grated Parmesan cheese*

Put one pancake on top of the other. Spread tomato sauce. Place mozzarella on top of sauce. Place thinly sliced tomatoes on mozzarella. Sprinkle with Parmesan cheese. Grill until Parmesan is golden.

You can make any pizza you like by adding your favorite things to the basic recipe.

TOTAL GRAMS 23.0
GRAMS PER SERVING 11.5

## Small Pancakes

2 servings

*40 g (1½ oz) soya flour*
*20 g (¾ oz) protein powder*
*3 eggs*
*120 ml (4 fl oz) sparkling mineral water*
*60 ml (2 fl oz) whipping cream*
*¼ teaspoon salt*
*120 ml (4 fl oz) cooking oil*
*soured cream, to serve*

Mix all ingredients except cooking oil and soured cream in food processor. The batter should be liquid enough to pour.

Heat heavy frying pan. Add 2 tablespoons oil. When oil is hot, add batter by the spoonful. Let it spread naturally. Cook on one side for about 2 minutes. Turn and cook other side.

When ready, put on a plate and keep warm in oven or serve immediately with lots of soured cream.

TOTAL GRAMS 14.6
GRAMS PER SERVING 7.3

# Desserts

## Rum Truffles

10 servings

*470 ml (17 fl oz) whipping cream*
*340 g (12 oz) plain unsweetened chocolate*
*16 teaspoon-equivalents sugar substitute\**
*3 tablespoons rum or cognac*
*60 g (2 oz) crushed pecans*

Bring cream to a boil. Add rum or cognac and simmer about 5 minutes.

Add chocolate and melt, stirring continuously for about 2–3 minutes. Add nuts. Mix in well. Turn off heat. Let cool for 10 minutes, then add sweeteners. Mix well.

Line baking sheet with greaseproof paper. Spread chocolate mixture evenly on sheet. Cover with foil and put in refrigerator. Let set for several hours or overnight.

When ready to serve, cut chocolate spread into squares and put in a tin.

\*See note on page 378.

TOTAL GRAMS 120.0
GRAMS PER SERVING 12.0

## Lemon Mousse

12 servings

*7 eggs, separated, at room temperature*
*360 ml (13 fl oz) whipping cream*
*juice from 3 large lemons*
*1 envelope unsweetened gelatin*
*3 tablespoons orange liqueur*
*10 teaspoon-equivalents sugar substitute\**

Cream sweeteners and egg yolks.

In a double boiler, or saucepan over simmering water, combine lemon juice with gelatin and melt. When melted, dribble in sweetened egg yolks, stirring constantly. Set aside.

Whip the cream. When stiff, fold in egg-gelatin mixture.

Beat egg whites until peaks form. Fold into cream.

Adjust sweetness.

Cover with foil and let it set in refrigerator for several hours.

\*See note on page 378.

TOTAL GRAMS 19.2
GRAMS PER SERVING 1.6

**Special Note:**
There are several brands of sweetener that come in granulated form and can be used in cooking, including Candarel, Hermesetas and Sweetex. A teaspoon of any of these three has the same sweetening power as a teaspoon of sugar. If you are using a different brand, check the label to find the sugar-equivalent. The more different sweeteners in a recipe, the greater the synergy of effect and the less is required. Remember, if heat is required, aspartame loses its effect. Adjust to your taste. The less sweetness that satisfies your palate, the better.

## Chocolate Truffles

10 servings

*340 g (12 oz) plain unsweetened plain chocolate*
*710 ml (1¼ pints) whipping cream*
*2 egg yolks*
*3 tablespoons rum*
*16 teaspoon-equivalents sugar substitute\**
*80 g (2½ oz) roasted almonds*

Simmer cream for about 5 minutes.
  Cream egg yolks and sweeteners. Add rum. Set aside.

*See note above.

Melt chocolate in cream. Turn off heat and very slowly dribble in egg yolks while stirring continuously. Add nuts and mix.

Line baking tray with greaseproof paper and spread chocolate mixture over it. Let set in refrigerator for several hours.

TOTAL GRAMS 124.0
GRAMS PER SERVING 12.4

## Walnut Butter Cookies

12 servings

*110 g (4 oz) ground walnuts*
*6 teaspoon-equivalents sugar substitute\**
*3 tablespoons rum*
*2 eggs, separated, at room temperature*
*90 g (3 oz) butter*
*40 g (1½ oz) walnuts, coarsely chopped*

Preheat oven to 180°C (350°F/gas mark 4).

Cream egg yolks with sugar substitute.

Beat egg whites until stiff and set aside.

Cream together all ingredients except coarsely chopped walnuts and fold in egg whites.

Put dough (1 tablespoon at a time) on buttered baking tray, place walnuts on top, and bake for about 40 minutes or until golden.

TOTAL GRAMS 27.5
GRAMS PER SERVING 2.3

*See note on page 378.

## Italian Sponge Cake

8 servings

*5 eggs, separated, at room temperature*
*8 teaspoon-equivalents sugar substitute\**
*4 teaspoons vanilla essence*
*½ teaspoon grated lemon rind*
*3 tablespoons soya flour*
*4 tablespoons whipping cream*
*½ teaspoon cream of tartar*

Preheat oven to 170°C (325°F/gas mark 3).

Grease a sponge tin with butter or oil.

Place egg yolks and sugar substitute in bowl. Beat with electric hand mixer until well blended. Add vanilla and lemon rind. Continue to beat and add soya flour 1 tablespoon at a time. Beat until well blended. Add cream.

Beat egg whites with cream of tartar until stiff. Fold yolk mixture into whites with an under-and-over movement. Be careful not to break down egg whites.

Turn into sponge tin and bake until done (about ½ hour).

TOTAL GRAMS 10.2
GRAMS PER SERVING 1.3

*See note on page 378.

## Zabaglione

6 servings

*230 ml (8 fl oz) whipping cream*
*3 eggs, separated*
*6 teaspoon-equivalents sugar substitute\**
*60 ml (2 fl oz) sherry*
*280 g (10 oz) strawberries, washed and hulled*

Scald cream (do not boil). Beat egg yolks with one half of the sugar substitute. Pour cream over egg yolks and beat with wire whisk until well blended.

Cook mixture in top of double boiler, or in a saucepan over simmering water, beating constantly with hand mixer or rotary beater until it begins to thicken. Cool.

Remove from heat and stir in sherry. Beat egg whites with remaining artificial sweetener until stiff. Fold into cream mixture carefully so that egg whites do not break down.

Refrigerate and serve with whole or sliced strawberries.

TOTAL GRAMS 33.0
GRAMS PER SERVING 5.5

*See note on page 378.

## Fruit Jelly*

8 servings

*2 sachets sugar-free raspberry jelly*
*100 g (3½ oz) sliced strawberries*
*120 ml (4 fl oz) whipping cream, whipped*

Prepare 1 sachet jelly according to instructions on packet. Add strawberries. Pour into mold. Chill until firm.

Prepare second sachet of jelly without cold water. Cool. Fold in whipped cream.

Pour on top of strawberry jelly. Refrigerate for at least two hours.

*To unmold*: Run a wet knife along edge. Dip bottom of mold in warm water. Turn over onto wet plate.

TOTAL GRAMS 9.2
GRAMS PER SERVING 1.2

## Blueberry Ice-cream

6 servings (approx. 120 ml [4 oz] each)

*5 egg yolks*
*3 teaspoons vanilla essence*
*8 teaspoon-equivalents sugar substitute***
*60 ml (2 fl oz) water*
*60 g (2 oz) frozen blueberries*
*470 ml (17 fl oz) whipping cream, whipped*

*Not suitable for aspartame-intolerant persons.
**See note on page 378.

Place yolks, vanilla essence, sugar substitute and water in liquidizer. Liquidize at medium speed for 30 seconds. Add blueberries. Liquidize for 10 more seconds.

Fold egg yolk mixture into whipped cream. Blend lightly until you have marbled effect. Pour into freezer container. Freeze.

TOTAL GRAMS 17.4
GRAMS PER SERVING 2.9

## Vanilla Ice-cream

950 ml (1⅔ pints) or 8 servings
(approx. 120 ml [4 oz] each)

*5 egg yolks*
*3 teaspoons vanilla essence*
*8 teaspoon-equivalents sugar substitute**
*60 ml (2 fl oz) water*
*230 ml (8 fl oz) whipping cream, whipped*

Place yolks, vanilla essence, sugar substitute and water in liquidizer. Liquidize at medium speed for 30 seconds.

Fold yolk mixture into whipped cream. Blend well, being careful not to break down volume of whipped cream. Empty into refrigerator tray. Freeze for 2 hours.

TOTAL GRAMS 8.8
GRAMS PER SERVING 1.1

*See note on page 378.

## Flan

4 servings

*5 eggs*
*230 ml (8 fl oz) whipping cream*
*230 ml (8 fl oz) water*
*4–6 teaspoon-equivalents sugar substitute\**
*1 cap almond essence*
*dash nutmeg or dash cinnamon*

Preheat oven to 180°C (350°F/gas mark 4). Beat first five ingredients in liquidizer for 3–4 minutes. Pour into large baking dish or individual dishes and sprinkle top with nutmeg or cinnamon. Bake in a bain-marie for 40 minutes or until set.

TOTAL GRAMS 4.0
GRAMS PER SERVING 1.0

\*See note on page 378.

# Carbohydrate Gram Counter

| Foods | Grams of Carbohydrate |
|---|---|

*Milk Products*

| | |
|---|---|
| Milk (whole, 230 ml [8 oz]) | 12 |
| Milk (semi-skimmed, 30 ml [1 oz]) | 1.3 |
| Cream (single, 30 ml [1 oz]) | 1 |
| (soured, 30 ml [1 oz]) | 1 |
| (whipping, 30 ml [1 oz]) | 1 |
| Soya milk (unsweetened, 230 ml [8 oz]) | 5 |
| Plain yoghurt (skimmed, 230 ml [8 oz]) | 13 |
| (whole, plain, 230 ml [8 oz]) | 12 |

*Cheese*

| | |
|---|---|
| Cheddar (30 g [1 oz]) | .6 |
| Swiss (Emmenthal, 30 g [1 oz]) | 1 |
| Cottage (plain, 230 g [8 oz]) | 8.3 |
| Cottage (reduced-fat, 230 g [8 oz]) | 9 |
| Cream cheese (30 g [1 oz]) | .5 |
| Camembert (30 g [1 oz]) | .5 |
| Feta (30 g [1 oz]) | 1 |

Gouda (30 g [1 oz])                                    1
Mozzarella (30 g [1 oz])                               1
Provolone (30 g [1 oz])                               .5
Roquefort (30 g [1 oz])                               .6


*Nuts*

Almond paste (30 g [1 oz])                            15
Almonds (30 g [1 oz])                                  5
        (12–15 nuts)                          4
Brazil (4 nuts)                                        2
Cashews (30 g [1 oz])                                  8
Coconut (60 g [2 oz])                                 12
Hazelnuts (30 g [1 oz])                                5
Macadamia (30 g [1 oz])                                3
Mixed (30 g [1 oz])                                    6
Peanuts (30 g [1 oz])                                  5
Peanut butter (30 g [1 oz])                            6
Pecans (10 halves)                                     4
Pine nuts (30 g [1 oz])                                3
Pistachios (30 g [1 oz])                               5
Pumpkin seeds (30 g [1 oz])                            4
Sesame seeds (30 g [1 oz])                             6
Soya beans (30 g [1 oz])                               7
Sunflower seeds (30 g [1 oz])                          6
Walnuts (30 g [1 oz])                                  4


*Grains*

Pumpernickel bread (1 slice)                          13
Wholemeal bread (1 slice)                             14
Bagel (1)                                             30
Pancake (using 30 g [1 oz] mix)                       20
Waffle                                                28
Rice: cooked (150 g [5½ oz])                          50
Rice: puffed (30 g [1 oz])                            13
Noodles (cooked, 110 g [4 oz])                        37

Muesli (sugar-free, 40 g 1½ oz])                              16
Popcorn (popped, 30 g [1 oz])                                 49
Porridge oats (cooked with water, 60 g [2 oz])               18

*Soups*

Chicken Consommé (230 ml [8 oz])                              2
Cream of Chicken (230 ml [8 oz])                              8
Chicken Gumbo (230 ml [8 oz])                                 9
Cream of Mushroom (230 ml [8 oz])                            10
Turkey Rice (230 ml [8 oz])                                  10

*Herbs and spices*

Allspice (1 tsp)                                              2
Basil (1 tsp)                                                 1
Caraway (1 tsp)                                               1
Celery seed (1 tsp)                                           1
Cinnamon (1 tsp)                                              2
Coriander (1 tsp)                                            ½
Dill seed (1 tsp)                                             1
Garlic clove (1)                                             1
Saffron (1 tsp)                                               1
Thyme (1 tsp)                                                 1
Tarragon (1 tsp)                                             ½
Vanilla (1 tsp)                                               3
Ginger root (fresh, 30 g [1 oz])                             3
Ginger root (ground, 1 tsp)                                  2

*Vegetables*

Asparagus (6 spears)                                         3
Beans, French (boiled, 50 g [1¾ oz])                       3.3
Beetroot (2, 5 cm [2 in] diameter)                        15.6
Broccoli (cooked, 60 g [2 oz])                               1
Brussels sprouts (4)                                         6

*Vegetables*

| | |
|---|---:|
| Cabbage (80 g [2½ oz]) | 4 |
| Carrot (18 cm [7 in]) | 6 |
| Cauliflower (cooked, 60 g [2 oz]) | 2 |
| Celery (3 pieces, 13 cm [5 in]) | 4 |
| Chicory (raw, 100 g [3½ oz]) | 3 |
| Coleslaw (sweetened, 110 g [4 oz]) | 16 |
| Cucumber (6 slices, 3 mm [⅛ in]) | 2 |
| Curly kale (cooked, 60 g [2 oz]) | 2 |
| Kohlrabi (cooked, 60 g [2 oz]) | 2 |
| Lettuce: cos (2 leaves) | 2 |
| round (1 head, 15 cm [6 in]) | 9 |
| iceberg (⅙ head) | 2 |
| Mushrooms (10 small or 4 large) | 4 |
| Okra (8) | 5 |
| Onion (60 cm [2 ½ in]) | 10 |
| Parsley (1 tbs) | 1 |
| Parsnips (1 tbs) | 18 |
| Peas, (cooked, 60 g [2 oz]) | 6 |
| Peppers: green (2 rings) | 1 |
| red (dried, 30 g [1 oz]) | 5 |
| Potato (baked, 12 x 6 cm [4¾ x 2½ in]) | 21 |
| Potato salad (60 g [2 oz]) | 15 |
| Pumpkin (100 g [3½ oz]) | 7 |
| Radish (4 medium) | 1 |
| Rhubarb (stewed, 100 g [3½ oz]) | 7 |
| Spinach (100 g [3½ oz]) | 4 |
| Spring greens (80 g [2½ oz]) | 9 |
| Squash: summer (1 small) | 7 |
| winter (1 small) | 16 |
| Swede (cooked, 60 g [2 oz]) | 5 |
| Sweetcorn (1 ear, 13 cm [5 in]) | 16 |
| Sweet potato (13 x 5 cm [5 x 2 in]) | 36 |

Tomato: raw (6 cm [2½ in])                       9
     cooked (60 g [2 oz])               6
     juice (20 ml [4 oz])               5
Turnips (cooked, 60 g [2 oz])                     4
Water chestnuts (30 g [1 oz])                     7


*Protein (fat or lean, without breading)*
Fish, poultry, meat, or eggs          0-trace amts.

*Fats/oils*
Olive, vegetable, butter, etc.                    0

*Beans (cooked)*
Haricot (200 g [7 oz])                           34
Black-eyed (200 g [7 oz])                        34
Split peas (230 g [8 oz])                        52
Broad (100 g [3½ oz]))                            6
Red kidney (100 g [3½ oz])                       30
Soya beans (cooked, 100 g [3½ oz])                5
Tofu/bean curd (100 g [3½ oz])                    7

*Fruit*
Apple (1 medium)                                 18
Apple sauce (unsweetened, 110 g [4 oz])          13
Apricots (3 fresh)                               14
Avocado (large)                                  16
Banana (1)                                       26
Blackberries (110 g [4 oz])                      12
Blackcurrants (110 g [4 oz])                      7
Blueberries (110 g [4 oz])                       17

*Fruit*

| | |
|---|---:|
| Raspberries (90 g [3 oz]) | 9 |
| Strawberries (110 g [4 oz]) | 7 |
| Cantaloupe (½ melon, 13 cm [5 in]) | 14 |
| Cherries (140 g [5 oz]) | 13 |
| Grapefruit (pink, ½) | 13 |
| Grapes (140 g [5 oz]) | 22 |
| Lemon | 6.1 |
| Lemon juice (230 ml [8 oz]) | 19.5 |
| Olive (10 green) | 1.0 |
| Peach (6 cm [2½ in]) | 10 |
| Pear (9 cm [3½ in]) | 25 |
| Pineapple (140 g [5 oz]) | 19 |
| Plum (1 medium) | 9 |
| Prunes (cooked, 60 g [2 oz]) | 39 |
| Honeydew (½ melon, 5 in) | 16 |
| Kiwi (1, medium) | 11 |
| Papaya (⅓, medium) | 10 |
| Mango (½, medium) | 17 |
| Orange (1, medium) | 18 |

*Samples of Carbohydrate "Fattening" Items*

| | |
|---|---:|
| Blueberry muffin (1 average) | 17 |
| Vanilla milkshake (1 average) | 50 |
| Banana Split | 91 |
| Taco | 14 |
| Cheeseburger (110 g [4 oz]) | 33 |
| Chicken tikka with pilau rice | 54 |
| Ice lolly | 17 |
| Waffles (plain homemade, 1) | 28 |
| Pancake (plain, buttermilk, 1) | 15 |

| | |
|---|---:|
| Bread pudding (100 g [3½ oz]) | 50 |
| Trifle (100 g [3½ oz]) | 22 |
| Apple pie (homemade, 1 slice) | 61 |
| Brownie (homemade, 1 average) | 15 |
| Jam (plum, 1 tbs) | 15 |
| Onion rings (fast food order) | 33 |
| Tapioca, cream (90 g [3 oz]) | 22 |
| Apple turnover | 30 |
| Pecan pie (homemade, 1 piece) | 41 |
| Doughnut (glazed, 1) | 22 |
| Hot dog with bun (1) | 24 |
| Tortelloni (cheese-filled, (100 g [3½ oz]) | 45 |
| Roast beef sandwich | 20 |
| French toast (2 slices) | 34 |
| Macaroni cheese (140 g [5 oz]) | 40 |
| Pizza (1 piece) | 24 |
| Spring roll (1) | 30 |
| Sorbet (lemon) | 45 |
| Sugared almonds (30 g [1 oz]) | 23 |
| White granulated sugar (30 g [1 oz]) | 28 |
| Marzipan (100 g [3½ oz]) | 50 |
| Marmalade (30 g [1 oz]) | 21 |
| Peanut brittle (30 g [1 oz]) | 23 |
| Honey (30 g [1 oz]) | 34 |
| Rolled oats (100 g [3½ oz] cooked with water) | 9 |
| Bran Flakes (30 g [1 oz]) | 18 |
| Chocolate éclair | 26 |
| Digestive biscuits (1) | 5 |
| chocolate covered (1) | 8 |
| Boiled sweets, fruit gums (30 g [1 oz]) | 25 |

# References

## Chapter 1

1. Yudkin, J. and Carey, M. "The treatment of obesity by the 'high-fat' diet. The inevitability of calories," *Lancet* 2 (1960), pp. 939–941.

## Chapter 2

1. Putnam, J. J. and Allshouse, J. E. *Food Consumption, Prices, and Expenditures, 1968–89*, United States Department of Agriculture, Statistical Bulletin No. 825, 1991, p. 61

## Chapter 3

1. Putnam, J. J. and Allshouse, J. E., op. cit., p. 61.

2. See especially the bibliography to Shafrir, E. "Effect of sucrose and fructose on carbohydrate and lipid metabolism and the resulting consequences," in Reitner, R., ed. *Regulation of Carbohydrate Metabolism*, vol. II, Boca Raton, Florida, CRC Press, 1985.

3. Dolnick, E. "Le Paradoxe Francais," *Hippocrates*, May/June, 1990, pp. 37–43.

**Chapter 4**

1. Bernstein, Richard K., *Diabetes Type II* (New York, Prentice Hall Press, 1990), pp. 32–33.

Also: Ferrannini, E., et al. "Essential hypertension: an insulin resistance state," *Journal of Cardiovascular Pharmacology*, 1990, 15(supplement 5), pp. S18-S25.

**Chapter 5**

1. Cahill, G. and Aoki, T. T. *Medical Times* 98(1970).

2. Grey, N. J. and Kipnis, D. M., "Effect of diet composition on the hyperinsulinism of obesity," *New England Journal of Medicine*, 1971, 285, p. 827. Also: Pfeiffer, E. F. and Laube, H., *Advances in Metabolic Disorders*, 1974, vol. 7.

Also: Muller, W. A. et al. "The influence of the antecedent diet upon glucagon and insulin secretion," *New England Journal of Medicine* 285(26) 1971, 1450–4.

3. Chalmers, T. M., Kekwick, A., Pawan, G. L. S., and Smith, I., "On the fat-mobilising activity of human urine," *Lancet*, 1 (1958), p. 866.

See also: Pawan, G. L. S., and Kekwick, A., "Fat-mobilising and ketogenic activity of urine extracts: relation to cortilcotrophin and growth hormone," *Lancet* 2 (1960), p. 6.

**Chapter 6**

1. Council on Foods and Nutrition, "A critique of low-carbohydrate ketogenic weight reduction regimens," *Journal of the American Medical Association* 224:10 (June 4, 1973), pp. 1415–1419.

2. Kekwick, A. and Pawan, G. L. S., "Calorie intake in relation to body weight changes in the obese," *Lancet* 2:155 (1956).

3. Kekwick, A. and Pawan, G. L. S., "Metabolic study in hu-

man obesity with isocaloric diets high in fat, protein or carbohydrate," *Metabolism* 6 (1957), pp. 447–460.

4. Pilkington, T. R. E., et al. "Diet and weight reduction in the obese," *Lancet* 1 (1960), pp. 856–858.

5. Kekwick, A. and Pawan, G. L. S., "The effect of high fat and high carbohydrate diets on rates of weight loss in mice," *Metabolism* 13:1 (1964), pp. 87–97.

6. Stevenson, J. A. F., et al., "A fat mobilising and anorectic substance in the urine of fasting rats," *Proceedings of the Society for Experimental Biological Medicine* 115(1964), p. 424. See also; Braun, T., et al., "Factor in human urine inhibiting lipid metabolism," *Experientia* 19 (1963), p. 319.

Also: Friesen, H., et al. "Metabolic effects of two peptides from the anterior pituitary gland," *Endocrinology* 70 (1962), p. 579.

Also: Li, C. H., "Lipotropin, a new active peptide from pituitary glands," *Nature* 201(1964), p. 924.

7. Olesen, E. S. and Quaade, F., "Fatty foods and obesity," *Lancet* 1(1960), pp. 1048–1051.

Also: Werner, S. C., "Comparison between weight reduction on a high calorie, high fat diet and on an isocaloric regimen high in carbohydrate," *New England Journal of Medicine* 252 (1955), pp. 661–665.

8. Benoit, F., et al. "Changes in body composition during weight reduction in obesity," *Archives of Internal Medicine* 63:4 (1965), pp. 604–612.

9. Grande, F., "Energy balance and body composition changes: a critical study of three recent publications," *Annals of Internal Medicine* 68 (1968), pp. 467–480.

10. Krehl, W. A., et al. "Some metabolic changes induced by low carbohydrate diets," *The American Journal of Clinical Nutrition* 20:2 (1967), pp. 139–148.

11. Young, C. M. et al. "Effect on body composition and other parameters in young men of carbohydrate level of reduction diet," *American Journal of Clinical Nutrition* 24 (1971), pp. 290–296.

12. Rabast, U. et al. "Comparative studies in obese subjects fed carbohydrate-restricted and high carbohydrate 1,000 calorie formula diets," *Nutritional Metabolism* 22(1978), pp. 269–277.

13. Kasper, H. et al. "Response of body weight to a low carbohydrate, high fat diet in normal and obese subjects," *The American Journal of Clinical Nutrition* 26(1973), pp. 197–204.

Also: Rabast, U. et al. "Therapy of adiposity using reduced-carbohydrate and high-carbohydrate isocaloric formula diets (comparative studies)," *Verhandlungen Der Deutschen Gesellschaft fur Innere Medizin* 81 (1975), pp. 1400–2.

Also: Rabast, U. et al. "Dietetic treatment of obesity with low and high carbohydrate diets," *International Journal of Obesity* 3(3) 1979, pp. 201–211.

Also: Reigler, E. "Weight reduction by a high protein, low carbohydrate diet," *Medizinische Klinik* 71(24) 1976, pp. 1051–6.

Also: Rabast, U. et al. "Loss of weight, sodium, and water in obese persons consuming a high or low carbohydrate diet," *Annals of Nutrition and Metabolism* 26(6) 1981, pp. 341–9.

**Chapter 12**

1. Ricketts, H. T. et al. "Biochemical studies of pre-diabetes," *Diabetes* 15(12) 1966, pp. 880–8.

2. Ezrin, Calvin and Kowalski, Robert. *The Endocrine Control Diet* (New York, Harper and Row, 1990).

3. Muller, W. A. et al. "The influence of the antecedent diet upon glucagon and insulin secretion," *New England Journal of Medicine* 285(1971), pp. 1450–4.

4. Cohen, A. M., Senate Hearings, April 30, 1973.

5. Jarrett, R. J. et al. "Glucose tolerance and blood pressure in two population samples: their relation to diabetes mellitus and hypertension," *International Journal of Epidemiology* 7(1978), pp. 15–24.

Also: Wright, D. W. et al. "Sucrose-induced insulin resistance in the rat: modulation by exercise and diet," *The American Journal of Clinical Nutrition* 38(1983), pp. 879–883.

Also: Reaven, G. M. et al. "Characterization of a model of dietary-induced hypertriglyceridemia in young, non-obese rats," *Journal of Lipid Research* 20(1970), pp. 371–378.

Also: Zavaroni, I, et al. "Effect of fructose feeding on insulin secretion and insulin action in the rat," *Metabolism* 29(1980), pp. 970–973.

Also: Hwang, I. S. et al. "Fructose-induced insulin and hypertension in rats," *Hypertension* 10 (1987), pp. 512–516.

Also: Reaven, G. M. "Insulin independent diabetes mellitus: metabolic characteristics," *Metabolism* 29 (1980), pp. 445–454.

6. Freund, H. et al. "Chromium deficiency during total parenteral nutrition," *Journal of the American Medical Association* 241(5) 1979, pp. 496–498.

Also: Liu, V. J. and Abernathy, R. P. "Chromium and insulin in young subjects with normal glucose tolerance," *American Journal of Clinical Nutrition* 25(4) 1982, pp. 661–667.

7. Solomon, S. J. and King, J. C. "Effect of low zinc intake on carbohydrate and fat metabolism in men," *Federal Proc.* 42(1983), p. 391.

Also: Tarui, S. "Studies of zinc metabolism: III. Effect of the diabetic state on zinc metabolism: A clinical aspect." *Endocrinol. Japan* 10(1963), pp. 9–15.

8. Coggeshall, J. C. et al. "Biotin status and plasma glucose in diabetics," *Annals of New York Academy of Science* 447(1985), pp. 389–92.

9. McNeill, J. H. "Insulinlike effects of sodium selenate in streptozocin-induced diabetic rats," *Diabetes* 48(12) 1991, pp. 1675–8.

Also: McNeill, J. H. et al. "Enhanced in vivo sensitivity of vanadyl-treated diabetic rats to insulin," *Canadian Journal of Physiology and Pharmacology* 68(4) 1990, pp. 486–91.

**Chapter 13**

1. Crook, W. G. *The Yeast Connection* (Jackson, Tennessee: Professional Books, 1985).

2. Svare, C. W. et al. "The effect of dental amalgams on mercury levels in expired air," *Journal of Dental Research* 60(9) 1981, pp. 1668–71.

**Chapter 14**

1. Egger, J. et al. "Is migraine food allergy? A double-blind controlled trial of oligoantigenic diet treatment," *Lancet* (October 29, 1984), pp. 719–21.

**Chapter 15**

1. Council on Foods and Nutrition, "A critique of low-carbohydrate ketogenic weight reduction regimens," *Journal of the American Medical Association* 224(10) 1973, pp. 1415–19.

2. Tolstoi, E. "The effect of an exclusive meat diet on the chemical constituents of the blood," *Journal of Biological Chemistry* 83(1929), pp. 753–758.

3. Reissel, P. K. et al. "Treatment of hypertriglyceridemia," *American Journal of Clinical Nutrition* 19(1966), pp. 84–98.

4. Krehl, W. A. et al. "Some metabolic changes induced by low carbohydrate diets," *The American Journal of Clinical Nutrition* 20(2) 1967, pp. 139–48.

5. Rabast, U. et al. "Outpatient treatment of obesity using a low-carbohydrate diet," *Medizinische Klinik* 73(2) 1978, pp. 55–59.

6. Riegler, E. "Weight reduction by a high protein, low carbohydrate diet," *Medizinische Klinik* 71(24) 1976, pp. 1051–6.

7. Rickman, F. et al. "Changes in serum cholesterol during the Stillman diet," *Journal of the American Medical Association* 228(1974), p. 54.

8. Phinney, S. D. et al. "The transient hypercholesterolemia

of major weight loss," *The American Journal of Clinical Nutrition* 53(1991), pp. 1404–10.

9. Newbold, H. L. "Reducing the serum cholesterol level with a diet high in animal fats," *Southern Medical Journal* 81(1988).

10. Kaplan, N. M. "The deadly quartet: upper-body obesity, glucose intolerance, hypertriglyceridemia, and hypertension," *Archives of Internal Medicine* 149(1989), pp. 1514–20.

11. Lichtenstein, M. J. et al. "Sex hormones, insulin, lipids, and prevalent ischemic heart disease," *American Journal of Epidemiology* 126(1987), pp. 647–57. Also: Pyorala, K. "Relationship of glucose tolerance and plasma insulin to the incidence of coronary heart disease: results from two population studies in Finland," *Diabetes Care* 701(1985), pp. 38–52. Also: Fontbonne, A. et al. "Coronary heart disease mortality risk: plasma insulin level is a more sensitive marker than hypertension or abnormal glucose tolerance in overweight males: the Paris prospective study," *International Journal of Obesity* 12(1988), pp. 557–65.

12. Manninen, V. "Joint effects of serum triglycerides and LDL cholesterol and HDL cholesterol on coronary heart disease in the Helsinki Heart Study. Implications for treatment." *Circulation* 85(1) 1992, pp. 365–7.

13. *Medical Tribune* 33(2), January 30, 1992.

14. Reiser, S. et al. "Serum insulin and glucose in hyperinsulinemic subjects fed three different levels of sucrose," The American Journal of Clinical Nutrition 34(1981), pp. 2348–58.

15. Reaven, G. M. et al. "Role of insulin in endogenous hypertriglyceridemia," *Journal of Clinical Investigation* 46(1967), pp. 1756–67.

See also: Coulston, A. M. et al. "Deleterious metabolic effects of high-carbohydrate, sucrose-containing diets in patients with non-insulin-dependent diabetes mellitus," *American Journal of Medicine* 82(1987), pp. 213–220.

16. See 37 references in Coulston, A. M. et al. "Original ar-

ticles: Persistence of hypertriglyceridemic effect of low-fat high-carbohydrate diets in NIDDM patients," *Diabetes Care* 12(2) 1989, pp. 94–101.

17. Reaven, G. M. et al. "Hypertension as a Disease of Carbohydrate and Lipoprotein Metabolism," *The American Journal of Medicine* 87(suppl. 6A) 1989, pp. 6A-2S—6A-6S.

18. Reaven, G. M. "The role of insulin resistance in human disease," *Diabetes* 37(1988), pp. 1595–1607.

19. Stout, R. W. "Hyperinsulinaemia—a possible risk factor for cardiovascular disease in diabetes mellitus," *Hormone and Metabolic Research* 15(1985), pp. 37–41.

20. Rocchini, A. P. "Proceedings of the council for high blood pressure research, 1990: insulin resistance and blood pressure regulation in obese and nonobese subjects: special lecture," *Hypertension* Supplement 1, 17(6) 1991, pp. 837–842.

21. Childs, M. T. et al. "The contrasting effects of a dietary soya-lecithin product and corn oil on lipoprotein lipids in normolipidemic and familial hypercholesterolemic subjects," *Atherosclerosis* 38(1981), pp. 217–228.

22. Horrobin, D. F. "The importance of gamma-linolenic acid and prostaglandin $E_1$ in human nutrition and medicine," *Journal of Holistic Medicine* 3(1981), pp. 118–39.

23. Saynor, R. "Effects of omega-3 fatty acids on serum lipids," *Lancet* 2(1984), pp. 696–7.

24. Railes, R. and Albrink, M. J. "Effect of chromium chloride supplementation on glucose tolerance and serum lipids including high density lipoprotein of adult men," *American Journal of Clinical Nutrition* 34(1981), pp. 2670–8.

25. Cattin, L. et al. "Treatment of hypercholesterolemia with pantetheine and fenofibrate: An open randomized study on 43 subjects," *Current Therapeutic Research* 38(3) 1985, pp. 386–95.

See also: "Pantetheine treatment of hyperlipidemia," *Clinical Therapy* 8(1986), pp. 537.

26. Grundy, S. M. et al. "Influence of nicotinic acid on meta-

bolism of cholesterol and triglycerides in man," *Journal of Lipid Research* 22(1981), pp. 24–36.

27. Bordia, A. "Effect of garlic on blood lipids in patients with coronary heart disease," *The American Journal of Clinical Nutrition* 34(1981), pp. 100–03.

Also: Ernst E. et al. "Garlic and blood lipids," *British Medical Journal* 291(1985), pp. 139.

28. Ferrari, R. et al. "The metabolical effects of L-carnitine in angina pectoris," *International Journal of Cardiology* 5(1984), pp. 213.

29. Simons, L. A. et al. "Long-term treatment of hypercholesterolaemia with a new palatable formulation of guar gum," *Atherosclerosis* 45(1) 1982, pp. 101–08.

Also: Kay, R. M. and Truswell, A. S. "Effect of citrus pectin on blood lipids and fecal steroid excretion," *The American Journal of Clinical Nutrition* 30(2) 1977, pp. 171–75.

## Chapter 16

1. Tremblay, A. et al. "Nutritional determinants of the increase in energy intake associated with a high-fat diet," *The American Journal of Clinical Nutrition* 53(1991), pp. 1134–37.

2. Cleave, T. L. *The Saccharine Disease* (New Canaan, Connecticut, Keats, 1978).

3. Masironi, P. *Bulletin of World Health Organization* 42(1970).

4. McGill, Jr., H. C. "The relationship of dietary cholesterol to serum cholesterol concentration and to atherosclerosis in man," *The American Journal of Clinical Nutrition* 32 (1979), pp. 2664–2702.

5. Masironi, op. cit.

6. Herrick, J. B. "Clinical features of sudden obstruction of the coronary arteries," *Journal of the American Medical Association*, 1912, LIX, 2105.

7. Willett, W. C. et al. "Relation of meat, fat, and fiber to the

risk of colon cancer in a prospective study among women," *The New England Journal of Medicine* 323(24) 1990, pp. 1664–72.

8. Willet, W. C. et al. "Original article: dietary fat and the risk of breast cancer," *The New England Journal of Medicine* 316(1) 1987, pp. 22–28.

9. Macquart-Moulin, G. et al. "Case-control study on colorectal cancer and diet in Marseilles," *International Journal of Cancer* 38(2) 1986, pp. 183–91. Also: Berta, J. L. et al. "Diet and rectocolonic cancers. Results of a case-control study," *Gastroenterologie Clinique et Biologique* 9(4) 1985, pp. 348–53.

Also: Haenszel, W. et al. "A case-control study of large bowel cancer in Japan," *Journal of the National Cancer Institute* 64(1) 1980, pp. 17–22.

Also: Tuyns, A. J. et al. "Colorectal cancer and the intake of nutrients: oligosaccharides are a risk factor, fats are not. A case-control study in Belgium," *Nutrition and Cancer* 10(4) 1987, pp. 181–96.

10. Warburg, Otto. *The Metabolism of Tumors* (London, Constable and Co., 1930)

11. Dilman, V. M. "Pathogenic approach to prevention of age associated increase of cancer incidence," *Annals of the New York Academy of Science* 621(1991), pp. 385–400.

12. *Federal Register* Department of Agriculture Document, 56(no. 229), November 27, 1991, pp. 60764 60824.

## Chapter 22

1. Evan, G. W. "The effects of chromium picolinate on insulin controlled parameters in humans," *International Journal of Biosocial Medical Research* 11(1989), pp. 163–80

2. Cattin, L. op. cit.

3. McNeill, J. H. op. cit.

4. Coggeshall, J. C. op. cit.

5. Naylor, G. J. et al. "A double-blind placebo controlled trial of ascorbic acid in obesity," Nutrition and Health 1985, p. 425.

6. Ferrari, R. op. cit.

7. Van Gall, L. et al. "Exploratory study of coenzyme $Q_{10}$ in obesity," in Folkers, K. and Yamamura, Y. eds. *Biomedical and Clinical Aspects of Coenzyme Q*, vol. 4, (Amsterdam, Elsevier Science Publishers, 1984), pp. 369–73.

8. Clinical use of glutamine at the Atkins Center for Complementary Medicine.

9. Clinical results obtained at the Atkins Center for Complementary Medicine.

10. Azuma, J. et al. "Therapeutic effect of taurine in congestive heart failure: a double blind crossover trial," *Clinical Cardiology* 8(1985), pp. 276–82.

11. Ellis, F. R. and Nasser, S. "A pilot study of vitamin $B_{12}$ in the treatment of tiredness," *British Journal of Nutrition* 30(1973), pp. 277–83.

12. Atkins, Robert C. *Dr. Atkins' Health Revolution* (Boston, Houghton Mifflin, 1988.)

13. Mohler, H. et al. "Nicotinamide is a brain constituent with benzodiazepinelike actions," *Nature* 278(1979), pp. 563–65.

Also: Yogman, M. and Zeisel, S. "Diet and sleep patterns in newborn infants," *The New England Journal of Medicine* 309(19) 1983, p. 1147.

14. Anderson, R. A. et al. "Chromium supplementation of humans with hypoglycemia," *Federal Proc.* 43(1984), p. 471.

Also: Curry, D. L. et al. "Magnesium modulation of glucose induced insulin secretion by the perfused rat pancreas," *Endocrinology* 101(1977), p. 203.

15. Coggeshall, J. C. op. cit.

Also: Liu, V. J. and Abernathy, R. P. "Chromium and insulin in young subjects with normal glucose tolerance," *The American Journal of Clinical Nutrition* 25(4) 1982, pp. 661–7.

Also: Ceriello, A. et al. "Hypomagnesemia in relation to diabetic retinopathy," *Diabetes Care* 5(1982), pp. 558–9.

Also: Shigeta, Y. et al. "Effect of coenzyme $Q_7$ treatment on blood sugar and ketone bodies of diabetics," *Journal of Vitaminology* 12(1966), p. 293.

16. Childs, op. cit.

Also: Horrobin, op. cit.; Saynor, op. cit.; Railes and Albrink, op. cit.; Cattin, op. cit.; Grundy, op. cit.; Bordia, op. cit.; Ernst, op. cit.; Simons, op. cit.; Day and Trueswell, op. cit.

17. Jamal, C. A. et al. "Gamma-linolenic acid in diabetic neuropathy," *Lancet* 1(1986), p. 1098.

See also: Ceriello, A. et al. "Hypomagnesemia in relation to diabetic retinopathy," *Diabetes Care* 5(1982), pp. 558–9.

18. Cohen, L. "Magnesium and hypertension," *Magnesium Bulletin* 8(1986), pp. 1847–9.

Also: Azuma, J. op. cit. Also: Norris, P. G. et al. "Effect of dietary supplementation with fish oil on systolic blood pressure in mild essential hypertension," *British Medical Journal* 293(1986), p. 104.

19. Kosolcharoen, P. et al. "Improved exercise tolerance after administration of carnitine," *Current Therapeutic Research* November 1981, pp. 753–64.

Also: Haeger, K. "Long-time treatment of intermittent claudication with vitamin E," *American Journal of Clinical Nutrition* 27(10) 1974, pp. 1179–81.

Also: Kamikawa, T. et al. "Effects of coenzyme $Q_{10}$ on exercise tolerance in chronic stable angina pectoris," *American Journal of Cardiology* 56(1985), p. 247.

Also: Taussig, S. J. and Nieper, H. A. "Bromelain: its use in prevention and treatment of cardiovascular disease: Present status," *Journal of International Academy of Preventive Medicine* 6(1) 1979.

Also: Bordia, op. cit.

20. Goebel, K. M. et al. "Intrasynovial orgotein therapy in rheumatoid arthritis," *Lancet* 1(1981), pp. 1015–7.

See also: Barton-Wright, E. C. and Elliott, W. A. "The pantothenic acid metabolism of rheutamoid arthritis," *Lancet* 2(1963), pp. 862–863.

Also: Roberts, P. et al. "Vitamin C and inflammation," *Medical Biology* 62(1984), p. 88.

Also: Sorenson, J. in *The Anti-inflammatory Activities of Copper Complexes, Metal Ions and Biological Systems* (Marcel Dekker, 1982, pp. 77–125.)

# Index

## *More Books from Vermilion*
The prices below were correct at the time of going to press.

| | | | |
|---|---|---|---|
| 0 09 181489 8 | **Mars and Venus Together Forever** | John Gray | £6.99 |
| 0 09 181529 0 | **Mars and Venus in the Bedroom** | John Gray | £6.99 |
| 0 09 181552 5 | **Mars and Venus on a Date** | John Gray | £7.99 |
| 0 09 181524 X | **Mars and Venus in Love** | John Gray | £6.99 |
| 0 09 180653 4 | **What Your Mother Couldn't Tell You and Your Father Didn't Know** | John Gray | £9.99 |
| 0 09 181696 3 | **Mars and Venus 365 Ways to Keep Your Lover** | John Gray | £1.99 |
| 0 09 181644 0 | **Earl Mindell's Secret Remedies** | Earl Mindell | £9.99 |
| 0 09 178287 2 | **The Herb Bible** | Earl Mindell | £8.99 |
| 0 09 181673 4 | **Gut Reaction** | Gudrun Jonsson | £7.99 |
| 0 09 181366 2 | **The Complete Guide to Stress Management** | Dr Chandra Patel | £12.99 |
| 0 09 180969 X | **How to Stop Smoking and Stay Stopped for Good** | Gillian Riley | £7.99 |
| 0 09 181031 0 | **Men's Health Matters** | Nicki Bradford | £10.99 |
| 0 09 178617 7 | **10 Day Clean-Up Plan** | Leslie Kenton | £6.99 |
| 0 09 178420 4 | **10 Day De-Stress Plan** | Leslie Kenton | £6.99 |
| 0 09 178444 1 | **New Biogenic Diet** | Leslie Kenton | £8.99 |
| 0 09 178510 3 | **New Raw Energy** | Leslie Kenton | £8.99 |
| 0 09 181604 1 | **Relate Guide to Better Relationships** | Sarah Litvinoff | £9.99 |

To order your copies from Vermilion (P&P free) call
TBS DIRECT on **01206 255800**.